Praise for *Dream Witchery*

"*Dream Witchery* invites readers on a captivating journey into the rich mystical dreaming traditions from Latin America. This enchanting book delves deep into the intricate tapestry of dream magic, offering an immersive exploration of spells, rituals, and recipes.... Leafar's expertly woven narratives unravel the threads of cultural heritage, unveiling the potent blend of spirituality and practicality that characterizes Latin American Witchcraft.... *Dream Witchery* is an invaluable guide for both novice and experienced practitioners, offering insights into dreaming practices that honor the spirits of the land and empower modern witches." —**Claudiney Prieto, author of** *Wicca: The Goddess Religion*

"A unique compendium of South American magic and spiritual practices grounded in an authentic, non-Western mindset that is refreshing and powerful. The diversity of voices and offerings contained in its pages make it stand out as a treasure of cultural celebration in the occult world." —**Rebecca Beyer, author of** *Wild Witchcraft* **and** *Mountain Magic*

"Elhoim Leafar's intention to teach magic from an often-overlooked perspective is made clear, and he delivers on that promise. Full of rituals, folklore, and simple spells, the essence of South American magic is infused into these pages as only a person indigenous to the practice can do. With several contributing spellcasters from walks of life well outside the typical colonizer regime, Leafar has authored a magical gem that many practitioners, myself included, can learn and grow from." —**Vincent Higginbotham, author of** *How Witchcraft Saved My Life* **and** *Thrifty Witchery*

"A beautiful collection of South American and Indigenous Witchcraft that focuses on the dreamer and dream world. In this book, Elhoim Leafar uses his expert knowledge of magic and witchcraft to guide you in various magical practices spanning from the waking world across the misty liminal realms and into the dream world. Filled with ways to deepen your dream practice, protect your dreams, and enhance your dreaming experience, Elhoim has created a beautiful tome that highlights the magic of the dream world." —**Annwyn Avalon, author of** *Water Witchcraft* **and** *The Way of the Water Priestess*

"*Dream Witchery* takes the reader on a journey to South America by exploring the origin of the authentic esoteric and indigenous magick of Hispanic practitioners. It is at once a deeply personal yet delightfully collaborative book; a mystical and introspective dive into the power and significance of dreams. If you have ever desired knowledge on how to harness your subconscious mind for empowerment in your magick, *Dream Witchery* contains exercises, recipes, and spells told from the necessary perspective of an author with a wealth of personal experience." —**Judy Ann Nock, author of** *The Modern Witchcraft Book of Crystal Magick* **and** *The Modern Witchcraft Guide to Magickal Herbs*

"Dreams have guided humanity in the most mysterious ways throughout time. Everyone has them. Everyone navigates them. But they remain mysterious valleys of our inner worlds that few know how to navigate. Even fewer know how to work them into our everyday lives. Here, Elhoim makes those pathways, gifting the reader with both historical wisdom and practical knowledge for working one's dreams, and bringing those nighttime worlds into deeper clarity." —**Jake Richards, author of** *Backwoods Witchcraft*

DREAM
WITCHERY

About the Author

Elhoim Leafar is a sorcerer, dowser, and urban spiritual worker who descends from a lineage of *curanderos* and old-time brujos from Venezuela. He has taken initiations in multiple traditions and mystical esoteric systems, including Espiritismo Tradicional Venezolano and La Corte de los Encantados, and in Afro-Caribbean traditions such as Candomblé and Santeria. His classes and books portray the Afro-Caribbean influence of his country and the Pagan spirituality of his tribe and family.

Visit Elhoim Leafar online at www.elhoimleafar.com or follow him on Instagram/Twitter @elhoimleafar.

About the Illustrator

David F. Dagnino is a mechanical engineer by profession and freelance illustrator. He graduated as a mechanical engineer with honors from Simon Bolivar University (Venezuela, 2011). His thesis received the award for the Best Engineering Thesis of Venezuela 2012. He graduated *summa cum laude* with a master's in mechanical engineering from the City College of New York (CCNY) and with a medal of merit from the Golden Key International Honor Society (United States, 2017).

DREAM WITCHERY

**FOLK MAGIC, RECIPES & SPELLS FROM
SOUTH AMERICA FOR WITCHES & BRUJAS**

ELHOIM LEAFAR

Llewellyn Publications
Woodbury, Minnesota

FIRST EDITION
First Printing, 2023

Book design by Christine Ha
Cover design by Kevin Brown
Interior art by David F. Dagnino (pages 15, 40, 62, 72, 88, 100, 106, 123, 137, 153, 155, 156, 165, 179, 192, 206, 221, 239, 267, 298, 310, 332)

Llewellyn Publications is a registered trademark of Llewellyn Worldwide Ltd.

Library of Congress Cataloging-in-Publication Data (Pending)
ISBN: 978-0-7387-7475-6

Llewellyn Worldwide Ltd. does not participate in, endorse, or have any authority or responsibility concerning private business transactions between our authors and the public.

All mail addressed to the author is forwarded but the publisher cannot, unless specifically instructed by the author, give out an address or phone number.

Any internet references contained in this work are current at publication time, but the publisher cannot guarantee that a specific location will continue to be maintained. Please refer to the publisher's website for links to authors' websites and other sources.

Llewellyn Publications
A Division of Llewellyn Worldwide Ltd.
2143 Wooddale Drive
Woodbury, MN 55125-2989
www.llewellyn.com

Printed in the United States of America

Hey, Tribu, each and every one of you.
This work is for you.

Dedication

To all those who have been marginalized, ignored, mocked, exiled, and trampled on—to all those who have ever felt cornered in fear—you are not alone, you are not a burden, you are not difficult to love, and you are not out of place. Do not let anyone make you doubt who you are or how valuable you are.

And to all those in my coven—extended, beautiful, sacred, and eternal family.

David, if I had to emigrate again, drop everything and start all over again, as long as it was with you, I wouldn't think twice.

Disclaimer

The publisher and author assume no liability for any injuries caused to the reader that may result from the reader's use of content contained in this publication and recommend common sense when contemplating the practices described in the work. In the following pages you will find recommendations for the use of certain essential oils, incense blends, and ritual items. If you are allergic to any items used in the rituals, please refrain from use. Magical work is not meant to replace the care of a qualified medical professional.

CONTENTS

EXERCISES & RECIPES

DREAM MAGIC INSIGHT
CONTRIBUTOR SPELLS

TRIBAL TALES

Disclaimer on Ethics & Morality

In modern witchcraft and magic, especially in Western magic, we have continual conversations about the ethics and use of esoteric arts for the benefit of others with regard to people's consent. An example of this is the saying "Don't cast a spell on someone, even to their benefit, without the person's prior consent."

In contrast, in Venezuela we say, "*Quien te mira en aprietos y ofrece ayudarte simplemente está esperando un no por respuesta, el que quiere ayudarte, va y te ayuda sin preguntar.*" This is translated as "Whoever looks at you in trouble and offers to help you is simply waiting for a no for an answer, whoever wants to help you goes and helps without asking."

As someone born and raised in South America, I wrote this book on the magic of dreams to reflect the perspective and tradition of our Hispanic people. In that tradition, consent regarding the use of spells and rituals, as long as they are done with good intentions, is not part of our discussions or traditions.

Receiving people's consent or "asking permission to help" is not something in our vocabulary or in our books. It is not part of our culture to ask someone in an overwhelming situation or in trouble whether or not they want our help. We would not ask someone who is thirsty if they want water and then simply sit idly by while the person collapses, dehydrated, in front of us if they refuse help.

Our Latin American and Caribbean esoteric traditions descend mostly from Indigenous peoples, native slaves, or pirates fleeing the system. Our magic is a reflection of those who made use of different spells and recipes to help anyone who might need it because, for them, there was a common enemy: the invading white European man and his ideas of racial identity, colonialism, and Christianity.

Throughout the book you will find language in the recipes such as "if you want to use this spell to help someone without the person knowing…" It is up to the reader, based on maturity and their individual ethics, whether or not to consult with the person affected or seeking help.

Once again, this book was not written to reflect contemporary American or Western aspects of modern magic and witchcraft but to share the authentic rituals and esoteric traditions of South America as they are performed by their sorcerers and brujos. Therefore, and to reiterate, asking someone if they need help is culturally and ethically considered rude.

Acknowledgments

To the incredible and talented team at Llewellyn for making this possible, for the trust in this work, for their enormous dedication and respect for my work, and for allowing me to make the book that I would have wanted to have in my hands when I was growing up, a book that will represent me and my people.

To Heather Greene and Stephanie Finne for helping me materialize this work that I spent so many years trying to get out there. Only those in the heavens know how difficult it must be to edit my complicated ideas and put them in order. You made it possible.

Infinitas Gracias!

INTRODUCTION

It was a terrible day at military school with the usual bullies. A couple of seniors locked me in one of the bathroom stalls; I couldn't fight them. I spent four hours locked in the cubicle before the kind janitor found me and let me out. Parents had already picked up their children from school, and those classmates who locked me in told my dad that I left early, so he left without picking me up.

I walked for hours, arriving home hungry and physically and mentally exhausted, without even the desire to cry. I just wanted to shower and go to sleep, and that's what I did.

The next morning, I wrote in my journal—an old blank notebook that I covered with some pieces of cloth from my mom's workshop:

> *I dreamed with many numbers last night. I don't know what they mean. I dreamed that I was flying very high among the clouds and my hands could stretch so much that I felt like I could touch the moon. It was a gigantic moon, and I was flying so high that I couldn't see the moon above me but at my same height. A long piece of cloth was tied around my neck, and looking down there was sea, water, waves, many waves. The water reflected the dark night and the full moon next to me.*
>
> *A lady with bronze or copper-colored skin danced on the waves, but I did not listen to the music. She danced with open arms and a huge circle of golden fire formed around her. She and the circle remained on the waves, and behind her I only saw clouds, many white clouds, as white as the moon.*

Naturally I thought that the copper and bronze lady was Yemaya, the goddess that my mother always invoked on the beach. I was only twelve years old, and I didn't know what it meant, but I guessed that a goddess was taking care of me.

Thirteen years later, I found myself in the United States, in what would become my new home, after a long, exhausting trip from Venezuela. It was around 7:00 p.m. after a busy day. I had already filled four pages of my diary (now virtual from my smartphone). I had barely eaten half a sandwich at the airport. A few hours before I was in Atlanta, Georgia, then I had to endure the most complicated transfer ever to take the flight to New York.

On the plane from Georgia, the man sitting next to me seemed to know all the flight attendants. He helped me put my luggage above the seat. He kindly offered me the window. I was happy because this was my first time traveling to the United States, and I wanted to enjoy the view.

Suddenly, everyone was looking out the windows. I was half asleep but still could hear everyone murmuring, and curiosity sucked me in. I looked out the window and was overtaken with awe. "Oh my Goddess," I thought. I had completely forgotten that it was the day of the lunar eclipse. You can't imagine how big the moon looked from the plane window. The man sitting next to me, who at that point I was guessing was the plane's marshal, was looking past me to see what the excitement was about too. I managed to tell him, in my limited English, "Lunar eclipse tonight." He responded with a curt, "Oh, thank you."

I looked at the moon and how impressive it was—right next to me. We seemed to be at the same height, and when I got a little closer to the glass, I could see the clouds below us and under the clouds a dark sea. At that moment, the flight attendant announced something on the plane's speaker. I couldn't hear what it was, but everyone seemed to be happy. Apparently, as I finally learned, we were going to arrive at the airport in good time. Was it possible that I had taken the only flight in the history of flights that did not suffer from a delay?

As we descended very slowly into New York City, I was once again surprised by the beautiful sight of the city, with its impressive bridges and huge lights. Then, I heard everyone murmuring once again with excitement. There, in the water, stood a beautiful lady with her huge crown and a torch in her hand. She looked forward with such an imposing presence. I wondered aloud what that statue represented. What was it? The man next to me told me that it was the Statue of Liberty, who welcomes the passengers.

Witches say that when you are looking for something, something is out there sitting and waiting for you. Clearly there was a goddess out there waiting for my arrival, sending moments and memories in the form of night visions to me. It was not the same goddess that I thought it would be but was instead another of the multiple manifestations of the universal feminine creative energy, who was the goddess of immigrants. She welcomed me with open arms in the middle of the night of the lunar eclipse in the Big Apple. Printed in bronze inside the statue's pedestal is the poem "The New Colossus," written by Emma Lazarus in 1883:

> Not like the brazen giant of Greek fame,
> With conquering limbs astride from land to land;
> Here at our sea-washed, sunset gates shall stand
> A mighty woman with a torch, whose flame
> Is the imprisoned lightning, and her name
> Mother of Exiles. From her beacon-hand
> Glows world-wide welcome; her mild eyes command
> The air-bridged harbor that twin cities frame.
> "Keep, ancient lands, your storied pomp!" cries she
> With silent lips. "Give me your tired, your poor,
> Your huddled masses yearning to breathe free,
> The wretched refuse of your teeming shore.
> Send these, the homeless, tempest-tost to me,
> I lift my lamp beside the golden door![1]

Eight years have passed since that trip, since that dream finally manifested into reality. Living in the United States has not only led me to learn a new language but also to discover other forms of witchcraft, to connect with other witches with different experiences and knowledge, and most importantly, it

....

1. A bronze plaque with "The New Colossus," written by Emma Lazarus (1849–1887), is inside the Statue of Liberty on Liberty Island, New York City.

has forced me to search and discover even deeper connections with my own craft, with my roots, and with my ancestors.

In the field of witchcraft, there are many books with vague references to what we practice in South America, which is my own way of encompassing the countries connected to the Amazon. They often discuss how witches in South America do this or that. However, these books are written by authors who don't speak our languages and have never set foot in our countries or only spent a few weeks of vacation there. This frustrates and angers me, which is always followed by another thought: authors write these books because they know that someone else wants to read it or someone else is curious about the subject. This last thought was the motivation for me sitting down for long hours to write between jobs, repeating to myself, "Okay. You guys want to read about this? Well, I'm going to make you read everything you don't know about our practices—starting with the dreamworld."

A Window to the World Beyond the World

In South America, our families, most of whom descended from Indigenous peoples and slaves, have developed enormous religious, mystical, and spiritual practices around the subject of dreams. Although this can be read as an overgeneralization, the truth is that many of our native practices are similar. Before colonial times, a large percentage of our Indigenous peoples were navigators in small canoes. Those native Indigenous groups, from which the Wayúu, Arawak, and Taino peoples originated from, to just mention a few, were not precisely limited to a single place. Their influence covered much of South America before the settlers arrived, and their religious and esoteric practices, as well as their initiation rites, found a way to prevail over time by adapting and hiding in folklore and oral tradition.

For the Indigenous and later the enslaved peoples, dreams were not limited to predicting future events. Instead, dreams were mostly a window to the "world beyond the world" where gods, ancestors, elemental spirits, and the souls of all those who had departed from their physical body finally dwelled together. For these peoples, dreams were a magical escape between labyrinths of illusions where they could communicate with their ancestors, hide secrets that could only be revealed from there, and even move between worlds and bodies. For example, brujas Wachi in Colombia possess the bodies of the youngest people while they sleep. There's also brujas Macici in Venezuela who, when sleeping, release their spirits through their mouths and travel by possessing the bodies of nocturnal birds and pumas in order to spy on their enemies and keep evil spirits away.

When you live most of your life in your country of origin, you learn and practice and become initiated into the esoteric practices and rites of that land, so it is only a matter of time before you begin to take certain things for granted. When you emigrate to another place, you discover that those items in your suitcase can get lost at the airport and the only thing that really matters, and has more value, is what you know, what you have lived, what you have learned. You then give greater value to these old teachings. That was what happened to me when I arrived in the United States. After several years, I understood that many of the experiences and much of the knowledge that I took for granted are for many the engine of their spiritual search.

The peoples of South America are a people who—like many others—were conquered and enslaved, and although the settlers forced their language and culture on us, we became independent. We tamed the language and made it our own. We enriched it, we nurtured it with our different accents and cultures, and we added our own words and our own pronunciation. Just as it happened with the language, it also happened with our religious practices. Catholicism was imposed by the evangelizers, but after several years, and thanks to religious secretism as well as to the modern decolonizers of our history, we have found the return to our roots, and this empowered us.

Even being so different from each other, Latin Americans master our language, our magic, our gastronomy, and our religious faith. This book was made to represent how rich our culture is and how powerful our roots are, which connect us directly with the Pachamama and with the spirits of the earth, with the deities of the mountain, with the gods that our ancestors venerated, and with the gods of the river that change shape and the goddesses of the stars that wear crowns of wheat and dresses made of feathers and fur.

About This Book

This is not just another dream book but rather a complete esoteric compendium on dream magic and its applications from a South American perspective. In those countries, witchcraft is not only seen as a magical religion based on fertility and the celebration of natural cycles but also a powerful tool that includes centuries of practice and learning from the hands of slaves, witches, outcasts, exiles, and priests of Indigenous tribes. Collectively these peoples have made use of these magical tools in the form of spells and amulets to liberate their families and communities against the colonizer, against the oppressor, and against the abusive monarch.

In the end, what is *brujeria* or witchcraft for our peoples? It is another way of telling our stories and myths masked as spells and perfumed with oils and powders to free the weak and the oppressed from abusive arms.

As you read this book, you will discover that I deal with the subject of dreams as an instrument of mediumship. It is an aspect of magic that is vitally important but not sufficiently investigated or studied in sorcery. I will go beyond the manuals of dream interpretation and spells that just put objects under the pillow. I will show how dreams are an essential means of divination, clairvoyance, and precognition for witches, warlocks, and sorcerers. I will also show, from the spiritualist perspective, that dreams are a vision of our subconscious self that allows us to distract the mind enough to free it from the physical body and allow the spiritualist's body to be possessed by a passing spirit that has been summoned.

As the book progresses, you will develop your own views on dreams and their magical applications in sorcery. You will also find many exercises and rituals, stories, folklore, legends, and a huge number of simple spells to perform at home or in a small patio, as well as rituals to be performed on specific dates in groups of two or more people. I also include concoctions, tisanes, and common herbal infusions to help you fall asleep and avoid insomnia, as well as instructions on making amulets at home.

Each chapter is punctuated with legends and short myths from different parts of South America, particularly those that have survived the oppression of Indigenous peoples by colonialism and the church. I gathered much of this information during conversations with priests, spiritual workers (shamans, healers, and witch doctors), as well as sorcerers from various parts of Argentina, Bolivia, Brazil, Chile, Colombia, Ecuador, Guyana, Paraguay, Peru, Suriname, Trinidad and Tobago, Uruguay, and Venezuela.

Contributors

May your craft always be a representation of your intelligence and experience, not just a verbatim copy of the books you've read. It is for this reason that I decided to do something for this book that is often not valued in society: I asked for help and advice.

My magical work is a mixed representation of the places I have lived and the traditions I have been initiated into, and I have learned in the process from many different masters. Inviting some of them to collaborate here with me has been of vital importance, and each contributor added something new, something different, and, in turn, something vital that enhances the cultural experience that you can read in each line of this book.

These contributions, as varied as they are vital, led me to expand the scope of this book in order to find the perfect space for them. Our esoteric community is erroneously led by authors—we apparently get all the fame—and the leaders are really the booksellers, bloggers, YouTubers, podcasters, editors, and even the occasional event organizer. They act as our anchors, our cultural and social glue, and several of them were invited to collaborate on this project.

A Note about the Illustrations

To preserve the folkloric aspect and the particular texture of the book, the illustrations were made by David Dagnino (Venezuelan) and curated together with Elhoim Leafar. They represent and illustrate various everyday rituals and esoteric aspects of oral and traditional folklore that are culturally shared by several countries from South America and various Indigenous tribes in the region.

Many of the images used throughout the chapters of this book are reproduced and captioned in an image description list. You can find it at the back of this book.

Spells to Get Started

In magic and sorcery, the intention is important, but the intention is not every-thing. The passage from theory to practice is what separates the experts from the amateurs. Although accumulating knowledge is important, the experience is gained with the daily practice. To get into practice, here are two easy but functional exercises.

EXERCISE
Ritual Cleansing Against All Evil

Sometimes the simplest methods are the most effective, and it is not always necessary to overelaborate to achieve the purpose we are seeking. In traditional spiritualism, we always say that before each ritual you must take a moment to carry out a spiritual cleansing, otherwise you will end up contaminating the entire ritual with your own energy. With that in mind, here is a simple cleansing ritual that you can carry out. My advice here is: if it is within your means, buy these ingredients in large quantities, store them in properly sealed glass bottles, and use them whenever you need them.

You will need:
- White or purple candle in candleholder
- Lavender incense cone
- Lighter
- One long willow stick that you can bend, between 1 to 2 feet (30.5 to 61 centimeters) long
- Hemp yarn (always have enough yarn at hand)
- Myrrh or frankincense essential oil
- Handful of pins
- Bouquet of dried chamomile flowers
- Bouquet of dried lavender flowers

Light the candle and incense. Then bend the willow stick into a huge hoop. Moisten the hemp yarn with the oil and use it to tie the hoop.

Pin the chamomile and lavender flowers along the hoop until it is completely covered. Now pass the hoop through the smoke of the incense several times.

Place the consecrated ring on the ground and stand in it. Close your eyes for a minute and take a deep breath. Take the ring with both hands and pass it over your body from bottom to top five times, reciting:

Enchanted circle, cure me of all evil.
Enchanted circle, protect me from all evil.
Enchanted circle, heal me from the inside out.
Enchanted circle, protect me from outside and inside.
So be it.

Keep the hoop near your altar or sacred space. Add more flowers to it every so often to strengthen its magic and reuse it.

My personal recommendation is to never put out the incense; let it burn out instead. Be careful with the candles, though. Use glass jars for candles when they are very large, or put them out a couple of hours after the ritual to prevent fires.

EXERCISE
Manifestation Spell

Suppose you are totally new to the esoteric field and this is one of your first metaphysical books. You do not call yourself a professional witch, and you do not have a large library full of books to show off on Instagram. You are a newbie, as we all are—even after about thirty years of practice. Try this exercise to manifest understanding in your path, to open your mind and identify those obstacles in the process of your magical work.

You will need:

- White or yellow candle in candleholder (The candle can be small and simple or long and exuberant; just make sure it is white or yellow. These are colors that, at first glance, remind us of the tone of light at home.)
- Lighter
- Pencil and sheet of paper
- Bay leaf
- Heat-resistant saucer or small cauldron

Light the candle. Then take the pencil and write on the sheet of paper five reasons you think it is important for you to master your magic and learn to perform spells. For example, "I feel that in this way I can connect more with divinity," "I want to be able to understand my dreams," or "I want to get a better job where my efforts are duly valued and rewarded."

Now place a bay leaf in the center of the paper. Yes, a simple and common bay leaf that you probably have in the kitchen. You don't need to look for the sacred laurel that only grows at midnight on the outskirts of a mountain.

Now fold the paper around the leaf, as if it were an envelope. Be creative. You can roll it up like a sheet of parchment or fold it into triangles and squares. The important thing is that the bay leaf is completely covered and stored inside the paper.

Close your eyes for a moment with paper in hand. Meditate on what you have written and visualize the shape and color of the candle flame. Keep this vision in your mind with your eyes closed. Breathe deeply and slowly a couple of times.

Now open your eyes, and very carefully light the sheet of paper using the flame of the candle. Let it burn on a heat-resistant saucer or a small cauldron that you have at home.

You have just (in a surprisingly simple way) manifested your intentions to the universe and your guiding and protecting spirits. What you have written is on the way to being fulfilled.

If you wish to extinguish the candle, do so in some way other than blowing. Nothing bad is going to happen because of it. You are not cursing anyone or attracting bad fortune. You are extinguishing a candle that you lit with your best intentions in a private ritual between you and your spiritual guides. This is between you and the universe, and no one else.

You can repeat this ritual as many times as you want, making use of the same candle. It will be interesting to see how you feel between the first time you perform this ritual and the next and to witness how your confidence in your process changes little by little.

PART I
THE EXPERIENCE
OF THE DREAM

CHAPTER 1

BRUJAS, WITCHES & DREAMS

Witches are able to find power, extract it, and transmute it for their own benefit or that of others from practically any element present in nature. There are witches who find their power in water or air, while others find their power in plants and herbs, in flowers and trees, in crystals and minerals, or in times and places—even in emotions and dreams lies enormous power. It is a power that connects us with superior forces and opens the doors to the understanding of a world that is entirely connected to our own inner world and yet remains vastly unknown.

Dreams are our way to communicate in a direct, intimate way with Mother Earth, with our ancestors, with the cosmos, and with the spiritual world. Dreams are a natural language among all species in this world—and those from otherworlds.

Dreams contain all kinds of symbolic, mystical, and predictive meanings. Some of these meanings can even represent the remainders of memories from past lives or messages sent to us by our ancestors from a different time than ours. In all the cultures of the world, dreams take on enormous symbolic and sometimes even religious weight. In the Yoruba culture of the Caribbean, dreams represent predictions of the future, while in the Yanomami culture of Venezuela and Brazil, dreams represent messages from our ancestors.

When we close our eyes, relax our extremities, and surrender ourselves in complete confidence to the world of sleep, our conscious mind takes a break, giving way to our unconscious being. Once we have released that false sense of control, we surrender to an inner force greater than ours: dreams.

Dreams are full of revelations and messages with all kinds of meanings. The amount of information we receive and simultaneously send night after night while we sleep is equal (or dare I say even higher) to the amount of information that we perceive and send during the day.

Dreams help us to reveal and break down every event, thought, and emotion of the day to its smallest parts, leading us to better understand each of those events and thoughts, hence perhaps the famous phrase "let me sleep on it." It is a way of admitting "I am not in complete control of this decision at the moment; let me fall asleep and tomorrow I will have a fresher head." During the night, our brain reviews the information received without our conscious self intervening to make decisions that can be influenced by our emotions, and in the morning, the information is more fluid, clearer, and without the emotional pressure of the day before.

While we sleep, we are capable of immersing ourselves in the world of spirits—one of the many worlds that surround us. From that existential plane, we can contact all kinds of astral and spiritual entities with greater ease. It is an energetic world that does not require any kind of language but instead communicates in symbols that are later remembered as words in the morning.

During the dream journey, we are more perceptive to the hidden world that surrounds us. In the world of dreams, we are no longer dependent on the senses that are connected to our physical organs and the earthly world of sensations, and without a physical body to disable many of our energetic senses, we are able to interact with esoteric entities. We are open to exploring a world of energy, light, and shadows that is permanently present in our environment but that we are only able to perceive without the senses and organs of our physical body.

Magic, Witchcraft, and Too Many Words

Whenever we try to define groups of people, we end up doing it wrong. The world is not black and white, and if we walk along the path of gray tones, we will quickly find an infinite variety of shadows and shades. Putting people in boxes under a tag is not a good pursuit, but just for healthy fun, or rather to maintain some order in this book, I am going to define from the outset some terms that I will use and that are not always interchangeable. Again, these definitions are my own and represent my individual vision, and ultimately people can fit into more than one category; this is simply for academic purposes.

Sorcerers Like Spiders

In the mountains of Sorte (Venezuela), we have this exercise that nearly everyone hates: the dance of the spider. It consists of placing a series of painted rocks in various places several meters apart, undressing until you are only in your underwear, then crouching down and walking with your feet and hands like spiders around the place. It's fun. Well, at least fun to see it, not so much to do it.

The goal is for the spider people to find a rock, pick it up with their mouth without making any use of the hands, and bring it to a specific point. The exercise does not end until all rocks have been collected.

The tradition is more of a malicious humility kick that elders force novices to perform because it always works to reveal from the first moment who is most humble. Those are the novices that, although they don't understand the reason for the practice, go and do it without question. The most arrogant novices will say, "I'm not going to take off my clothes for no reason, and this is very stupid." The exercise is not mandatory, but those who do it later receive better treatment. What is the lesson? When dealing with the world of spirits, there will be times when you cannot say no to those you are working with, or things will get out of control. You must be humble and remember this is not about you. It is about keeping alive the traditions and, through these traditions, teaching our stories and folklore to the next generations, just as they were taught to us.

As a sorcerer, your job is not to take control over things; it is to understand why these things happen and find a way, either by esoteric or energetic means, to shift the situation into your favor or in favor of someone else. Being a sorcerer, or brujo, is like being able to control the weather—as much as you can have the power to do so—and your methods may or may not work to bring rain or snow, but it is not your responsibility to do it. It is not correct to play with Mother Nature; disturbing those cycles is unnatural. It is okay for the sorcerer to predict the weather in order to warn others and thus lessen the implications and consequences of a disproportionate rain or a heavy snowfall, which can easily ruin a harvest. As you can understand, the sorcerer is using their power, their deep knowledge and understanding of the cycles of nature in favor of something bigger, in benefit of the whole community.

While the purpose of the spider exercise is to separate the humble from the arrogant, it can also be used to describe magic workers. Once, my godfather Alexander said:

**This is how witches work, like silent spiders from their corner,
silently weaving their webs to catch and attract with their spells
everything they want, even to catch their enemies and all those**

who seek to harm their own. The witches weave their webs day
after day and night after night, and once something is within reach
of their webs—a would-be lover, a stroke of good luck, a spirit ally,
an omen of good fortune, a vision of the future—the witches feel it
like spiders feel the fine vibration of something that has fallen into
their web, and then they catch it silently and walk toward it with
all elegance and without making much noise. That's how witches
are: they are like powerful weaver spiders.

Now, if witches, brujos, and sorcerers are spiders, I might venture to
think that magic is like a spiderweb. What is a spiderweb made of? Spiders
feed on other smaller insects, sometimes even insects larger than them. After
feasting, the spider, inside its tiny body, transforms these various nutrients
and elements into the threads it releases and uses these threads to weave a
network.

Is magic then like the webs of the spider? Possibly it is. Witches make use
of all the elements they find in their environment—from feathers they find
in the streets, candles they buy in the market, shells and snails they find on
the beach, rocks they source from a river, a lock of hair they take from their
loved one or an enemy, even the wildflowers they find growing next to the
parking lot. They mix all these elements in their little refuge at home in a
small but powerful altar and then craft a powerful spell to attract everything
that is within reach: their network.

Magic has many interpretations and manifestations, but it is ultimately
a multifaceted, transformative essence that witches and wizards find in all
things around them.

Sorcery, Brujeria, Witchcraft? Which Is Which?

These days we use the terms *witchcraft, sorcery, magic,* and *spiritism* inter-
changeably or see them as different faces of the same character. However, it is
important to differentiate these practices because when you use these terms out
of context, you omit centuries of slavery, culture, and history that has defined
witchcraft in Latin America. In the United States, for example, *witchcraft* is a
term used for a modern religious or magical practice that mostly seeks to keep
alive European folk practices and similar ancient religious practices, along

with celebrating natural cycles. That is not the case in Latin America. While the term *brujeria* is translated into English literally as "witchcraft," when we refer to the practice of brujeria, we talk about those rituals, prayers, and spells that grandmothers practiced, many of which were under a strong influence of Spanish religious practices and Indigenous Latin American tribes. These rituals, prayers, and spells range from simple tricks, such as putting eucalyptus leaves in your shoes so you don't lose work or placing coriander sprigs over your ears to focus your attention, to piercing a red rose with a needle on a new moon night so your lover doesn't get an erection when he tries to be unfaithful.

In brujeria, there is enormous cultural context that goes beyond venerating nature and its cycles as it occurs in traditional and modern witchcraft. Our Latin American ancestors unearthed the secrets of nature to empower themselves and survive during times of war, to cure themselves of poisons or to poison their enemies. Certain modern British witchcraft traditions under the influence of Wicca practice the beliefs of "do no harm to yourself or anyone" and "do not work with the energy of others without their permission," while for Latin American witches, cursing others is practically a daily routine, and they learn all kinds of curses and *sortilegios* (spells) to prevent others from surpassing them in some aspect of their life or perform *ensalmos* and *santiguar* with water of mint to a child, even without the permission of the parents, so that the evil eye does not make the child sick and cost them their life.[2]

The term *sorcery* is commonly used to define the study of all esoteric sciences and forms of magic. For me, as a good Capricorn, I am always particularly obsessed with lists and order. I like to distinguish the occultists (those people who are highly academic and collect books like there is no tomorrow) from the kinds of people who dance under the full moon or perform spells and rituals. I call these people occultists, although they mostly call

....

2. Ensalmos is a form of magical spell that consists of making use of biblical psalms to bless and/or protect a child. It is frequently used by *ensalmeros* (*sanadores, brujos, curanderos, hechiceros*) who practice folk-Catholic magic.

In Latin America, *santiguar* is used to refer to the specific action when a brujo/a/x draws a cross with the use of their hands over a sick, ill, poisoned, or cursed person while praying for healing and protection.

themselves witches, because they are the respected esoteric academics who are out there absorbing knowledge for tomorrow.

I define sorcerers, spellworkers, or spellcasters as those people who craft different spells and rituals from time to time. You know, like those witchy friends who buy a couple of books on spellcasting, craft a spell for love or good luck every three months, but continue going to church. They do not practice any kind of devotional spiritual work, don't search for initiations in magic, and are not clairvoyant.

But what about witches? We have multiple definitions of what witchcraft is, and all of those definitions are valid. In the United States, witches are often members of a British initiatory tradition that is part of a revival religion that venerates the mother goddess and the cycles of nature. However, there is another broader—and I might venture to say more widely accepted—definition that states that witches follow an esoteric path in which they focus on gathering knowledge and making practical use of it, making contact and contracts with spirits, studying and practicing spells (including curses and *amarres*, or love spells), and learning various methods of divination.

It is important not to confuse witchcraft with brujeria, although the English-Spanish dictionary translates them as the same. *Brujeria* is the term that, in America Latina, we use to refer to our own esoteric religious practices, which are not directly mixed with the cycles of nature but rather focused on venerating the ancestors, nature in all its forms (with cycles or without them), and all kinds of spells with the purpose to improve aspects of life (love, money, health) or empower minorities and the marginalized against colonialism, patriarchy, and those abusive leaders of our peoples.

Brujeria has a long history of being the tool of the marginalized and of those who feel more vulnerable, so it is important not to confuse the term with *witchcraft*. Throughout Latin America, we use the same term of *brujeria*,[3] but in some countries brujeria can be part of an initiatory or hereditary path, while in others it is the linguistic umbrella for all those who practice some form of Afro-Caribbean esoteric religion (Umbanda, Candomblé, Lucumi, etc.) called brujos.[4]

....

3. Cross, *American Brujeria*, xix–xx.
4. Davila, *Mexican Sorcery*, xvi–xviii.

All these terms can be easily confused with each other, especially as their meanings have changed throughout the passing years. For example, until about a decade ago, *warlock* was a negative term that referred to a man practicing the occult arts. It was a sorcerer who made use of his knowledge and powers to cause harm to others—an oath breaker. However, today the term is gaining some acceptance in LGBTQIA circles, where it is well used by magical individuals to define themselves with a term other than *witch*. Although language seems to change and adapt to the times and to the styles of each individual, it is of great help to maintain a certain distance between some of the words so as not to omit their historical and cultural context.

For the use and understanding of this book, the terms that will be used most often are:

brujos: In my land, we use the term *brujos* for all those who practice some form of healing, magic, or divination. However, for the benefit of the reader and the modern practitioner, I like to define *brujo*, or *bruja*, as the practitioner of any form of the occult arts who exercises them under a Latin-Hispanic context or under a magical practice from Latin America. Although the term is translated into English as "witch," the linguistic origin of both words is completely different, and the cultural weight of each one is also different. The problem with assuming that *brujo* should simply be translated as "witch" is that traditional and modern witchcraft are heavily influenced by early British Paganism, while the practice of brujeria brings together magical, religious, native, cultural, and Indigenous pre- and post-colonization practices and beliefs. Assuming that "all brujos are witches" erases and dismisses centuries of slavery, cultural whitening, religious imposition, and generational trauma.

Energy workers or magic workers: This term applies to holistic therapists, healers, acupuncturists, and chiropractors. These are people who work in different ways with energy and its manifestation but do not resort to the use of spells and amulets, which work as common tools in sorcery.

Hechiceros, sorcerers, and spellworkers: These are individuals who practice any form of magic and sorcery without the commitment to be initiated into an esoteric path or to be part of a witchcraft cult or religion. According to Alexis Arredondo and Eric Labrado in their book *Magia Magia: Invoking Mexican Magic,* "Where hechiceria and Brujeria differ, is that the former focuses solely on spells, while brujeria is a more involved practice of Magic."[5]

Mediums: These are individuals with psychic-spiritual abilities that are used to contact the world of spirits, either by themselves or with the help of various items and practices. In Venezuela, it is said, "We do not need to be a medium to be a witch," while specifically in the Amazon, it is said, "It is not the obligation of the medium to act as an intermediary for everyone, but he has a gift that should not be wasted."

Occultists: You have one of those friends who is very into the subject of witchcraft, carries amulets, accumulates magic and occult books, and knows a little about everything in relation to the esoteric but does not practice spells or rituals of any style. They don't celebrate the phases of the moon or the changes of the seasons, and they have probably never seen a ghost in their life. That is the occultist. They are accumulators of knowledge, and they have a wide understanding of the esoteric, but they are not the people you are going to ask for assistance performing a spell, commission to make an amulet, or pay for a tarot reading.

Spiritists: In Latin America, we have a certain division regarding the term *spiritism* that is not mentioned in English books. There are those who practice traditional spiritualism (a form of magic, divination, and mediumship linked entirely to the world of spirits), and then there are the Kardesians, who practice Allan Kardec's

....

5. Arredondo and Labrado, *Magia Magia,* v.

    Hechiceria (sorcery) is the term used in various Latin American countries to refer to two types of esoteric practices (depending on each country). It may very well be the practice of a spellcaster or the practice of someone who deals and make contracts with spirits, an example being Saint Cyprian the Magician.

spiritualism. Although Kardec is one of the most respected authors on the subject, he was not Latin American, and he was not a medium. Instead, he was a good researcher, and his perspective on the subject is quite far from modern practice.

Warlocks: Although the term *warlock* derives from Old English and can be translated as an "oath breaker" or a "fibber," in Latin America many male practitioners use this term to refer to themselves as a male sorcerer not initiated in any esoteric path and who lives under his own rules. For many years, this term has been used to represent "male witches"; however, today this term has gained popularity in the LGBTQIA community to refer to a gay, bi, or queer witch.

Witches: Although *witch* is the term that I prefer to use for those who have been initiated into the religion of Witchcraft or Wicca, it is also an umbrella term to agglomerate and generalize all the previous ones under a single nickname. There are many types of witches; some follow traditional British witchcraft, while others are followers of modern American witchcraft. However, at least for me as a practitioner, the two main types are:

> *Coven witches:* These are witches who are part of a coven or a group of witches that gathers to perform spells and rituals and usually works magic or celebrates the sabbats as a team.
>
> *Solitary witches:* These are witches who operate in the field of witchcraft in an eclectic way, without being tied to a group, sacred oath, or an initiatory ceremony.

Definitions of Dreams

Similar to *witchcraft*, we can also find many different meanings for the term *dreams*. While writing this book, I consulted at least twelve different encyclopedias, a couple of Freud's books (which really weren't much help), and the local New York bookstore. At some point, I must confess that I broke down and went to the easiest source for any modern research: Wikipedia. I didn't like its definition of dreams either. So, I opted for my favorite definition from the *American Heritage Dictionary*:

A dream is a succession of images, ideas, emotions, and sensations that usually occur involuntarily in the mind during certain stages of sleep.[6]

I really like this definition. It is complete, understandable, and brief. Starting with this definition, we can now work from a more individual vision. What are dreams? Or rather, what are dreams for a sorcerer or energy worker?

Dreams are a complex summary of images, concepts, sensations, memories, visions, messages, and experiences that occur in our minds in a mostly involuntary way while we sleep. I say mostly involuntary because today there is the term *dream incubation*, which refers to what's become a very popular method to induce ideas and images in our subconscious. For example, watching a marathon of horror movies can lead us to have interesting nightmares, or reading romance poems before bed can lead us to have happy dreams.

Dreams act like short movies that play in our heads and later become experiences that are easy to forget. The dream experience can be so vivid and so complete that while we sleep, we convince ourselves that we are living such an experience and confuse it with reality, but when we wake up, we only remember some fragments of that experience, like pieces of a puzzle. The problem is, we don't remember what the complete puzzle looks like—we don't even remember the cover on the box. We only remember a few pieces of it.

Dreams are full of messages that arrive in one way or another. They come as visions of the past and future, memories and photographs of various moments in our lives, as well as future alerts and warnings of upcoming events.

Dreams can act as a manifestation of our psychic energy, allowing us to move between worlds and experiences, even navigating between the dreams of others and their minds, or they can act as an interesting source of power.

During our waking hours, we are mostly aware of our actions. We are naturally active in all our senses, perceiving information from the entire environment as colors, shapes, distances, dates, numbers, names, aromas,

....
6. "Dream," The American Heritage Dictionary of the English Language, Fourth Edition, 2000, retrieved October 1, 2022, https://www.ahdictionary.com.

sensations, textures, temperatures, etc. It is incredible the amount of information that our brain is perceiving hour after hour.

Once we go to sleep, the brain has the opportunity to process all this information and rest. Touch is limited to perceiving those comfortable sheets and that expensive mattress; your ears are mostly at rest because you are not (at least not voluntarily and consciously) listening to music or conversing with someone; and your other senses, including taste and vision, are completely at rest. Your brain is now only perceiving a minimum of information, such as certain sounds that put you on alert or the feeling that someone else may be in the room and wake you up suddenly.

While your brain is operating and your senses are mostly at rest, your intuition and all the senses of your astral or spiritual body are active—now more than ever. They continue to perceive, process, send, and receive information such as sensations, emotions, conversations, visions, experiences, etc.

This information manifests as visions of places you have never visited before or conversations with a loved one who has passed away. So much information is being processed in the form of dreams, and those dreams are loaded with enormous symbolism and power.

For a person outside the magical spectrum, dreams may simply be an occasional vision that becomes an interesting topic of conversation in the workplace. For the common occultist or the most curious, dreams carry messages that must be deciphered with one of their dream interpretation manuals. For those of us who move within the magical spectrum, those who practice the occult arts, dreams are more than precognitions or visions of the future or the present that can be interpreted. For us, dreams are powerful visions of enormous meaning. Their symbols can be loaded with all kinds of hidden messages that can be given all kinds of interpretations. A dream can be a clear vision of a traumatic event from the past that can help us understand the events of the present; a warning about events close to happening in the future that are preventable or sometimes simply unavoidable; or, as it always happens to my mother, a visit from the familiar sorcerers who have gone before us and come to give you all kinds of spells and magical secrets.

For a sorcerer, dreams can play a pivotal role in crafting. They can answer questions that we have not yet been able to answer with a tarot deck. They can also be an instrument of powerful sorcery and a way to enter the dreams of a loved one and conquer them or enter the dreams of an enemy to exhaust them and weaken them from their rest (psychic attack).

Dreams can be used as a bridge for the sorcerer to move between different worlds, realities, and timelines through astral projection; to connect and make pacts with all kinds of spirits and entities, such as done within spiritualism and conjuring; to move back into the past and understand familiar situations like retrocognitions; or to even temporarily let go of their spirit and possess human and animal bodies at night as with shapeshifting.

Different Dreams and Different Magic

In this section, I am going to consciously define, identify, and separate various forms of sleep and their basic characteristics. This will be very useful to you as the book progresses and you put into practice the various exercises in it.

Common Dreams

These are those ordinary dreams where your role is limited to being an observer of events and moments. They are perhaps the most common, or at least we assume so due to lack of evidence to the contrary. They are the easiest dreams to interpret. They commonly represent a summary of recent events in quite familiar surroundings.

Vivid Dreams

Vivid dreams, which I will define fully later in this book, are part of the active dreaming family along with lucid dreaming. These dreams are full of information about events that have happened to us either recently or far back in the past. They are those dreams that allow us to reflect on the past and our decisions. They also lead us to remember old memories that, for some reason or another, we buried in the unconscious.

Lucid Dreams

Lucid dreams are another form of active dreaming. In these dreams, we are able to perceive information with our senses as if we were conscious. In a minority of cases, people remember it as one lucid dream in which they were conscious, but for the majority dreamers, these dreams present themselves as ordinary dreams in which some event or trigger leads the individual to wake up within the same dream and react, and once they are aware, they can act within the dream and verify its origin or purpose.

Lucid dreams are the most complex and difficult to interpret because once our consciousness takes power within them, most events, objects, and people present in the dream are influenced by our conscious mind. This spoils any type of subsequent interpretation of them.

Nightmares

Nightmares can be caused by stress, anxiety disorders, post-traumatic stress disorder, sleep apnea, or abuse of hallucinogenic substances. Nightmares are dreams worthy of being interpreted by experts. In these disturbing visions, we find symbolism associated with memories that we prefer to ignore for our own well-being; traumatic situations that are often related to our own childhood; or visions of events that have not happened but still cause us anxiety, such as dreaming of an earthquake occurring in your city or the death of a loved one.

In esoteric culture, nightmares are commonly considered a prediction of something abominable about to happen that we must prevent.

Day Dreams

There are two modern holistic views regarding day dreams. The first concludes that the dreams that occur during the day are influenced by the sun and the search for truth and light. This is in contrast to the dreams that occur at night, which are linked to the moon and its movements, allowing us to investigate nocturnal visions that take us to the depths of our subconscious being.

The second day dream belief has been greatly influenced by native tribes of Latin America. In this view, day dreams share messages from the living, those who still walk in the light of day, and they are unconsciously shared visions of daily events.

For the interpreter, dreams are pure information and are extremely important. The importance lies not just within the dream, though; the hour of day or night when the vision takes place can have a powerful significance for the dreamer and the interpreter. If a person holds a night job or for any other reason sleeps and has dreams during the hours of the day, between sunrise and sunset, their dreams are considered day dreams. They are different from dreams had at night. Note that this is not daydreaming, which is defined further in the following section.

Daydreams

Daydreams are dreams that occur while we are conscious and can happen unexpectedly. These dreams are mostly influenced by fantasies, dreams, personal goals, or frustrations that suddenly lead us to disconnect from reality. They can be used as a defense system to make us feel good when we need it or to motivate us to achieve certain goals.

Collective Dreams

Collective dreams occur when two or more people share a dream vision during rest. They can occur as a result of a cultural, religious, esoteric, or genetic link.

Common Dreaming versus Active Dreaming

In holistic terms there are two general types of manifestation of the dream: *common dreaming* and *active dreaming*. Common dreaming is an entirely unconscious and passive process. During these dreams, we surrender to guidance and continuous omens and allow ourselves to be carried directly by the dream states. Since we are in our most submissive state, we perceive and receive without any struggle from the conscious mind to understand the omens and signals.

Active dreaming is when we are able to direct the dream and act as our own guide. This process requires enormous practice and constant training. Individuals must be patient and dedicated because although some master this process within a few weeks, many take months to achieve it, and it may take years for many more.

The hours of sleep and the regularity of it have a huge influence on the active dreaming process. If your sleep hours are irregular due to work issues or constant schedule changes, or if you suffer from any type of complication related to sleeping hours, achieving active dreaming will be more difficult. Mastering this process typically requires a long period of rest without interruptions. Even if you have mastered it for a long time, if your sleep schedule begins to suffer from irregular changes, results can be affected and you can throw back several months of training.

The hours of sleep can always vary from one person to another depending on their level of stress and daily effort, personal relationships, diet, and work. On average, most people sleep about eight hours a day. Personally, I never sleep more than seven hours. In fact, I usually go to sleep between 1 and 2 a.m. and sleep five to six hours. I make up for it with a roughly thirty-minute nap during the day. It has always been like that. If I try to sleep longer, inevitably I only manage to lie in bed with my eyes closed, pretending to be asleep. It simply doesn't happen. My brain just won't accept sleeping longer.

However, active dreaming still works for me despite what could be considered getting only a few hours of sleep. It also works for my sister Neyber, and she sleeps almost twice as much as I do, making it clear that it is not the quantity but the quality of the rest time that really matters here.

It is necessary to understand the differences between common dreaming and living an active dream. Common dreaming is an entirely unconscious process during which we are certainly limited to being guided between dreams by a hand that we do not see. Active dreaming consists entirely of an active process, which can be moderately or entirely conscious. During this process, we take control of the dream, and we are able to make decisions within it and move with greater freedom.

Am I Having an Active Dream?

Here are the most common signs that you are experiencing an active dream. If you perceive one of these signs consciously during sleep or you wake up and remember having witnessed one or more of these signs, make notes about it for yourself. This will be useful in future practices.

- You remember being able to see your reflection on some surface during sleep. This is a conscious action that your mental body performs to be sure that you are living a dream and are fully present in it.
- You look at your hands during sleep. This action is a natural reaction of the mental body once it realizes that it is in another place

and not feeling physical changes. Looking at the hands is an immediate natural reaction to understand that we are inhabiting the body.

- You remember clear conversations with someone else, either someone you know or a stranger. If it is not a conscious dream, you will only remember having spoken with someone and not remember the actual conversation.

- You have extremely cold hands upon waking—especially if the rest of the body is at a different temperature. This may indicate that the body was facing a process similar to the near-death experience and was starting to cool down because the heartbeat has decreased. This is not a warning of dream danger; it is simply common for those who practice astral projection to wake up with incredibly cold hands in the morning.

- You remember simple geometric shapes that are very specific (golden triangles, silver circles, blue hexagons, etc.). Remembering them is a voluntary and conscious action of the mental body to somehow "mark" the path traveled during the process.

- You dream of specific places from your past where you experienced a traumatic or empowering situation. This is an indication of an active dream and/or awakening. During the dream process, our spiritual guides can lead us to relive these kinds of situations to understand the cause and consequences. In this way, they help us to shed more of the past and let go of old memories that are no longer useful to us.

Consciously Falling Out of Sleep

The feeling of falling, perhaps the most popular of all lucid dreaming experiences, is often confused with sleep myoclonus, or hypnic jerking, which occurs when the body jerks due to muscle contractions while we sleep. Often those spasms give a similar feeling to falling; however, you can differentiate between these unconscious spasms and consciously falling from lucid sleep with two easy-to-distinguish signs.

- You feel like you are falling, and when you wake up, the sensation prevails for a few seconds and is accompanied by a very rapid heartbeat, cold sweating, and the feeling of having very cold hands.
- You feel like you are falling, and when you wake up, you perceive certain sounds or aromas related to what you were dreaming about. An example would be dreaming you are in a field of violets or lavender and waking up to discover your room has a floral fragrance, despite not finding any flowers or similar perfume nearby.

If you identify these signs on a regular basis, chances are you are often in the process of active dreaming and you are entering lucid dreaming, either consciously or unconsciously.

There are many holistic methods related to the mystical art of dreams. If you want to train for active dreaming, although this is a function that usually occurs by itself in some individuals with years of psychic training, there are several complementary exercises that you can carry out once or twice a month, and some of these are included in this book. You can later increase the frequency of how often you perform them up to a maximum of two times a week. The most important thing during this process is to keep notes of everything you are doing in a notebook.

Dream Exercises

The following are two exercises of my own creation to perform at home. These exercises are made to help you to connect with your physical and spiritual environment and, in turn, lead you to work on developing a core, an internal energy system strong enough to support you with all kinds of medium, mystical practices in the future.

EXERCISE
Conscious Bilocation

This first working is based on a yoga exercise that was very useful for and complementarily to my individual practice years ago.

You will need:
- Cone of sandalwood or myrrh incense
- Censer, small cauldron, or heat-resistant plate
- Lighter or matches
- Comfortable cushion to sit on (optional)

Place the cone of incense in its holder, light it, and place the holder in a space close to you; it should be close enough to smell the amazing fragrance but distant enough to not bother you with the smoke. On the floor or on a cushion on the floor, sit cross-legged with relaxed arms extended and your hands resting on your knees (this is called lotus position in yoga). Close your eyes and take a deep breath.

Fix your closed eyes on nothing. Understand what you are not seeing. Your eyes are sealed, but they could see if you had not closed them. What they observe in these moments, just like when you are sleeping, is the complete lack of light.

Now, with your eyes still closed, perform two visualizations. First, visualize your environment. Visualize each and every one of the objects that surround you—plants, books, furniture, colors, appliances. Now visualize yourself. Take all the time you need; this will lead you to exercise your dream memory, which is the unconscious mind that comes into action while you sleep. In this way, you can develop the ability to visualize your own dreams and delve into them with more ease. When you end this visualization, breathe deeply and open your eyes.

The second visualization can be performed either just after the previous one or on another day. If it's another day, light another cone of incense in the censer, assume lotus position, and then shut your eyes as before. With your eyes closed, visualize a reflection of yourself forming right in front of you. Do not be afraid to be distracted by the details; give them the time they need. Visualize and project in this reflection everything you know and see about yourself, from the position in which you are sitting to the clothes and shoes that you're wearing, your hairstyle, and your way of breathing. Try to synchronize your breathing with the breathing of your reflection. Visualize how both breathe at the same time and in the same way. Now, it is time to hinder this visualization and take it to the next level.

Keep your eyes closed, keep your breathing deep, and keep visualizing this reflection of yourself. For an instant, both of you stop breathing. Hold the air for a moment and, while your reflection continues to hold, release the air. With your reflection still holding, take a deep breath again. As you hold the air, visualize your other self releasing the air. From this moment, count in complete silence up to twenty breaths, and while you exhale, your other self inhales. While you inhale, your other self exhales, and so on until you have both completed twenty breaths.

Once you have mastered this part of the exercise and carried it to perfection, you may move to the next level. If you feel that you have not yet mastered this exercise completely, do not advance. Instead, try the exercise again after a few hours or on the next day. If you advance to the next part of this exercise without having been able to fully visualize this breathing cycle, it can have consequences on your sleep hours during the following days. You will also end up blocking your own ability to visualize dreams properly.

If you have fully mastered this exercise, the next step is to repeat the simultaneous breathing between you and your visualized self for fifty breaths. After both you and your other self have finished breathing fifty breaths, inhale again. Slowly open your eyes and visualize your other self exhaling in front of you. Continue breathing and take another twenty breaths. As you breathe, do not stop staring into the eyes of this projection of yourself. Once you've reached twenty breaths, say aloud to your other self, "Thank you for making yourself present." Close your eyes, take a deep and slow breath, visualize your other self covered in light, and vanish in it while you hold your breath. Once this other you has disappeared, open your eyes. You will notice that it is no longer there. Now just get up, stretch, drink some water, and wait at least a week or two to repeat the exercise.

EXERCISE
The Maze

This exercise was something that I personally learned through practice in the dream world. This exercise is done to develop a clearer vision and per-spective of the dreams we witness. With constant practice, it will lead us to have clearer dreams, as well as to identify the signs in them and to under-stand the origin of our nightmares. For this ritual, we will use a dream jour-nal, or a diary exclusively intended to store your dreams and notes about them. This topic is covered in chapter 9, "Dream Journal."

You will need:
- Comfortable cushion to sit on
- 4 tablespoons coarse salt
- Colored paper (It can be yellow, blue, or purple, but not white.)
- Pen or pencil
- Lighter or matches
- Blue or white candle in candleholder
- Myrrh incense stick
- Incense holder
- Glass of water
- Dream journal

During any time between midnight and noon, place the cushion on the floor and use the coarse salt, which is a purifier, to mark four small dots on the floor around the cushion. On the paper, draw a series of lines to form a small map. Add lines to form corridors, and turn the map into a small maze of your own creation. Mark a point in the center of the maze (this is you). Once the maze is ready, proceed to light the candle and incense. Place the glass of water in front of you and sit on the cushion.

Do not read the rest of this exercise if you have not done the drawing, otherwise you will be much more aware of the activity, and you will not be able to let your subconscious do the work properly.

When ready, hold the map with one hand and hold the glass of water in the other hand. Visualize the map for several minutes in complete silence and without any kind of distraction. Take a sip of the water, close your eyes, and try to remember and visualize the map in your mind. Focus on it as long as you consider necessary, and do not open your eyes.

When you feel that you have the map completely made in your head, open your eyes and look at the map in your hand in great detail. It does not matter if it looks exactly the same as you imagined—that is also part of the exercise. Next, place the glass of water on the ground and hold the map with both hands.

Hold the map between you and the candle so that you perceive the light through the paper without seeing the fire. Now continue to study the maze you drew in detail. Observe the direction and form of the lines. Hold this focus for two minutes. Now lower your hands and close your eyes.

In the space of your mind, draw the map again. Remember the shapes and lines and their directions. Decipher the shapes and sequences that you used unconsciously to draw the map. Place and visualize the symbols that formed these lines, see which roads they are heading toward. Remember: You are in the center of this labyrinth. All roads lead to you, and all roads are molded around you.

Open your eyes again, place the map on the ground, and meditate. Breathing deeply and in complete silence, decipher which direction is the right one for you. Memorize those lines and paths. This map/maze is a manifestation of your subconscious and the paths of your mind and your dreams, so memorizing it is key to being able to move between dreams with greater freedom.

At the end of this meditation (five to ten minutes), fold the drawing and keep it in your dream journal near your bed. In your journal, take note of the day you performed this exercise. Wait about six months to do it again, drawing a new map. This exercise can be repeated every six months or done once a year.

Short-term results of this ritual: clearer dreams; less tendency to have nightmares; greater number of identifiable signs, faces, and symbols in dreams.

Long-term results of this ritual: a more active presence in your own dreams and deeper and longer dream states.

Dream Magic Insight
RESTFUL SLEEP TEA
BY DAWN AURORA HUNT

I am someone who struggles with sleep. A fast-paced life and a bit of anxiety often make sleep an elusive nighttime partner. Over the years, I have employed many strategies to help me sleep, not just to rest my body but also so that in the depth of sleep, dreams, guides, and spirits can reach my conscious and subconscious mind. Lucid dreaming is all good, but if your body cannot get enough sleep to dream in the first place, you will be out of luck.

Finding peace before your head hits the pillow may help you get to a deeper sleep sooner and stay there longer. The following is a recipe for a nighttime tea and my simple nighttime ritual to help you fill your mind with gratitude before drifting off. Be sure to use only organic herbs for consumption (not herbs treated with pesticides or dried improperly). When preparing this tea and spell before bed, it is a good practice to turn off or put away your phone and other devices before doing the work; do not recheck them until morning for the best results.

You will need:
- 2 tablespoons dried peppermint leaves
- 2 tablespoons dried passionflower
- 2 tablespoons dried chamomile
- 2 tablespoons dried valerian root
- 2 tablespoons dried lavender
- Large bowl
- Mixing spoon
- Airtight, opaque container
- Water
- Disposable paper tea bag
- Edible marker pen (usually used for decorating cakes and cookies)

- Large mug
- Honey (to your taste)
- Spoon

To make the loose-leaf tea, simply add all ingredients and stir them together in a large bowl so the herbs are evenly distributed. Once that is done, you can store the tea in an airtight, opaque container for up to a year.

About thirty minutes before you plan to go to bed, bring water to a boil. While the water is coming to a boil, prepare the tea bag. Using your edible marker pen, write three things you are grateful for on the paper tea bag. These can be as simple as "heat," "food," or "my cat" if you can't think of anything else. Scoop your desired amount of loose tea into the bag, seal it properly, and place it in the mug. At this point, add the honey. As you drizzle or scoop the honey, envision the sweetness of the things you are grateful for and how they enrich your life.

Once the water boils, pour the hot water into the mug. Stir your tea clockwise until the honey dissolves and the writing on the tea bag disappears. Steep the tea for no less than three minutes. Remove the tea bag and dispose of it.

Sip your tea mindfully, thinking about how grateful you are for the things you have. If you have time or feel called to, write one page in a journal describing why you are grateful for the things you wrote on the tea bag. Let these thoughts be the last before you enter into a deep, peaceful slumber after you have drank all the tea filled with gratitude.

TRIBAL TALES
THE WAYÚU PEOPLE AND GUAJIRO PEOPLE

The Wayúu and Guajiro peoples live mostly between Colombia and Venezuela. They are part of the Arawak ethnic group. This group is divided into more than a dozen clans among more than sixty territories. They are the largest Indigenous ethnic group in Colombia and one of the largest Indigenous ethnic groups in Venezuela, where almost three hundred thousand members live.

Much of their religion and many of their myths revolve around Maleiwa, the creator of everything, especially everything that moves, lives, and breathes, as well as the founder of society and order. His companions (or children, according to some versions), Pulowi and Juya, represent the balance that inhabits all living things. Pulowi is femininity, the devastating wind, and the breeze, while Juya is masculinity, manifesting as a wild and nomadic hunter. Both are presented together as a married couple, symbolizing procreation, continuity, and life. A part of both inhabits everything that exists.

Juya usually appears in dreams as a native hunter dressed in colored skins with his face painted black. He acts as a guard so that no one enters dreams, including the deceased that were cremated and not buried (which differentiates them from most of the Amazon tribes, as they still bury their bodies) or the Javi, who act as nocturnal demons made of shadow and animal blood.

When Pulowi is not present in dreams, Wanülu, the spirit that embodies evil, envy, disease, and death, is allowed to enter dreams. This creates all kinds of nightmares and horrendous visions, thus depriving humans of sleep and creating further physical discomfort, which can lead to illness, irritability, and insanity.

Lapü means "dream" in Wayuunaiki, the language of the Wayúu. This term is used to identify two things. First, Lapü is the native deity or spirit that transmits dreams from one individual to another. Second, the term identifies all those visions that move between the liminality of the material world and the dream world. That is why, in Venezuela and Colombia, the Guajira Peninsula is considered the magical and dreamlike territory where dreams are born and sent to the rest of the world. It is also the most popular place to find the famous Wajes, or interpreters of dreams who are descendants of the Wayúu.

For the Wayúu, dreaming of the soul of a deceased person means that their tomb is not consecrated or the rites of the same were not completed. It means the body must be exhumed, perfumed, and prepared to receive a second grave on a night when the moon is not in the sky.

It is of vital importance to follow the mandates of the Oütshii, Outsu, or Jarima—a woman of the tribe who is prepared and trained to be the traditional doctor and herbalist. She is the one who best knows the art of curing with herbs and can heal against all kinds of poisons. She also knows how to interpret dreams and decides who will be the next in the order.

Usually the Piachi and the Alijunas (young maidens of the tribe who move around the city, although both terms often also apply to small children and the elderly) receive signs from their ancestors through dreams. Once they narrate these dreams to the Jarima (considered in these cases a high priestess), she will know who has been chosen. According to tradition, they all receive the same dream with the same message, and this message is passed from generation to generation through dreams.

For the descendants of the Wayúu people, especially those who still practice the old traditional religion, the *alapujawaa* (sleeping action) does not only refer to closing the eyes and resting until the next morning. It is also the transit of *aa in* (the soul) through the Japu, or Japira, (world of dreams) while our body rests, and from there we have the virtue of communicating with our spirit guides and with each and every one of our ancestors.

For the Wayúu who interprets dreams, there are six questions that must be asked, always in the same order. They represent the six steps that the soul takes from the world of dreams before waking up again in the world of the living:

1. How was your most recent dream?
2. Have you had that same dream before?
3. Is there anything that seems familiar to you in that dream?
4. Did you see yourself or a deceased relative in the dream?
5. What do you think this dream means and why?
6. What do you think you are ignoring or forgetting about that dream?

CHAPTER 2

THE BIGGEST REALM

Dreams guide you to discover your true magical potential; in them lie all the memories of your spiritual powers from past lives. The dream world is your biggest realm. Dreams act like wild creatures that come and go without our control over them. They are nocturnal creatures, visitors of instinct that move between worlds without the need for permission. When we force them to come, they laugh and escape, and for that reason, a witch should never try to take control over lucid dreaming—just flow with it. They try to understand them and pursue them, to invoke and study them, but never to control them. In fact, trying to control dreams is like trying to control the ocean with one hand. Magic, in truth, is to immerse yourself within the experience—as you do in both dreams and the ocean.

No one can teach you to dream, just as no one can teach you to feel love. Dreams are sensations that come and go, like passengers, and we must let them come, hug them when they are here, and give thanks when we see them leave. They are never static; they are changing, alchemical, internal transmutators that can influence your mood and your day simply by manifesting as a beautiful vision or as a fearsome nightmare.

What you can control are the visions you choose to have within the dream once it arrives. With some practice, you can immerse yourself in it, prolong it, make it clearer, and even move within it more easily, but you are never going to have control over everything that is the dream. The process is where your power lies.

Many people believe that our brain turns off to sleep, but it is the opposite. Once the sleep mechanism is activated, the brain goes through a series of very elaborate organic operations within which two things occur.

First, your brain processes and stores all the information that was received during the day. Once you are asleep, completely unconscious, your brain can work without any distraction.

Second, your brain deals with all kinds of emotional situations that happened during the day. I believe there is nothing better than a good nap between one day and another to help you make a decision because during the sleep processes, our unconscious is finally dealing with reality and deciding what to do. When you wake up in the morning, even after a stressful night or busy day, you feel much better and much less tense because your brain has processed an enormous amount of information and emotions, which leads you to generate better decisions, leading you to better results.

Processing Stimuli

Unless you are an experienced medium or psychic, you will notice that it is practically impossible for you to receive signals and pick up on certain omens while you are awake, even if you are clearly looking for them. Your mind is sharp when you are awake, so your senses are processing all the stimuli from the external world and sending all that information to your brain. The brain is capturing and storing everything while you deal with your emotions and reactions to these stimuli. All of that is happening every second that you are awake. It is difficult to pick up a signal this way.

When you are asleep and visiting your inner self in the world of dreams, your eyes remain closed, your senses of touch and taste are practically at rest, and therefore you can only perceive some outside sensations and sounds. Your brain is still working but your conscious self is resting, or at least working less. It is then that you, your innermost I, that individual entity that moves between the conscious self and the unconscious self, can enter the world of dreams and then receive and interpret all kinds of messages and signals.

Once you are immersed in the dream process, all the information you receive is from the unconscious, so you are fully able to receive omens and all kinds of wisdom coming from other realms. These realms all connect with the world of dreams, and it is important that you understand that these worlds are inhabited by all kinds of messengers. There are spirits that, once they manifest, are easily mistaken for angels, fairies, nymphs, dryads, mermaids, and even goblins, plus many creatures of our kingdom. Many of them are, but many are from other dream worlds and realms, so keep your mind open. Instead of being scared by what you see or trying to understand why these creatures and beings look the way they do, just flow with them.

You are living many lives at once in many different worlds. Don't forget that as you wake up in this world, you are simply asleep in the others.

The Kingdom of Dreams

The kingdom of dreams works like a train station. All other kingdoms connect with it, as it is the central pillar that ties them all together. Have you ever practiced astral projection or doubling? If so, have you ever seen those rapid tunnels of light at the beginning that you must eventually detach yourself from in order to advance?

Whether you have seen them or not, that is the transit you are doing. Those tunnels are part of the intermediate realm, the world of dream walkers, where souls awaken after dying and before moving to any other realm where they belong.

The realm of dreams acts as the intermediate realm for the simple reason that consciousness is able to enter there with practically no effort. The spirits and souls of the deceased, once they are unconscious, enter there at the first attempt. Other realms, such as the astral realm or the realm of spirits, require much more work and determination to breach.

This kingdom is perhaps also the most confusing of all because everyone passes through there at some point, even animals. Have you ever dreamed of a dog, cat, or bird? They are not always just visions; many times they are souls that cross each other in dreams. Dreams are full of signs, stories, memories and experiences, deceased souls, gods, and, as mentioned, all kinds of spirits, such as angels and fairies and others that only inhabit these realms, making them difficult to learn about in books.

Conscious access to this realm while we remain asleep will lead us into contact with all kinds of spiritual guides and teachers. Many of them are waiting for a disciple to whom they'll grant the mystical and esoteric secrets never revealed in life. Other teachers are waiting for someone specific, and they will not reveal their secrets to you no matter how much you insist.

It is in dreams that our psychic power probably reaches its greatest potential. Once your conscious mind is free from all distractions and resting, your subconscious is able to operate at its maximum power, and for that reason, psychic attacks occur mostly at night. The people who seek to harm you through the use of spells, amulets, or buried magical works are going to take advantage of this and attack you while you sleep.

This energy will feel stronger at night for many reasons, including the basic factors mentioned in many witchcraft books such as people realizing hexing and cursing at midnight or summoning spirits and working with demons and other spirits at night. There may also be people who wish to harm you by entering your dreams. These people will wait until a point in the night when you are supposed to be asleep and unaware of what is happening around you.

If your mind does not have the proper training, it is quite easy to receive these attacks in your hours of rest. This is another reason why we should focus on learning to master the way our energy manifests itself, even while we are sleeping. You can use the energy that your body emanates during the night to charge amulets, use energy shields, and perform certain spells that you carry out before sleeping.

Great past-life scholars, who work with the subject of regressions, understand that a past-life regression involves pushing one's consciousness into the intermediate world. During this regression process, an experienced individual can use their knowledge to push your mind/consciousness beyond the limits of the physical plane and into the intermediate world. It is only a matter of waiting a short period of time to make you connect with your past lives. However, this energetic process is exhausting for both of you, and it may require multiple sessions to fully connect with a complete vision of your past self.

Dreamland and Dream Walking

We all connect with the magical world of dreams, visions, and illusions regardless of age, gender, sexual orientation, ethnicity, location, or language. We are all tiny particles of existence. From the youngest babies to the oldest elders, once we enter the world of dreams, we are all participants in this majestic adventure.

My parents told me that dreams were the doors to the spirit world, a world of visions and memories that only the most dedicated could understand. I grew up agreeing with this vision for many years, but after a certain age, I began to disagree. I realized that dreams were not doors or portals to the world of spirits but the keys to many different worlds and planes of existence. I understood, after much study and dedication, that the world of dreams works as a transfer station, like those between trains. You arrive, buy your ticket, locate the corresponding rail, and board your train in the correct direction.

Before understanding this, I only saw the world of dreams as a paradisiac valley of flowers with a thick, cloudy sky. Now the world of dreams reminds me more of Grand Central Terminal in New York City. If you have ever been to Manhattan, you may have visited this place, and surely, like many, you were impressed with the wild creativity of its architecture. It is one of the largest train stations in the world with gigantic granite walls, cream and pink marble decorations between platforms and floors, sumptuous staircases and arches, and platforms and corridors that blend together. At the entrance, there are statues of the Pagan gods Vulcan and Minerva watching a naked Mercury rise above them, holding his caduceus and stepping on a large gold clock on an arch of glory. Other statues and huge steel eagles act as guardians at certain points of the station. And let me not neglect the central star, a bluish barrel vault ceiling covered with bright stars depicting the constellations that are visible during winter. Of course newer visitors and less frequent passengers stop to gaze at this enchanting sky and lose themselves in its stars, often forgetting the passage of time—just like in a dream.

Similarly, when you go to sleep, you find yourself in a world so diverse that words cannot describe it. When you awake, you might try to put everything into words, detail by detail, but as many times as you visualize it and make the effort to remember it, the dream changes. Sometimes you even begin to recall and observe details that were, perhaps, not even there at first.

Entering the world of dreams is not and has never been an easy task. In fact, it is much easier to fall into frustration in the attempt. This is not because you cannot do it, though, but because we are used to getting things faster. We order food because it is faster than cooking; we order clothes online because it is easier and faster than going shopping at the store. When you finally immerse yourself in a world where time is not conditioned by your mind and you accept that most of the time you are not going to be in control of what happens, it's natural for frustration to arise. The secret is to get carried away by the dream. The dream knows perfectly where it needs to take you. It is not controlling you. It is guiding you.

Remember, again, that dreams are not one place. They are the keys that open the doors to different worlds: the unconscious, the world of memories, the dark world where you store your traumas and sorrows from the past, the future through visions, the world of spirits, and the astral world. That latter world is perhaps the largest of all, and that is because it is not a world at all—it is a conglomeration and reflection of all worlds, made of pure energy and constantly expanding.

I wrote the following lines and titled the poem "The Ayahuasca Goddess" after a visit to the Orinoco River. It was inspired by the presence of Curigjui, the wisest goddess of the land, who communicates with humans through the plants.

Her eyes were made of river and moonlight
Her hair was woven of night and stars
Her skin was made of salt and coal

Among men and animals she walked barefoot
All of them knelt at her arrival
Her feet made fertile the land she walked on
Her breasts overflowing with milk nourished the soil at dusk

When the last perdition crossed the great river
And great clouds laden with death rode the waves
Her name was hidden in the mouth of the last serpent
And her precious name cut her serpent's tongue in two
So no one else could ever summon her

She hid in the depths of the earth
Her hair grew to cover the forests and to cover the rivers
And the intoxicating aroma of her hair would open the doors
to a world that the souls could not reach without her blessing.

Religious Insight

Multiple cultures have considered dreams sacred beyond their association with the night and subsequent awakenings. This is due to their connection to a superior divinity and with the realms of death—with the transformation process that we call mortality. For long periods of time, dreams were considered something to be thankful for in the mornings. This was because you never know with total certainty that you will wake up after closing your eyes to sleep.

Venezuelan Indigenous Communities

Among the descendants of the Arawaks, who basically make up approximately 1.5 percent of the Venezuelan population, dreams constitute an escape to the divine world, a world made up of aquatic beings and deities. It is an underwater world to which only spirits and ancestors have access, meaning the seas and rivers are a reflection of it in the earthly world. For them—or, more specifically, for the ethnic groups of the Amazon that include the Kurripako, the Wanikua, the Wenaiwika or Piapoco, the Warekena, and the Bari—dreams are a mysterious way that the ancestors send messages from beyond and remind us that they are there, waiting for us.

Extinct Indigenous Ethnic Groups of the Amazon

The extinct peoples and evangelized ethnic groups of the Jirajara, the Ayoman, the Gayones, the Waikerí, and the Máku (the latter coming from Brazil) had folklore rich in natural elements that contemplated parts of life as aspects of divinity. Among these various mestizo peoples, including descendants of the Waraos and the Jirajaras, dreams formed a detailed system of religious study that was duly interpreted by priests and whose secrets and methods were transmitted orally from a priest to an initiate to keep the secrets to themselves.

Although these ethnic groups and their languages are extinct, there is much that is told about them in the history books. They were fishers, warriors, and farmers who interpreted dreams as omens of destiny and as memories of their ancestors transmitted from generation to generation.

Christianity

Among the followers of Christianity, dreams are seen both as prophetic and as a representation of the divine connection between human beings and God. The Bible mentions dreams and alludes to them as mystical visions full of messages from God in at least twenty-four verses, and I've included a few just to mention some of the sacred visions.

Genesis 20:3

But God came to Abimelech in a dream by night and said to him, Behold, thou art but a dead man, for the woman which thou hast taken; for she is a man's wife.

Genesis 28:12–14

12 And he dreamed, and behold a ladder set up on the earth, and the top of it reached to heaven: and behold the angels of God ascending and descending on it.

13 And, behold, the Lord stood above it, and said, I am the Lord God of Abraham thy father, and the God of Isaac: the land whereon thou liest, to thee will I give it, and to thy seed;

14 And thy seed shall be as the dust of the earth, and thou shalt spread abroad to the west, and to the east, and to the north, and to the south: and in thee and in thy seed shall all the families of the earth be blessed.

For those interested in knowing more about these sources in the biblical aspect, I invite you to consult Genesis 37:5–10 and Matthew 1:20.

Hindu Philosophy

According to the Indian physician Charaka (first to second century AD) and the editor behind the *Charaka Samhita* and *Susruta Samjita*, which are the fundamental texts of Ayurveda medicine (the traditional medicine of India), dreams, or Swapna, are a fundamental part of human life. We, as human beings, immerse ourselves in a dream world that reflects a large part of our conscious activities.[7]

According to the sacred teachings of Charaka, there are a total of seven classes of dreams, and the signs within them can be of good fortune or misfortune. The classes are as follows:

1. *Dṛṣṭa:* The sleeper dreams of something that they have seen in their daily life.
2. *Śruta:* The sleeper dreams of something that has entered their mind through the auditory pathway.
3. *Anubhūta:* The dreams are generated by external sensations picked up while sleeping.
4. *Prārthita:* The dreams are created or influenced by internal desires.
5. *Kalpita:* The dreams are fantasies generated by the mind.

....

7. Eranimos and Funkhouser, "The Concept of Dreams and Dreaming."

6. *Bhāvita:* The dreams are premonitory dreams.

7. *Doṣaja:* The dreams are caused by an altered state of mind. This type can be further divided into physical (*phala*) or psychological (*aphala*).[8]

Jewish Thought

According to the Talmud, dreams are of enormous importance among Jewish people. They are proof of the existence of the afterlife, as well as a place where the medium is able to communicate with others. Here is an example of this belief as described in the article "Dreams in the Talmud and in Depth Psychology" by Susan Vorhand, PhD:

> There is an idea within the Talmud that all spiritual realities have a counterpart in the physical world so that we can experience a taste of them. Accordingly, Talmudic sages claim that "Sleep is one-sixtieth of death" and "Dreams are one-sixtieth of prophecy." (Babylonian Talmud, Berachot, 57b). The body at rest abdicates control, while the soul separates a bit and roams free. Immediately upon awakening each morning the pious Jew recites the following prayer: "I am grateful to You, O living and eternal King, for You have returned my soul within me with compassion—abundant is Your graciousness." (Siddur, 1984 p. 2).[9]

Among the followers of the mystical path of the Qabalah, meeting face-to-face with the deceased is not possible because these meetings do not occur face-to-face but soul-to-soul. For this reason, the medium is trained to meet them and converse with them through dreams.[10]

The Talmud tells the story of a rabbi who walks among dreams, and in them, a sage appears. The wise old man speaks to the rabbi in his dreams and

....

8. Varela, *Sleeping, Dreaming, and Dying.*

9. Vorhand, "Dreams in the Talmud and in Depth Psychology."

10. Jewish Kabbalah emerged as a religious form of mysticism based on the study of the Torah, while mystical Qabalah, spelled with a Q, is a hermetic practice that explores different aspects of life, magic, alchemy, and the cosmos.

informs him of things that he would not know or that he would be unable to find out in the world of the living.[11]

Among the Jews during the medieval era, dreams were taken to be of such importance that they could be used to break or modify the law, as shown in this following example:

> In Havre, in 1637, the city court declared a child legitimate when the mother swore that her husband, missing for four years, had embraced her in a dream. To such fantastic lengths Jewish belief did not go. Yet a vow or a decree of excommunication pronounced in a dream was held to be real and binding, even more so than one uttered during waking hours, for the latter could be voided before a court of three men, while the former required a full congregation of ten, the idea being that since the deity had somehow been involved in the dream action, only a minyan, over which the Shechinah presided, had the power to release the dreamer.[12]

But the Talmud also says, "Nothing happens to a man, good or ill, before he has beheld some intimation of it in a dream." This is to briefly mention that everything that happens for good or bad is—and has always been—announced in dreams as a prophecy and codified for the unique understanding and interpretation of the wisest and most knowledgeable sages.[13]

Magic and Dreams

Magic and spells linked to the world of dreams are highly relevant for those who practice divination or those who are blessed with the gift of clairvoyance. Mediums and witches can benefit from using the symbols and messages hidden in dreams to anchor their own magic between dreams and reality and to predict the future and even understand the past. In this particular field, if you learn to work with your dreams, to move more comfortably

....

11. The Talmud is an ancient collection of texts that form the heart and core of Jewish religious law and theology; it is also known as Babylonian Talmud.
12. Trachtenberg, *Jewish Magic and Superstition*.
13. Epstein, *Babylonian Talmud*.

within them, and to remember them, you will have many great tools at your fingertips.

Dreams are an infinite source of information, and they connect you with the deepest wisdom. Once you are inside them, you are able to access worlds from which you can collect all kinds of information about yourself, your life, the universe, and the past and the future. For the experts, it is even possible to collect information about past lives.

What you see as dreams are often just very light veils through which you observe other worlds. It's a thin curtain that keeps your subconscious in a safe area, telling you "do not pass this line" to prevent you from getting lost. It is for this reason that in this book you will learn how to channel a guide in the world of dreams to take you by the hand.

With constant practice, you will learn to sleep better, delve into dreams more quickly, develop more clarity and understanding within them, direct your course within them, and walk through old memories of past lives. The most advanced practitioners will then learn how to carefully delve into the dreams of other individuals, protect themselves against psychic and magical attacks that may occur while they sleep, and unfold themselves in these ethereal worlds, manifesting their own energy body within them.

The Intermediate World

Another reason I call the dream world the intermediate world is because it functions as the perfect rest area. In it, you can mediate between the various other worlds, which helps you to make contact with various spirits. There are three reasons why meditating in the dream world is an important practice:

1. The intermediate world is the most easily accessible place among all the worlds, as was already stated in the previous chapter. It allows the living to contact beings from other worlds, including the dead.
2. It is the fastest way to find and make a pact with spirit guides and guardian spirits. Although we are more vulnerable in the intermediate world, we are safer there than in the astral plane or other energy worlds, which require more states of consciousness.

3. Meditating in the intermediate world leads you to expand your senses beyond your body, and once this happens, you are able to develop senses corresponding to the spiritual body.

Sailing Accompanied

Navigating the world of dreams on your own can feel very complicated the first few times. Between meditation and other exercises, it takes constant work, and it often takes several weeks to months before you achieve the results you expect. I say this without any intention of discouraging the reader but because we live in a society where we appreciate quick results, even if they are mediocre results, and feel enormous contempt toward constant work and the commitment of realization. However, when it comes to magic and science, the commitment is what brings true results.

As you progress, you will feel that you are learning to swim much faster, and after some time, you will stop swimming in the pool, so to speak, and graduate to swimming in rivers and beaches without even knowing when you made the change.

That being said, it is important for you to know the dangers that are there, in those waters, and the problems that may come up. Here is what you can expect:

- In the least of the cases, you will get a strong, constant headache.
- A much more common problem is coming across various kinds of illusions, such as specters and projections, which are there to scare you and drive you away.
- In some of the worst cases, you may find yourself face-to-face with non-gentle spirits and specters that take all kinds of forms to deceive you, such as the form of a loved one or someone whom you personally idealize very much.

It is after at least two or three months of constant practice and meditation that you should advance to the next level, which is to summon a guardian spirit. You can carry out this practice entirely alone. You do not need a formal teacher.

With a guardian spirit on your side, you will have an entity that will take you practically by the hand and guide you intuitively all the way. Although many will not see the spirit guide projecting itself in their dreams or meditations, it remains there, hovering and moving stealthily to act and protect if the situation arises.

The guardian is never chosen, although we all would probably like to conjure what seems to be the most powerful of all guardians. The rituals performed to conjure a guardian work mostly as a powerful magnet, attracting a spirit willing to offer you support and guidance in your processes, rituals, and constant practices, which, in turn, lead you to anchor your own individual connection with said spirit so that you perceive its presence closer and closer.

While anyone could take a ritual and modify it, or even rewrite it entirely, to seek to attract a much stronger spiritual guardian than is really necessary (as some books and their authors encourage you to do), it is much more appropriate to act calmly, wisely, and with discipline and understand that the guardian spirit that comes to you is at your level of learning or slightly above. It should not be a spirit that can take control over you or energetically abuse you, forcing you to do their work.

The Profound Wisdom of Dreams

Beyond connecting us with spirits, dreams also connect us with the profound wisdom of creation and with divinity (by whatever name you call it). While access to dreams allows us to clarify certain emotions and situations, the understanding that is acquired through them allows us to delve deeper into these fields of magic and wisdom and understand the reason behind all the situations that occur in our environment. This includes emotions that remain blocked and seek to manifest themselves, karmic situations that are forcing events around us, promises from the past that seek to be fulfilled, and even spells and hexes performed by a magician who seeks to move certain circumstances in their favor.

All conscious individuals are capable of sounding and entering these worlds, and all of us have access to a great variety of energy tools in these worlds. However, it requires enormous practice and dedication to achieve these journeys, especially to be able to understand dreams, interpret messages that come with them, and retain clear memories of them.

Magic is perhaps the most direct way to delve into the understanding of the subconscious's processes. While modern science focuses on explaining the processes of sleep and their states, the great philosophers and thinkers have given us centuries of advantage in seeking to understand dreams, their purpose and reason for being, and their origins.

The dreams, daydreams, and visions that we receive during the day, especially during meditation, are ways of making these inward journeys, right where the doors to these otherworlds are. The key to entering the world of dreams, as well as the world of spirits, is to stop looking for these worlds outside; the access to them is inside.

An old legend of Venezuelan Wayúu folklore, which I have translated here, says:

> **Then, after finishing the work, painting the last sunset with their blood, piling up mountains and rivers with their own hands, the great creative spirit departed. They rose to the heavens where they set the sun. They continued on, carrying the moon made of fire, mud, mother's milk, and rock. They continued to rise up high, high above the sun, high like the stars, where they then created other worlds, and more worlds that danced between these worlds.**

This old legend, of which there are many modern interpretations, talks about how the great creative spirit sacrificed himself after his last dream. Once he woke up, he painted the world and the heavens and rose up to them to create other worlds, which can only be reached when sleeping.

The Dream World and the Astral Plane

The dream world is an intermediary world and one world among many. In contrast to popular belief, it is not the same as the astral plane, just as the United States of America is not all of the Americas. It is only a small part of everything that the energetic universe comprises.

More information exists in our Indigenous South American communities about the world of dreams than about the astral world, which is frequently discussed in magical circles. We dream at different levels but never consciously enter the astral plane. Unlike dreaming, those who work on the astral plane remember their experiences.

Of the two, however, the dream world, or the intermediate world, as I call it, is the world we enter more easily, either during deep meditation in the morning or sleeping soundly at night. To help clarify, imagine that you live in an apartment and want to go out to the market. Once you leave your apartment, you find yourself in a long corridor with many doors. Once you get on the elevator at the end of the corridor and arrive at the main floor, you go to the front door of the building. Once you cross it, you find yourself on the street, which represents the entire energy universe, or a series of planes of existence that coexist with each other in almost perfect harmony. However, the corridors on various floors of your building represent the many astral planes, which are accessible from many places and from many dimensions. The elevator is your dream span, a small underworld that allows you to enter all the others. It is the oneiric, intermediate world, the world of dreams, the one that connects them all to each other.

Those who have more experience or connection with the astral plane go through these dream worlds without even realizing it, without paying much attention to details. Those who are constantly practicing to achieve their conscious awakening in the astral worlds briefly walk through these long corridors that connect virtually with the dreams of others. In this way, these corridors allow us to be fully connected while we rest.

Multiple Astral Planes

The energetic universe is built entirely of energy; it is essentially energy and frequency. Within the energetic universe are the astral worlds, which are these uncountable. They are infinite, although human beings only access three of them in our processes of mediumship.

First, there is the "higher" astral plane. This plane is not called "higher" because it is above but simply because of a misconception that has grown over the centuries about relating the sky with the good and the lower worlds with the bad. The higher astral plane is a place of infinite light and energy; it feels like sailing inside a rainbow. The amount of light is such that it can result in an experience as addictive as it is overwhelming for simple human beings. This plane is the place where the spiritual beings of light live (angels and very ancient creator gods), as well as ascended masters. We could say that in a certain way Jesus, Buddha, and the great teachers, such as Saint Germain and Serapis Bey, belong to this plane.

The intermediate astral plane is in every aspect the astral plane that many of us know and about which we read in books. It is an eternal and ancient place made entirely of energy, where all kinds of creatures and beings converge, from ghosts and spirits to divinities, teachers, and the so-called astral larvae, which are minor entities without consciousness that usually escape from these planes and act as larvae that adhere to and steal our energy. This astral plane is energetically linked to the dream world, and they are slightly separated from each other by what seems to be a subtle network, which is described by teachers and spirits as a curtain woven like a fishing net with a fine golden thread. Once you discover it, you will feel as if you have walked all over the world with a transparent bandage over your eyes and hadn't even noticed it.

The lower astral plane, misinterpreted by the modern Christian conception of the underworld, which was borrowed from the Pagan myths of ancient Greece, is the third astral plane that humans can access. It is known as the sacred precinct of the otherworld. Here live all the individuals who had a very traumatic life and who were not presented with the opportunity to work on it (or never took such an opportunity when it was presented). These are individuals who lived so full of regret, hatred, and sadness that when they died, they did not manage to advance in the spiritual world because all of these chains that keep them tied to the physical world. After some time, they end up submerged in the lower plane, like heavy rocks that sink in the sea and, after some time, are crushed by the deep weight of the ocean.

My mother, who has more than forty years of practice of brujeria and traditional Venezuelan spiritualism, said that when you tried to communicate with the afterlife and conjure a specific soul but only saw darkness or felt a terrible weight on the shoulders, it meant the soul corresponded to someone who had died in disgrace or had a very hard life until the end. She advises to pray to the spirits of light and Saint Michael the Archangel to free these people and help them ascend. But she also told me that helping those souls required much more commitment than a few prayers and a couple of candles.

There are infinite planes of existence, or astral worlds, to which only other (nonhuman) beings can access because they are more spiritually advanced beings. They are more disconnected from the physical world, and these beings are more enlightened than us and our race.

A Convergence of Beings

Because the dream world connects all these planes, it is a place where all conscious beings can converge, and if there is a conscious mind there, then there is also an unconscious side, a deep place within the mind where memories, emotions, information, and experiences are stored. Therefore, if it is conscious in this or in some otherworld, in this or in another life, it must also have an unconscious being that manifests itself in the dream world—an energetic extension of itself.

While the physical world is inhabited by human beings, plants, animals, and bacteria (and perhaps aliens, but that is a task for another author), the astral worlds are inhabited by other species, species that, unlike us, are not made of carbon but of other entirely different elements. Just as angels were forged from light and djinns from fire in pre-Islamic Arab belief, each and every one of their worlds must have been forged as well.

Something that is taught in modern metaphysics, especially in the schools of Saint Germain or contemporary metaphysics and Conny Méndez or Christian metaphysics, is that the physical world that we know is the world to which we have adapted. According to this belief system, the world is seen from two different perspectives.

Just as dreams are free of physical rules, our physical world is governed by a series of rules and characteristics, such as gravity, time, space, matter, and temperature. These rules determine practically everything that surrounds us, while dreams are independent of these guidelines that force our vision and perspective.

Humans, as walking beings, have learned to see the world horizontally, and I dare to say we even think horizontally, probably as a result of being subject to the force of gravity. If we try to see and understand the word from a spiritual perspective, which is the vision of fairies and other spiritual beings, we can understand the freedom of the dreams. When you understand something so simple like that, dreams immediately turn into a powerful ally for you as a witch. These beings can have a vertical and deep perspective of the world, and therefore in many esoteric traditions, including the tradition of *La Corte de las Brujas* (the witch's court), one of the native traditions in Venezuela, the world is interpreted from a vertical vision with planes of existence above and below, which rise and descend in different energetic frequencies.

- *Example 1:* When you drive and park a car, you are not looking down and up. Instead, you are sitting behind the wheel, and a set of mirrors properly located on the sides and in front of you serve as a guide to understand your surroundings at all times, or at least your horizontal environment. When driving down a large multilane bridge, you are not worrying about colliding with the roof because you know that the roof is up. What worries you are the cars on both sides of you.

- *Example 2:* You are going to rent or buy a property. When was the last time that the seller or the owner of the property mentioned the height of the ceiling? For sure they mentioned the horizontal measurements of the apartment, house, or bedroom, the distance between one wall and another, and based on those measurements you might have looked for a bed, table, or other piece of furniture suitable for the space. But again, in all these conversations, no one probably mentioned or asked about the height of the ceiling. Unless you're thinking of hanging that gigantic 200-bulb Victorian chandelier you inherited from your grandma's huge fortune, just knowing the height of the ceiling probably doesn't seem to be relevant to you.

This is not all to say that height is not important, but this example is to make you understand that the rules that govern the physical field that surrounds you do not govern or act on the dream world. Even when you are awake, it also surrounds you. Just as humanity discovered that the earth is round, our oldest masters discovered that the planes of existence all obey their own rules. They just mostly lack our own rules.

In Christian metaphysics, for example, according to the Venezuelan author, poet, and folklorist Conny Méndez, the physical universe is more like an experimental field of study where rules—human rules and laws—are fundamental to our existence, as well as rules of physics and the laws of chemistry.[14] "Nothing is created, nothing is destroyed, everything is transformed" is a phrase attributed to the French alchemist Antoine Lavoisier that indicates that all the elements in the universe, including water, simply change their molecular structure to pass from one form to another.[15]

In turn, the followers of Méndez's metaphysical perspective seriously reinterpret her words, using this as lore to complement the Indigenous conception that other universes could exist in between, such as the astral plane and the dream world, just to mention some, which makes it different from all other universes.[16] This model of thought coincides not only with the spiritual traditions and oral folklore of the Indigenous natives, who consider the otherworld to be a world made of water and spirit, but also with the teachings attributed to the ascended master Saint Germain.[17] Saint Germain was a European alchemist who became famous for constantly appearing and disappearing from different places without using doors, even appearing in several places at the same time, and for his anecdotes of trips to the future and the past, indicating that the laws of physics, mainly those of time and space, were alien to him. He had a great understanding of the universe and the astral worlds.

The planes of existence end up looking like a *matryoshka*, or a Russian doll, which is hollow and contains another doll inside it that, in turn, contains another doll and so on, going on to have five or more dolls inside (always ending in an odd number). The planes of existence closely mirror these dolls. Each plane exists on top of another. Our physical world, being one of the youngest internal planes, remains covered by another plane, and this plane, in turn, is covered by others. Examining the planes of existence is more of an inside out thinking model, not top down or left to right.

The planes of existence are all connected to each other, and outside of them there is only the primordial nothingness, a silent and eternal darkness that envelops everything to the ends. Meanwhile, the universes continue

....
14. Méndez, *El Librito Azul*.
15. "1783. Lavoisier y los estudios sobre combustión animal," *Editorial Médica Panamericana*.
16. Méndez, *Metafísica al alcance de todos*.
17. Méndez, *El libro de oro de Saint Germain*.

expanding between them. The astral planes and worlds continue to be born one after another, covering each other like new skin, as if placing the Russian doll inside a newer one each time.

As clarified previously, the dream world is the place where everyone converges, and this gives us the power to interact with all kinds of deities in the same place. In short, the dream world is a place that all sentient beings are able to access.

Metaphysical Concepts

During the nineteenth century, British Theosophist Alfred Percy Sinnett and his collaborator William Scott-Elliot shared in their metaphysical writings the idea that our physical world resulted in a conglomeration of inhabitants that went beyond humans. They wrote that this world we inhabit was being shared simultaneously with multiple nonphysical beings, visitors from different planes of existence, who appeared under the most diverse forms. These forms were able to take possession of small beings, such as plants and some domestic animals, until manifesting in the form of highly intelligent human beings who were commonly confused with mediums, clairvoyants, and sorcerers.

Sinnett, who dedicated himself to studying the world from the esoteric perspective and with a fairly broad vision, established that the various worlds and planes of existence converge between them simultaneously and in such a subtle way that we don't even realize it. For example, whenever you sit alone in a room, it is important to remember that you are not there alone but constantly surrounded by various individuals from various worlds. Many of them are probably aware of what's happening and many others not.

The esoteric ideas and concepts of Sinnett and Scott-Elliot, which developed around the year 1900, were, in turn, supported by Rudolf Steiner, an Austrian esoteric and philosopher who worked closely for several years with Charles Webster Leadbeater on research related to clairvoyance and reading the auras. Sinnett, who would soon be respected as a firm and concise voice on esoteric issues, believed and promoted that our world was simultaneously shared with many others and that dream worlds (plural) were the bridge through which we could access other worlds. However, people must first learn to find the bridge and later be skillful and cautious enough to be able to cross it.

The ideas put forth by these philosophers, researchers, and occultists were truly great and advanced for their time. All of them only failed in a minute detail, most of them not being experienced clairvoyants or magical workers, by simply assuming (as many do) that human beings were the only conscious beings in the formula, the only ones capable of seeing, feeling, perceiving, and understanding the subtle worlds that surrounded us. The truth is that in most planes of existence, a notorious number of beings that inhabit them are often in the same situation of not understanding where they are.

A Short Anecdote

Once I had the opportunity to write a short article for a local magazine in Caracas, Venezuela. In the article I wrote:

> **When you cry for someone who has passed away, remember that someone is also crying from the other side. That someone is the one who left you here, and probably that someone is scared because they don't understand, because they can't understand why they feel lonely, sad, cold, and abandoned, in a desolate immaterial world where time does not pass and all the figures look like distant memories of an old dream, and unlike any Hollywood movie, no familiar figure wrapped in light has come to collect him.[18]**

In general, most of my writings tend to get feedback, but this particular article connected with more readers than usual. Soon after publication, readers contacted me by mail to tell me about their medium-mystical experiences and ask questions about their dreams or about their loved ones who had left this world but were, in a way, still present at home and did not seem to know how to leave or how to move forward. Most of these emails repeated the sentiment of "Since he died, he has not stopped appearing in dreams and visions" with slight variations.

This brief period of time between death and the ascension to another time plane usually varies, always according to different emotional and metaphysical factors. During that period of time, it is common for the souls of the deceased to feel confused, sad, desolate, and anxious because it is obviously a new experience.

....
18. Leafar, "Elhoim's Column. "

Dying does not come with an instruction manual. Once the soul leaves the body, dreams are the easiest way for the deceased to access, in a certain way, the world of the living and manifest, but that process does not come with instructions either. It can cost the departed enormous effort, time, and energy, and the dream world is, for them, the easiest door to open.

EXERCISE
A Spell Bag to Guide Your (and Other People's) Dreams

Make use of this traditional spell to incubate a dream in yourself or someone else. This spell can be repeated and modified to suit the needs of the sorcerer. This spell, as simple as it is effective, leads the sorcerer to gain experience moving between the worlds of night visions, thus allowing them to work their energy while they sleep.

You will need:
- Paper
- Scissors
- Pencil
- Square piece of purple cloth no bigger than your hand
- Piece of onyx or smoky quartz
- Fresh sprig of coriander
- Pinch of salt, rosemary, white pepper, cinnamon powder, and anise powder
- Pinch of earth (optional; use if you want to recreate a vision in relation to a specific site that you have previously visited)
- Silver, purple, or black thread

At any time between sunset and midnight, cut the paper in the shape of a five-pointed star, write your name in the center of the figure, and draw an arrow from your name to the tips of the figure (as shown in the drawing).

Holding this small talisman in your hands, recite three times:

In all directions I want to go I move,
In all the worlds that I seek to walk I tread,
The four cardinal points guide my hand,
They take me to know what I need to know,
They take me to look, wherever I want to look.

Place the talisman in the middle of the fabric. Now, while you visualize in your mind the dream that you want to have or remember, or the dream that you want to give to someone else, place all the other ingredients next to the talisman one by one. Do this calmly while you continue to visualize that vision that you are looking for.

Once you have added all the elements of your spell to the cloth, recite the previous incantation once more. Proceed to close the cloth, bringing up the corners to make a small bag. Tie this charm bag closed, making seven knots with the thread.

Place this bag under the bed or on the nightstand and touch it with your fingertips before going to sleep. It is unlikely that the talisman will begin to work during the first night, but from the second night on, the vision should begin to appear as fragments.

Dream Magic Insight
THE ART OF DREAM/
ASTRAL TRAVEL OF THE MASQUES
BY ONCLE BEN

In the region where I live (Provence, southeast France), we name witches "Masco/a"—in standard French *Masque*, which can translate as "Mask." If they are good, we call them *Desmacaire* (Who removes the Mask), and if they are bad, we call them *Emmascaires* (Who wears the Mask). The Masco/a have the ability to travel in the astral world or dream world to go to the sabbat or to cast spells. This practice/belief is present everywhere in Southern Europe. The Masco/a can also visit sleeping people. This is called the *vesita* in the Provençale language and translates as "the visit."

The Visit Spell, a Southern French Spell of Astral Travel

So, the visit is a particular art of the astral/dream journey of the Masco/a. It allows you to come and visit a sleeping person to help them by performing prayers and healing gestures on them or in evil by cursing them. This spell needs to be performed when the person you want to visit is asleep (you need to know their bedtime habits in advance).

You will need:
- Protective objects of your choosing
- Populeum ointment
- Salt water
- Hazel wand
- Photo of or personal object belonging to the person you wish to visit
- Censer
- Incense composed of camphor, anise, poppy, celery seed, and Artemisia

- White candle in candleholder
- Sprig of fennel if you wish to do goodwill, or sprig of sorghum if you wish to do harm
- Lighter or matches

For this spell, you must first set up a sacred space. According to tradition, you must have some protective objects around you, and you must anoint yourself with populeum ointment. Purify the room before performing any work. To do this, go around the room three times, sprinkling with salt water, saying:

Heregot Gomet Hunc Gueridans Sesserant Deliberant Amei.

Then cast a circle in this space around you with a hazel wand. Trace it three times and say:

Eloïm, Essaïm, Frugativi et Appelavi.

Followed by:

O Almighty Father!
O most tender mother of mothers!
O admirable example of the sentiments of the tenderness of mothers!
O son, the flower of all sons!
O form of all forms!
Soul, spirit, harmony, and number of all things!
Conserve us, protect us, lead us, and be propitious to us.

(Ô Père tout puissant!
Ô Mère la plus tendre des mères!
Ô exemplaire admirable des sentiments de la tendresse des mères!
Ô fils la fleur de tous les fils!
Ô forme de toutes les formes!
Âme, esprit, harmonie et nombre de toutes choses!
Conservez-nous, protégez-nous, conduisez-nous et soyez nous propice.)

Then say three Our Fathers (the Lord's Prayer), three Ave Marias, and three Glorias.

Sit on the floor in the center of the circle you cast, facing the direction of the person you wish to visit (for example, if they sleep in a city to the south-east of you, face the southeast).

Place the photo or personal object in front of you along with the censer with incense and the white candle.

Between your hands, hold the sprig of fennel or sorghum, depending on your intention.

Light the candle and burn the incense mixture in the censer.

Hold the photo or personal object in your hand and knock on the floor three times and say:

> **By the Devil and by God, let the rite be accomplished.**
> **May my spirit fly and twirl toward _____ (name of the person).**
>
> *(Par le Diable et par Dieu, que le rite s'accomplisse.*
> *Que mon esprit vole et virevolte vers _____ Nom de la personne.)*

Stare at the candle until your eyes naturally close. Visualize yourself flying out of your body and into the sky, traveling through a window or a chimney.

Hold this visualization and see yourself flying to the person you wish to visit. If you feel you are losing focus, simply repeat:

> **By the Devil and by God, let the journey be accomplished.**
> **May my spirit fly and twirl toward _____ (Name of the person).**
>
> *(Par le Diable et par Dieu, que le voyage s'accomplisse*
> *Que mon esprit vole et virevolte vers _____Nom de la personne.)*

Fly to where the person lives, then travel through the roof, the window, or the door of their bedroom. See them lying down, sleeping peacefully. Sit next to them, on their bed, and say in a soft, calm, and serene way:

> **_____ (name of the person), stay calm, it's me _____ (your name),**
> **Trust me, you can stay asleep,**
> **I am just a sweet and pleasant dream,**
> **I'm here just to visit you,**
> **I am just a sweet and pleasant dream,**
> **Stay asleep because you trust me,**
> **I am just a sweet and pleasant dream,**

You know I'm only here for your good,
I am just a sweet and pleasant dream,
And this is all just a sweet and pleasant dream.

(_____ NN, reste calme, c'est moi _____ votre nom,
Ais confiance, tu peux rester endormis,
Je ne suis qu'un rêve doux et agréable,
Je suis ici simplement pour te rendre visiter,
Je ne suis qu'un rêve doux et agréable,
Reste endormis car tu as confiance en moi,
Je ne suis qu'un rêve, doux et agréable,
Tu sais que je suis là que pour ton bien,
Je ne suis qu'un rêve, doux et agréable,
Et tous cela n'est simplement qu'un rêve, doux et agréable)

Now say your healing prayers or whatever it is you wish from them. Tell them what you want them to do for you, give them the message you want them to keep in their unconscious mind. Indeed, you can ask them something in their sleep that their subconscious will remember and that they will execute when they wake up.

Repeat your request several times in a calm and repetitive manner, repeating their name and the wish several times.

When you're done, say goodbye and fly outward, taking the path you took to enter. Come home to your body. Stay still until you feel yourself inside.

Open your eyes, knock the floor three times while saying:

By the Devil and by God, the rite is accomplished.
Let this room get back its original function.

(Par le Diable et par Dieu, Le rite c'est accompli.
Que ce lieu reprend sa fonction initiale.)

Blow out the candle and purify the room again.

TRIBAL TALES
THE INITIATION RITES OF THE AMAZON (*OS RITOS INICIÁTICOS DA AMAZÔNIA*)

When they ask you about initiations, remember that the day you were born was your first initiation and the most powerful, valid one. You came from a gestation period of nine months, where you were nourished directly from the womb of an earth goddess. All subsequent initiations are only chosen, beautiful complements.

Many tribes live in the Amazon. The actual number is practically countless since dozens of tribes refer to themselves under different names that turn out to be specific to each locality, which is why investigations often end up listing one or another tribe more than once. Sometimes small tribes emerge on the fringes as a result of new families being formed by exiles from other smaller tribes.

While finding the tribes that insist on staying hidden is a difficult task for those who come from outside, it is not impossible, especially when you have contact with other local tribes whose main mission is to keep those tribes and ethnic groups protected.

The Lost Initiation of the Yuri

One of these groups living in the Amazon is the Yuri ethnic group (Yuriinas), which comes from the lands of the Amazon that are currently part of Colombia. The Yuri are closely associated with other local tribes, such as the Ticuna (from which they originally came), the Passee (from which they split), and the Uainuma (into which they have rejoined for religious and cultural reasons).

The Yuri are made up of less than three hundred inhabitants, and their protection is considered a priority for numerous Amazon tribes. The Yuri have this distinctive dark brown tattoo that extends from the top of the mouth to the ears. They are usually naked, especially the women, who do not wear clothes except for religious celebrations.

During religious celebrations, Carojeoje (the priests of the tribe) wear the Agague, a long crown made of small feathers that extends to cover the entire back. They are decorated with Arojie, necklaces made of wild animal teeth, and Jabbe, bells made of teeth and seeds are tied to the ankles to create all kinds of sounds while they dance around the ritual fire.

The rites of the Yuri are not secret or forbidden. These are performed openly and are held for long days to celebrate the arrival of the first period in women, who will now be givers of life, and to honor young men who are already in parenting age (three full moons after the man's first voluntary ejaculation).

One of these rituals in which the outsiders are invited to participate, especially if they come from the local tribes, is the Araje Ujann Ujae (the dream of the deceased who returns). It is an initiation rite in which all the priests of the people or the tribe are destined to participate.

A young man of fathering age, who has already gone hunting on multiple occasions and has slept on the outskirts of the tribe for six nights in a row, is symbolically invited to return. Over the course of those six nights, the man must have found a place to sleep, hunt, fish, train, and eat. This place must be across a thick river and where a selection of local plants have been planted every full moon for months.

After spending six nights sleeping outside, the young man returns completely naked. He carries only three long strips of skin with hanging bells on his left leg and a long necklace of bones that extends from the neck to below the limb.

A huge hole in the ground awaits the young man. In it, he will be buried alive. A line of priests stands on each side, forming a wide path to guide the young man with chants and small skin drums as he walks between them. The priests cover the eyes of the young man with a long piece of dark skin that has been dried in the sun on the branches of a sacred tree for several days. Once his eyes are blindfolded, the young man is supported by three priests and placed in the hole, where he lies down lengthwise and is completely covered in earth from the neck to the feet.

The ground is then covered with flowers picked that very morning by a virgin maiden who has (or has recently had) her period. The naked young woman dances over the buried body, spilling flowers over it. Then the priests moisten the ground with a sweet and sour liquor made of herbs and fruits, an earthy flavored liquor, and alcohol with honey with a taste so bitter that it burns your throat.

The priests get the blindfolded young man to drink this liquor. They then continue to pour more of it on his body, symbolizing the bitter rain that falls when those we love most die.

A long ritual dance to the rhythm of the drums crosses over the young man in all directions. From dusk to dawn (last light of day to first light of the next), the young man remains immobile, drinking the bitter liquor the priest gives him from a bowl made from a coconut shell and carved with ritual symbols representing Kio (the first man to emerge from the mountain) and Ajg (the great spirit of the night who created the stars). Ajg taught Kio the art of reading the stars at night and the clouds during the day; he taught him to heal with herbs, make liquor, summon fire, hunt animals, and move at night without being noticed by the clouds, which are the souls of the deceased, thus forging the one who would be the first priest of the first tribe of the first mountain.

At dawn, between ritual songs and drums, the young man is unearthed. He is now intoxicated by the liquor and has been symbolically brought from the world of the dead. From the world of the dead, he has brought the secrets of the old language, the secrets to cure the sick. He has gained Kugjo (also Jukgo or Kojgo), the symbolic language of the spirit world that is used to interpret dreams.

The images that appeared in his head during the last hours are considered divine messages sent by the ancestors. Now, the young man has the mission of keeping these messages and symbols until the last of his days, using these secrets to his advantage, without ever revealing them.

During the following nights, and until the next initiation is performed on another young man, all dreams that visit the initiate will be considered divine omens. He must hide in the woods and draw these dream symbols in the lower parts of the trees—so close to the roots that the earth covers them so their secrets will wait hidden for him for the moment in which he dies again. The initiate will pass these secrets on to the next priest and so on and on. The magical secrets of the tribe's religion are thus preserved generation after generation without these mysteries ever being revealed.

CHAPTER 3

THE FINE ART OF DREAM INTERPRETATION

Dreams have been a matter of investigation and interpretation for millennia, and each culture and each civilization interpret them in their own way. Psychoanalysts Sigmund Freud and Carl Jung found their own interpretation of the world of dreams and its symbolism, but even their deepest studies and analysis were limited for two clear reasons: the cultural barrier, which clearly did not allow them to understand what certain symbols and present elements can mean for other individuals in different cultures, and scientific studies limited to their time that simply did not allow them to go deeper in their own analysis.

On that note, science is usually limited to proving what the scientist seeks to prove and nothing further. For example, if the scientist is seeking to prove that coal can become diamonds, they can easily overlook the fact that next to the coal mine there is a cave full of gold, silver, and other precious stones, because their focus is narrowed to one purpose: to prove that coal can become diamonds.

Dreams have been interpreted in multiple cultures as warnings of destiny, as omens of the future, and also as memories of past lives. In some cultures, they are even treated as a divine language that transmits the designs and wishes of gods, as was previously mentioned in chapter 2.

The Language of Dreams in South America

In the spiritualist cults of South America (Colombia, Brazil, Venezuela), dreams are a unique and individual language that connects us with the high spiritual courts and with their wishes and warnings for the future. They are also a means of communication with the world of the spirits, with ancestors, and with our witch's familiar.

In Colombia, for example, it is common to find witches creating all kinds of spells and amulets that make use of the magic of dreams to protect themselves during the night and to win the favor of the spirits. They will place an odd number of gold or silver coins under the pillow to keep their fortune and house protected, embroider the names of their ancestors on the back of the pillowcase to get protection while they sleep, or drink various kinds of tonics and herbal teas before bedtime to sleep without inconveniences and to have happy dreams. They may serve a cup of chamomile tea with some flowers of the chamomile plant in the tea, swirling the cup seven times before taking the first sip to move the energy and bring good omens at night.

Although dream interpretation is a common enough topic of everyday conversation in the big cities, magic related to dreams in Venezuela is certainly limited to witches and sorcerers who work in the mountains, such as in the famous reservoir *La Mariposa* in the vicinity of the capital city or around *la montaña de Sorte*, which is dedicated to the goddess María Lionza. In these places, the relationship between dreams and witches goes beyond interpretation, and the witches focus more on performing enchantments with mountain fairies to attract happy dreams and, in these idealized dreams, find certain omens and future warnings.

In the local botanic and esoteric stores of Barquisimeto and Caracas, you can commonly find all kinds of hanging amulets to place on the frame of the bed at night to help one dream of the lottery numbers. There are also small gold medals with red threads to hide under the pillow of a loved one to make them have happy dreams with the image of the witch who hid the amulet. Small bags full of aromatic herbs are sold that can be placed between the sheets to protect yourself against nocturnal psychic attacks. Another popular amulet that is easy to find in the city's botanicas consists of a brown or dark blue cloth bag (a charm bag) filled with earth collected from a recent grave and herbs collected from the entrance of a nearby cemetery. These are mixed with a pinch of white pepper and a pinch of sea salt to balance and purify. This amulet is placed inside the pillow to keep away evil spirits and ghosts that have been sent to do evil by order of some witch.

If the students of dreams in Latin America have something in common, it is that dreams are a manifestation of a language that is both universal and individual. In other words, dreams are a visible manifestation of a universal language that connects us with other worlds, other times, and other realities, but they are, in turn, also part of an individual language. Dreams act as messengers, and they deliver each message in a language that the interpreter/dreamer can understand.

It is because of this that we commonly dream of things, places, and people that are familiar because we know them from this or other lives and from this or possibly other alternative realities. When we dream and immerse ourselves in this internal world, which connects us all, it is common for the dreams to try to make a connection with you, sending and receiving messages. Once we wake up, even after having dreamed of the face of someone we think we don't know, we always have that feeling of "that face looks familiar to me" or "I think I know them from somewhere."

The Universal Language of Dreams

As mentioned, dreams are the messengers in a universal language, and the things we dream of are related not only to ourselves but also to all the fragments of the universe that surround us and its entire reality. When gods, goddesses, Orixás, spirits, ascended masters, angels, and other beings from higher or lower planes try to contact us for any reason, dreams work like the internet does, connecting us to one another.

Messages travel over long periods of time, and those dreams that you dream today may have taken centuries, millennia, or eons to be woven before reaching you. They may have been sent years or eons ago or centuries in the future as footsteps and guides for us.

Writing this reminds me of my mom commenting on her dreams to my dad in the morning. This was the daily routine at home. We didn't need an alarm clock, or at least I didn't, because every morning, before preparing coffee, my mom talked to my dad from bed about what she had dreamed during the night. Her voice woke us all up at home. My sisters and I, from the other bedroom, would laugh, saying, "Will there be a day that Mom doesn't wake up in the morning with a dream to tell and let us sleep?"

Dreams are a manifestation of various activities occurring in your subconscious. These dreams are, in turn, aligned with three different types of messages: messages from the internal world, messages from the intermediate world, and messages from the spirit world. These are explained in more detail in the following sections.

Internal World

Messages from past lives are left as signals related to your purpose of incarnation, sort of like a dream time capsule. Once we die and we can make a summary of what our life was, especially what we did and did not do, we have the opportunity to leave some messages in the form of visions and sensations, which allow us to try again in the distant future.

These messages from the past, or retrocognition, function as time capsules as they have remained stored in the dream world for decades, centuries, or millennia, properly marinating in old and new energy. This allows them to manifest both in the form of daytime and nocturnal visions, even leading you to embrace a certain feeling of nostalgia, sadness, or joy. Once you come across a place or a situation that is linked to a message that is stored in the internal world, such as when you visit a place where you think that you have walked before or when you come across someone on the street whom you could swear you know from somewhere, you will get a vision. The latter has happened to me more than a hundred times, I swear, especially with clients who come to me for a tarot reading or a magical bath and immediately ask me where they know me best from.

Messages from other moments in time (past and future) are the type of message that you can easily align yourself with in the world of dreams. These messages do not simply arrive. In fact, in magic, nothing happens without a proper reason; something or someone sent that message to you as a precaution, and many times it was yourself.

Intermediate World

Being a sorcerer or a magician, or any form of energy worker practicing any esoteric exercise, your desires and your mindset will be charged with a high power. Your power grows with constant practice, like a muscle, and it tends to lose progress that has already been made if you stop working for some time, requiring that you start over from scratch. Imagine trying to contact a spirit ally for help, which you have not contacted or provided any attention to for more than two years, or trying to put into practice a certain protection spell, which you have not performed for more than ten years and can vaguely remember.

If you regret any of the decisions you made or some of the steps you took during a situation that was created or generated by you, it would not be strange for your past self to pay a visit to your subconscious and leave a message there. The message is clearly not going to be timely enough to change the facts, but it will offer you a rare déjà vu feeling of "this was just what I dreamed about." In the end, in the intermediate world that dreams inhabit, it is important to remember that the laws of physics do not apply and neither do time, space, gravity, form, and matter as in our world.

Look at this as a corridor or as a puzzle with multiple pieces of memories, dreams, regrets, and emotions—all of them trying to fit together. You are trying to understand them, but for that, you need put them all together.

Spirit World

We all enter the world of dreams, but not everyone is able to enter that small piece of dream land where your dreams rule. Only you can—unless someone has a good spell for it. It's just as no one can or should enter your house without your authorization. Only two kinds of beings can leave messages for you in dreams: one is you, as mentioned previously, and the other kind is spiritual beings and ancestral guides. If, for some reason, the spiritual beings or guides must leave a message, your subconscious decides whether those messages should be delivered to you.

A message in your dreams may have been left there by your spirit guides to warn you of something or because you have been consciously asking for signs. When this happens, your spiritual body reacts to the messages as a kind of intervention. We may well call it a divine intervention or simply a message from beyond.

These messages are highly perceptible during the nights around the new moon, when the gravitational and energetic influence of the moon feels less powerful in our subtle body—the moment when even (according to esoteric spiritism) spirits and ghosts enjoy greater freedom to move, present, and manifest among the living. These messages serve as a guide for a specific purpose: to help us make a decision, to take action, or to indicate that we should get away from something or someone. In short, these messages are usually as a necessary precaution in our favor and benefit.

Checking These Signals

When you are trying to interpret a dream, be it yours or someone else's, there are three main factors that you must analyze: the symbols and people present in the dream, the moment and phase of the moon involved in the dream, and the emotions recently experienced that may have had an influence on the dream.

The symbols and people represent the message and its direction. The moment (day or night, beginning of the morning or end of the day) and the phase of the moon (new, waxing, full, waning) can represent a beginning, an intermediate time, or an end toward which your dream is moving. Finally, recent emotions can have a great influence on the dreams. For example, a traumatic experience can lead to nightmares and having a great and joyful day can lead to happy dreams.

These three aspects are important to analyze when we try to interpret a dream. You can also try drawing and detailing the dream in writing, telling the dream carefully to an expert, or meditating in front of a crystal ball trying to visualize the dream in it. While these fairly common methods can be effective, they often focus solely on guessing the future that the dream is portending, and that may be ignoring the reasons for the dream and deeper symbolism.

Roaches and Weddings: The Cultural Context of Dreams

Since my arrival in the United States, I have understood that for many occultists and dream interpreters living here, dreaming of mice, cockroaches, and other insects is a sign of disease; it represents that an illness has come to the home. By contrast, in Venezuela dreaming of cockroaches is normally a sign of wealth and good luck. It means money is seeking to enter the corners of the house, but out of fear, we are keeping it away.

My mother once dreamed of cockroaches. Specifically, she dreamed that a large number of these insects were on the faces of my nephews. My mother spent a whole week repeating over and over again how scared she was about it. Nine days after having that dream, one of my nephews, who was only six years old at the time, pulled a pot of boiling water off the table, and it fell on him and burned his face. It took about seven years of medical visits and dermatological treatments to repair this situation to the point of leaving the best possible marks on it.

What we would have normally expected was not fulfilled, but what the dream could have predicted for another person in another place did come true. This dream showed that what we know and what we think we know is little compared to what we still have to learn.

Another example is dreaming of weddings. Although many people in the United States could easily see a young woman's dream of marrying in an elegant white gown as a positive sign, for us, in countries such as Venezuela, Chile, Peru, and Colombia at least, dreaming of a wedding represents an omen of death, while dreaming of a funeral is a positive omen that represents change, commitment, and ascension.

One of my sisters, Jennifer, is always dreaming different situations about the people closest to her, and most of the premonitions in these dreams tend to happen. She has become the fortune teller of the house. On a certain occasion, I have called my mother, and she told me that she had been talking to my sister, who lives in the same country but in another city. This time, my mother was dreaming something horrible about my sister. In her words, "I dream something dreadful. I hope all the saints take care of it."

She did not give me many details, so I decided to call my sister Jennifer. My sister told me that she had dreamed of herself attending a wedding with a long white dress covered with beautiful embroidery and long sleeves with pearl details and *nácar* (mother-of-pearl). She had a long veil with so many decorations that she had to remove it to walk to the altar because the veil did not let her see the way. She tried to see the groom, but she could not see his face. In her words, "His face was blurred, as if it were a mass that melts under water." She saw in his hands this beautiful bouquet of six huge white roses and five long bows. In front of them stood a woman dressed in blue with her face covered with flowers, and behind her the shone resplendent full moon. That last reminded me of the letter from the High Priestess in the tarot deck. My sister then heard the sound similar to an old telephone being hung up and woke up.

About three weeks later, on June 5, 2020, a night with a bright full moon, I got a call telling me that my grandmother had ascended (she had passed away). The most curious thing is that my mother had just finished talking to her on the phone. Twenty minutes after saying goodbye, my aunt called my mom back from the same phone, crying and telling her that Grandma hung up the call, dropped the phone to the ground, and stopped breathing. They had already called the emergency room, but my aunt knew that it was her time and there was no turning back.

The interpretation of dreams goes beyond the interpretation of the symbols and multiple external factors, including cultural factors, as explained in the previous point. The symbols can influence the way in which dreams are presented, and these are there to be deciphered and understood; that is why all external factors must be considered, as external factors (culture, history, place) can play a fundamental role in the way a person interprets the symbols in their dreams.

I suggest you get a book on the interpretation of symbols and your dream agenda. It is important to take into account that the universe (god, gods, goddesses, angels, fairies, and other beings) seeks to communicate in an energetic language rather than in a verbal or written language. Those signals or messages, once they are received in our unconscious, are translated into a language that we can understand.

The astral realms, as well as the world of dreams, are realms of emotion and energy. Language is a form of communication that human beings use to transmit ideas, questions, and solutions, but it is a language that corresponds to the physical body. In the realms that are made of energy, the messages can move and transmit in this way, but they could also be shown as two birds exchanging messages through the movement that their wings make in the wind. It is something that totally escapes our physical plane, and for this reason, dreams tend to be translated, adapted, and even interpreted for our understanding.

Different Interpretations for Different Cultures

Different cultures have offered us different means of interpreting dreams, ranging from meditating on them while drinking a cup of tea to writing them down on paper and burning them in the window.

The Problem of Time

In these worlds of energy, the notion of time is practically nonexistent, while for us humans the conception of time is a linear fact (past, present, future). The spiritual world is entirely timeless, and this can cause certain misunderstandings when dreams are interpreted.

Dreams travel in the form of emotions made of energy, and once they reach our energy field (in the unconscious), these messages are taken, deconstructed, and reinterpreted in a way that we can understand them. Once the message takes the proper form to be understood, such as images, events, sounds, and sensations, it can be perceived by us. Because your dreams are a shared space between your present self and all your other selves, including your past lives, it is normal that these messages are often not understood.

If this energetic space that you share with all the other versions of yourself is where all these messages come together, do not doubt your own understanding when suddenly you dream of people you do not know or of places that you do not remember ever having visited. Often your past self may have left a warning in your subconscious for you, such as "be careful with this person" or "we promised to help this person and we have not done it." In your head, you have the image of the last physical form that soul took when it came to earth. After many decades, or perhaps centuries, you have reincarnated and you have the message there, but you may not even know who that person is now in this new life and at this different moment in time.

Therefore, perhaps the best advice I can give you to understand dreams and the art of their interpretation is to start interpreting your own dreams and understanding your own language and culture. This will help you to understand that your dreams probably wouldn't symbolize the same thing for another person. Inquire about yourself, seek professional therapy at some point in your life, and explore past life regression sessions to understand more about yourself. These methods will be very helpful to understanding the language that your dreams are using to communicate past, current, and future messages with you.

Behind each dream is a teaching, a message, a memory, or a guide that we have been requesting consciously or unconsciously. That is why it is vitally important to understand what you dream, and it is also vitally important that you keep a note of these dreams for their proper interpretation. Look for the signs in each dream. What memories does it bring you? What feelings does it bring you? How did you feel in the dream? Were you alone or accompanied? And if someone else was there, by whom were you accompanied?

Use Your Intuition

Learning to interpret our dreams is as important of a priority as learning a second language when moving to a foreign country. Dreams are our direct path to other worlds. A witch who is not capable of interpreting their own dreams is like a tree that does not know how to move water from its roots to nourish its leaves. Start with books, and investigate your past and your inner self, as I suggested previously. But know that the best tool to guide you through the interpretation process is your intuition.

Once you trust your intuition, you will be able to understand what other psychoanalysts do not capture in dreams. While some books lead you to understand the meaning of a symbol or the reason for the presence of the symbol, your intuition can tell you how that symbol got there, why it's appearing now, and where it came from.

The books dedicated to the interpretation of dreams are a good complement for the study of our psyche, but they should not be taken as our main tool. Many of these books were written from an analytical and individual perspective that completely ignores cultural, individual, and religious elements that can have a huge influence on the way your dreams take shape.

Using your intuition daily to analyze those night visions, you will be able to not only put into practice your own psychic ability every day but see beyond what is evident and understand hidden meanings in each symbol, each moment, and each small detail present in the dream.

Greek philosophers and scholars saw the dream as an oneiric vision made up of three parts: the scene or visible place in the dream, the inanimate objects or plants and animals present in the dream, and the individual present to recreate the dream with symbols or words. Consider these words from Ovid in *Metamorphoses Book XI*:

> There is no door in all the house, lest some turning hinge should creak; no guardian on the threshold. But in the cavern's central space there is a high couch of ebony, downy-soft, black-hued, spread with a dusky coverlet. There lies the god himself, his limbs relaxed in languorous repose. Around him on all sides lie empty dream-shapes, mimicking many forms, many as ears of grain in harvest-time, as leaves upon the trees, as sands cast on the shore.[19]

Remembering Your Dreams

The first step to interpretation is remembering your dreams. Here is an incense recipe and spell to help you do that. It uses the new moon, which is associated in magic with the understanding of the new beginnings and processes. It is also associated with our darker side, with the work of shadows, and with the full action of plunging into darkness to understand what it is that inhabits it and remains hidden there.

....
19. Ovid, *Metamorphoses*.

EXERCISE
Moon Incense to Remember Dreams

Remembering dreams is quite a difficult task for many. I, for example, must take note of them immediately, because after a few hours I don't even remember having a dream. I have tried all kinds of remedies, incenses, charms, and little rituals to help me remember. Many have failed, a few have been highly effective, and the following recipe is one of those that worked wonderfully well for me.

You will need:
- Lighter or matches
- White candle in candleholder
- Black candle in candleholder
- Heat-resistant plate or small cauldron
- Dried flowers (use jasmine, chamomile, poppy, and rose bulbs)
- Piece of charcoal
- Long wooden wand or kitchen spoon

Recommended moon phase: New moon

Begin by lighting the white candle (clarity, understanding) and the black candle (inner cleansing, purification). On a heat-resistant plate or inside a cauldron, prepare a mixture of equal parts dried flowers associated with sleep and the moon, including jasmine, chamomile, poppy, and rose bulbs.

Carefully light a piece of charcoal (easy to find at your local esoteric store) and place the hot charcoal over the dried flower blend. With the help of the long wooden wand or kitchen spoon, move this mixture inside the cauldron with a firm hand, maintaining a constant but slow movement in order to move all the parts of this incense and allow the smoke to emanate properly.

Repeat this ritual two to three times a week to start developing a better memory regarding your dreams.

Dream Magic Insight
DREAM INTERPRETATION SPELL
BY TEMPERANCE ALDEN

Dreams are the windows to our subconscious mind, a realm where the hidden truths and desires reside. In this spell, we will use the magical properties of mugwort, mullein, and mint to create an incense blend that will aid us in interpreting our dreams.

You will need:
- Lighter or matches
- Charcoal disc
- Heat-resistant container
- Dried mugwort, mullein, and mint
- Mortar and pestle
- Pen and paper or dream journal

Before starting the ritual, find a quiet and comfortable place where you won't be disturbed. Take a moment to ground yourself and set your intention. Then light the charcoal disc and place it in the heat-resistant container. Crush the mugwort, mullein, and mint using the mortar and pestle, and sprinkle them onto the charcoal disc. As the incense begins to burn, inhale deeply and allow the smoke to envelop you and unfurl in the space you are sitting in.

Recite the following spell, inspired by the power of the herbs and the mystical nature of dream interpretation:

Mugwort, mullein, and mint's incense blend,
A mystic key, their magic transcends,
Revealing dreams that dance and bend,
A world of meaning to comprehend.

With this incense, I set my mind,
To traverse the realms of the undefined,
Guided by the herbs' alchemy divine,
My soul takes flight, to worlds unconfined.

Mint's clarity, a razor-sharp sight,
Slicing through the veil of night,
Mullein's protection, a shield so tight,
Guiding me through the dreams' wild flight.

Through the veil of sleep and shadow,
Mugwort, mullein, and mint's potent flow,
Unlocks the secrets of my soul,
A tapestry of dreams, my life's whole.

With this spell, I embrace the unknown,
Interpreting the dreams that have grown,
Mugwort, mullein, and mint, your magic be,
As I seek the truth, so mote it be.

As you recite the spell, allow your mind to focus on your intention to interpret your dreams. After the incense has burned out, take a moment to record your dreams in your journal or on a piece of paper.

Reflect on the symbols, emotions, and events that occurred in your dreams, and try to interpret their meaning. Remember, dream interpretation is a personal process and can vary from person to person, so trust your instincts and intuition!

To complete the ritual, extinguish the charcoal disc with water (or let it burn out naturally) and dispose of it safely once it is completely cooled. Take a moment to thank the spirit of the herbs for their aid and the insights they have provided.

TRIBAL TALES
THE CIPARACOTO /
LOS INDIOS DE LA COSTA

The Ciparacoto are among the least known Indige-
nous people of Venezuela. Although it is common to find their descendants
living today in the states of Yaracuy and Merida (Venezuela), they are only
mentioned in a couple of books, including *El Dorado and the Quest for Fortune and Glory in South America* by Peter Koch and *The Witch's Dream: A
Healer's Way of Knowledge* by Florinda Donner-Grau, which are both conveniently of esoteric character.

The Ciparacoto is a tribe of Native Americans from the Carib family. They
were commonly found living in the coastal areas of the Falcon and Carabobo
states in Venezuela. They were great farmers (cassava and corn) and mer-
chants (salt, fish, pearls, corn). Their fermented drinks based on corn and
cassava had a ritual purpose that connected them with the ancestral spirits
and allowed them to carry and bring messages from other worlds.

Their weapons (bows and arrows and clubs) were commonly poisoned
with an herbal solution that acted as a paralyzer. They were also cannibals, and for them cannibalism was also a sacred ritual through which they
devoured enemies to absorb their strength, their courage, and the spirits of
their ancestors.

The elders are highly respected as the leaders of the tribe, not because of
their strength and physical prowess but because of their wisdom and experience gained over the years. The elders serve as healers and sorcerers for the
community and interpret the hidden signs in the language of the clouds and
in the guts of serpents. They also predict pregnancies and deaths by observing the surface of the water and teach how to create herbal poisons and communicate with the spirit world for advice and assistance.

For them, dreams are direct messages from beyond sent by the Obeba,
the spirits of ancestors so old that they are about to be reborn. The dreams
are always full of signs and must always be interpreted by an elder. A dream
that is not interpreted or that has been forgotten is a bad omen. If a dream is
forgotten, the individual who has forgotten it or has forgotten to go with the

old man to make the interpretation must sleep under the trees and outside the hut until they receive the dream again and can then have it interpreted.

For the Ciparacoto, one of the most conventional methods to perform the interpretation of dreams is to look at the surface of the water. However, there is a procedure that is more elaborate. First, you (the dreamer) should not eat anything from dawn until noon and only drink water and fruit juice. Then the interpreter should use a long arrow to draw a circle on the ground in front of the well, river, or sea. The dreamer should sit inside it to meditate and wait there until noon without being disturbed.

At noon, the individual drinks a fermented cassava-based or sometimes corn-based beverage. They continue drinking and looking at the surface of the water during the midday hours when the golden light of the sun is perceived as more intense on the surface of the water. The signs and visions to interpret the dream will be revealed.

Subsequently, the individual leaves the circle, thanking Parahuayo (the light of the sun or the sun god itself). They meet again with the interpreter or the elder of the tribe so that together they can interpret the symbols and visions of the dream, as well as the symbols found in the water. The signs that they find in the water act as tools to complement dreams, and without these spiritual tools, the dream cannot be fully interpreted.

For this Indigenous culture, practically lost today, dreams are interpreted not only by reading the dream but also by looking for signs and omens in the water. That is because the water's surface is considered sacred. It separates the three worlds: the world of birds, the world of people and other animals, and the world of waters.

CHAPTER 4

DREAM SPIRIT GUIDES

The world we inhabit is full of all kinds of living and nonliving beings, including the so-called spirits. The world of spirits is inhabited by ghosts of those who have passed away, specters, and all kinds of apparitions that move between both worlds, including poltergeists and a huge variety of spirits that transcend everything that we have written about them. It is a fascinating world in which all these individuals move and live, and the world of dreams is one of the intermediate worlds in which we can get in touch with them.

There is a variety of spirits as diverse as the variety of plants in our world: there are beneficent spirits, malevolent spirits, neutral spirits, divine-class spirits (slightly below deities), and ancestral spirits that transcend all concepts about good and evil. Working with them requires enormous practice (as does everything in magic), devotion (many times you will meet spirits that seek to receive affection, or even some kind of validation), respect (understand that they do not work for you and vice versa), and a lot of dedication. The deeper you go into your own power, the greater the variety of spirits you can work with.

Although our own world (the physical plane) is inhabited by an infinite number of these beings, not all of them are within our reach. Many of these spirits transcend the reach of all our senses (physical and mystical), and they are not so easily seen. As part of their spiritualistic practice, the traditional shamans of Peru and Guatemala ensure and teach that many spirits are in planes of existence so high that they transcended ours and no longer even remember the existence of our world more than as a vague memory of some very distant dream. In the *The Gospel According to Spiritism* author Allan Kardec writes:

Prayer is an invocation through which, by means of thought, Man enters into communication with the being to whom he directed himself. This may be for the purpose of asking for something, giving thanks, or as a glorification. We may pray for ourselves or for others, for the living or for the dead. Prayers addressed to God are heard by those Spirits who are charged with the execution of His will. All those addressed to good Spirits are referred to God. When someone prays to beings other than God, these are serving as mediators or intercessors, because nothing can happen without God's wishes.[20]

Certain old-school philosophers suggest in their prayers and rituals that when contacting the spirit world, we must insist to be heard or attended. Many times, you can spend hours praying to the spirits without being heard entirely, obviously depending on the spirit in question, and this something that constant practice leads you to resolve.

20. Kardec, *The Gospel According to Spiritism*.

Working with the Spirits

If the world of dreams is connected to the world of spirits like a bridge, it is normal to expect that spirits, ancestors, and guardians will be present in our dreams. After all, these spirits, just as we are, are passing through, moving between worlds and learning how to move between them—just as it is normal to expect that a deer will cross the roads built between parks since the parks are its natural habitat.

Multiple spirits can be present in our dreams. This list, which is not exclusive, includes:

- *Ghosts:* Souls or consciences of those who have left but maintain an unfinished business in the terrestrial world or who have suffered a tragic or perhaps even traumatic death, which does not allow them to advance in the spiritual world and keeps them tied to the place of their death. These are often the ones who end up existing in so-called haunted mansions and places of spiritualist worship.
- *Spirits:* Beings that embody the consciousness and memory of those who have left their body on the physical plane. Unlike ghosts, they are not tied to a physical place and can move freely between different worlds.

   In some Asian cultures, it is common to find folklore and tales about spirits that can end up becoming kami (animistic deities), who act as caretakers for shrines, torii, temples, and mountains.[21]

   In the local Indigenous culture of the Amazon, specifically among the Aboriginal ethnic groups of the Guajibo, Ye'kwana, Baniwa, Werekena, and Piapoco (who descend directly from the Arawak), spirits commonly come from the aquatic world and act as mediators between humans and the gods or high deities.
- *Guardian animals:* Guardian entities, either of a location or a person, that take the form of an animal native to the area.
- *Familiar spirits:* Guardian entities linked to a specific ethnic or family group that act as guardians and guides for the members of said group. They can often be spirits of the family's ancestors, a native

....

21. Ballaster, *Fables of the East.*
   Gould, *Youkai and Kaidan.*

guardian spirit that accompanies a nomadic group, or (in Amazonian Aboriginal tradition) the soul or consciousness of an unborn
individual that remains close to the family group.[22]

- *Divine spirits:* Depending on the group or religious tradition, these
high spirits can be angels, fairies, ancestors, ascended masters of the
New Age, or others. They act as mediators and messengers between
the high Divinity and humanity, delivering their messages in the
form of visions, dreams, premonitions, or omens.

Inhabiting a plane made entirely of energy, spirits are able to move more
easily in these planes, which they access from the world of spirits. For us
living beings, who are passing through the earthly plane and temporarily anointed by a body of flesh and blood, we are presented with a certain
difficulty in entering these parallel worlds. This premise is what makes the
constant practice of meditation and various methods of unfolding and astral
projection so popular among modern witches. Through the implementa-
tion of these various techniques, a witch, a magician, or a sorcerer is able to
move between these worlds with greater ease, allowing themselves not only
to access the dreams of others, assuming they have the necessary experience,
and their own for various purposes but also to interact with various spirits
and beings from the parallel world. They may communicate with these entities to make pacts or to request all kinds of magical and spiritual favors.

Guardian Spirits

Guardian spirits are there to be your allies and travel companions. Once you
are working with them, you will experience the huge feeling of being protected at all times. This feeling is accompanied by a massive responsibility. At
the end of the day, feeling protected by these spirits and other entities does
not always come free of charge. Usually they will expect the same attention
as a result, anticipating offerings and dedications of time and space (prayers
and altars) to help them to proceed to the next step of your spiritual evolution. There are many ways to work with guardian spirits, and there are
hundreds of spells and rituals written for it, but it is important to remember
three things that I had the opportunity to learn in the Amazon:

....
22. Van Cott, "Andean Indigenous Movements and Constitutional Transformation."

1. Your guardian spirits are exactly that—spirits. They move between worlds, anchoring themselves to you to stay close to this world. They are guardians who assist and protect you when necessary. They are not pets, and they are not trophies.

2. Guardian spirits require constant attention, beyond being greeted daily in the morning. They need to feel respected by you, who invoked them, and require (and enjoy) being cared for and treated as the guardians that they are.

3. A spiritual worker is only as powerful as their guardian spirit and vice versa. Spirits live a long time, perhaps too long, and they do not grow at the same rate as humans. Instead, they transcend and evolve at an entirely different speed. Acquiring power also takes a long time. Therefore, as a sorcerer, shaman, or magician advances in their practice, it is important to gain new guardians over time. These new guardians will reflect the level of your practice, and little by little you will have a small alliance of guardians working with you (not for you).

The difference between a guiding spirit and a guardian spirit (a difference that took me years of learning to understand personally) is that the former acts independently of you and your desires. They show up when they feel the time is right and guide you in the mystical processes that they consider to be useful. Once a guiding spirit has completed its teachings, they tend to disappear from your cycle and dedicate themselves to teaching others. After having closed the cycle, it is very difficult, almost impossible, to meet them again.

Guardian spirits, on the other hand, are there to provide assistance when required and to guide and protect you. The latter is their priority. Agreeing to any kind of deal with you allows them to move out of their world and thus move toward ours.

Don't get too immersed in the idea of conjuring a guardian spirit as if it is something you are going to do only once in your life. On the contrary, you will do it many times. A guardian responds to your level of power, and as we would say in New Age terms, it responds to your frequency, to your vibration. No matter how powerful you want your guardian to be, they will respond to your call according to the level of power that you are capable of manifesting.

As you progress through the meditations in this book, you might feel that you need a new guardian to keep you company. This need can manifest itself in many ways, such as a feeling of impending danger during your meditations, chills followed by a momentary blurred vision when you wake up from a session of magical work or meditation, or simply feeling that it is taking more time to advance in your practice. The latter is because you are immersing yourself in increasingly deep and complex worlds where at times you lose your connection with your senses and begin to feel an enormous weight on you. It is there a new guardian spirit will be of help to you and your magical work—to help you reconnect and deal with these sensations, as well as to protect you within these worlds.

Once you have started working with a guardian spirit and have created an ongoing working relationship with them, that spirit will be within reach whenever it is required to provide assistance and guidance to its summoner or sorcerer, and it is of the utmost importance not to take it for granted. Their work and presence when they are present, the support of the spirits as intermediaries between us and the spiritual worlds, can make a huge difference in the life of a sorcerer.

EXERCISE
Summoning a Guardian Spirit

Many times, it is in dreams that we receive the guidance we are waiting for, get answers from the oracles to our requests, and talk with our loved ones who have left. I invite you to customize this ritual in your own way if you wish to do so.

You will need:
- Handmade figure that can act as a totem or channeling body for the spirit
- Between 12 to 19.5 inches (30 to 50 centimeters) of blue fabric ribbon with seven knots tied around the figure as a symbol of alliance
- White candle in candleholder

- Lighter or matches
- Charcoal
- Censer
- Glass with equal parts of water and honey and a touch of fruit liqueur
- Incense blend made from myrrh, frankincense, dried mint leaves, eucalyptus, verbena, and rose petals
- Sheet of paper with the name that is going to be assigned to the guardian spirit written on it
- Dish with a small offering of fresh flowers and nuts (almonds, walnuts, pistachios, peanuts, hazelnuts, chestnuts, etc.)

Time: This can be performed on any day at a time between sunset and midnight, but a Monday (a day associated with the moon and ghosts, spirits, and other apparitions) is preferable.

Begin by placing the figure or totem facing you. Place all other elements except the incense blend intuitively around the figure, forming a small altar or devotional space.

Light the candle and the coal. Once the coal looks intensely red or white, proceed to pour the incense on it in small portions. Recite the following incantation three times:

> **OOOH, great avatars and blessed spirits,**
> **Hear my humble call and be welcome.**
> **Send to this sacred place and time a protective spirit.**
> **Send a strong and conscious spirit to watch over me at all times.**
> **Make come the one who is destined to guard my dreams.**
> **Let nothing and no one disturb my rest or my energy.**
> **Let nothing and no one interfere with the manifestation of my dreams.**
> **Here I wait for you to work with this once it arrives.**
> **May it be so, today, tomorrow, and always,**
> **So be it.**

Then take the paper with the name to be assigned. Proceed to burn it from the corners in the candle flame, and let it burn over the incense while reciting:

Welcome, you are here, oh great guardian spirit,
from today your name will be our secret and in our secret is our
contract.
And your name from now on will be (insert name). *(repeat three
times)*
And then it will be you who sleeps while I wake up.
And then it will be you who wakes up and takes care of me while I
sleep.
And it will be you then, (insert name), *(repeat the name three times)*
who guards that nothing and no one disturbs my dreams.
And from tonight you will be the one who accompanies my travel-
ing spirit in all its adventures and endeavors.
May it be so, today, tomorrow, and always.
So be it.

Moisten your fingers with the water from the cup and splash the figurine and the four corners of your workspace three times. Touch your lips
with two fingers of your left hand and say:

Oh (insert name), you are welcome to this place.

Then touch with these two fingers the figure (which from now on will
be the totem), close your eyes for a short moment, and take three deep
breaths.

Open your eyes, get up, and extinguish the candle without blowing (it
can be done with your fingers). Be sure to keep the candle and the rest of
the incense in a separate place. These now belong to your guardian spirit
and will only be used in the future when you or your guardian consider it
necessary.

Pick up the figure and place it where it can see the door in the room.
Every night before going to sleep, kiss the two fingers you consecrated the
figure with and then touch them to the totem to indicate that it should
wake up.

Ritual Care

You can prepare more of the incense mixture by combining equal parts
of the ingredients and burn it from time to time inside the room with the
totem. You can also serve a small cup of warm tea next to the totem and
dispose of the beverage the next morning.

Nullification of the Ritual

If, for some reason, it is your wish in the future to release this spirit from your contract and end this ritual, you must recreate the ritual with all its elements. Using the original candle with which you made the initial invocation, recite the following incantation, and let the candle burn until the end.

O mighty spirit, (insert name),
our deal and our contract has been powerful,
your time has come to leave.
I release you from our tasks together.
I let you go free of all responsibility.
I appreciate your presence and your strength at all times.
I let you go, (insert name), you are free to go.
Blessed be your presence always.
So be it.

Little Spirits

The *kabis*, or *aggiyis*, are a kind of minor spirit that lives in forests, fields, parks, and around lakes in the Amazon region. These conscious and individual manifestations of nature usually appear as figures as tiny as small larvae that float in the air or as big as aloe leaves. The kabis never appear one at a time; they always arrive in small groups similar to herds. Some seers claim to see these little spirits as fast-moving lights that move around them like fast fireflies. Although they are spirits of nature and emerge from it, they lack other skills or knowledge beyond protecting everything that is green and alive. They are not the strongest spirits. They are, according to more modern or progressive practitioners, spirits made from the residual energy of older spirits, and for this reason, they lack morals, knowledge, or even character of their own beyond acting on their own intuition.

There are many spirits of nature. The kabis, unlike other essential spirits, such as the *kabimaras* (spirits of the waters and rivers), the *ozunbi* (spirits of the rocks and the earth), or *jiojio* (spirits of the campfire), are a class of lesser spirits, often underestimated in local folklore. Because their presence is still and silent, they are adept at moving between people's minds and dreams, carrying messages in the form of sounds and images from one place to another.

According to the urban folklore of the villages of the Venezuelan Amazon, a skilled sorcerer with a strong relationship with the kabis is capable of conjuring fire and rain, seeing past lives through dreams, cursing long nights of insomnia to their enemies to drive them to madness and despair, or possessing animal spirits through the kabis. These minor spirits are traditionally invoked as a practice by sorcerers and priests. They can be a powerful ally in large numbers, but it takes time to master this skill, like everything in the field of sorcery, and without constant practice and discipline, you get nowhere.

The kabis spirits are permanently faithful to the sorcerer. When the sorcerer dies, the kabis accompany the sorcerer on their journey between worlds since they have bonded with the spiritual energy of the sorcerer, not with their physical presence.

It is common among us to hear "The kabis take care of you," when a person survives an accident or some mysterious situation occurs. It is assumed that these spirits are taking care of the sorcerer.

Dream Guardian Spirits: Laaki and Lunera

Luna bonita, lunita, lunerá, custodia mis sueños y guarda mis noches, cuentame cuentos con regocijo y derroche. (Pretty moon, little moon, moonlight, guard my dreams and keep my nights, tell me stories with flamboyance and joy.)

So says a traditional Venezuelan lullaby. This song is a translation of a lullaby that was originally sung by the Lokonos[23] in Maipure,[24] the Arawak language, and this is the only fragment of that song preserved today. The lullaby acted more as a prayer to the moon in the three forms it took for the natives: Atabey, the moon as a deity; Karaya, the moon as a physical element; and Akti, the moonlight that represents its spirit.

These days this lullaby is sung very softly while using one hand to cover the child's eyes and the other hand to uncover a small carved wooden figurine, called Laaki, with three eyes painted in oil on it. This figurine is a totem that acts as a guardian to stop evil spirits and nightmares from entering the dreams of the child while they sleep.

....

23. *Lokono* means "people" in Arawak.
24. Maipure as a language is closer to the Western Arawak spoken in Venezuela, Guyana, and Suriname than the Eastern Arawak spoken in French Guiana.

Laaki is what we know in traditional spiritualism as an anchor. We use it to connect the dreams of the baby with the guardian and also to harness the power of the dreams.

If a child has a frightful nightmare or vision, or any apparition occurs in the room, Laaki is covered with a piece of dark cloth to blind them. It is believed that the anxious spirit will then go mad and do violent mischief to dispel any negative entity in the vicinity.

A more modern method, in which the Laaki or spirit is treated with more respect, is to serve them a cup of sweet coffee and light a candle in their honor to wake them up and invite them to guard the room.

Laaki is not a single spirit; they are a guardian of the neighborhoods and the crossroads who acts as the child's protector. In return, the child, as they grow up, will be able to act as the anchor to harness the spirit in the world of the living, allowing the spirit to be among us for a longer time.

The measures to create the Laaki totem are not specific. Although most of these statuettes are traditionally made with practically any type of wood, some more traditional sorcerers believe that the figurine must be made from a piece of the root of the tree or from the forest where the wood was extracted to build the child's hut or cabin. Other less traditional followers of folklore simply buy these statuettes in the *guajiro* market (a type of market for traditional and Indigenous crafts that is quite common in countries such as Venezuela, Colombia, and Argentina).

Lunera represents a powerful allied talisman that can be used in witch-craft as a way for witches to harness the power of their own dreams at night. According to oral tradition, this spirit devours nightmares and chokes on curses that they find in the surroundings. The spirit grows to be as big as long trees and acquires such an imposing appearance that other lesser spirits feel intimidated.

EXERCISE
Conjuring the Kabis

This is an exercise to conjure the kabis as it is carried out in the Amazon. There are two variations of the same ritual: one of them is a closed and completely hermetic practice only for those who are born or live in the area, and the second is the version that I teach you here. It is usually put into practice with some tourists from time to time. This ritual essentially requires constant practice because the first times you do it, you experience fairly short effects.

The kabis communicate through a language that is based more on emotions shared through sound than on words and their literal meaning. That is why even if some of these words are pronounced incorrectly, they will understand the intention behind them; the words are simply a vehicle to carry the intention.

This reminds me of one of my many masters in the past (RIP) Javier Alexander Cabas, a native sorcerer and priest from Amazonas, who said, "The spirits speak many languages, languages that we still do not know on earth, languages that it is not their priority to teach us, therefore the symbolism and the sounds must represent our intentions."

Once they have been conjured, the kabis are present on the spot, and this time of silent interaction allows them to acknowledge the authority of the sorcerer who summoned them. Although this is entirely different from the more commercial version of sorcery, where the conjurer summons an unknown spirit and immediately gives it orders, this is the way we work in the Amazon lands. The relationship with spirits is based on respect and working together, so we spend more time conjuring various spirits to form alliances with rather than simply giving orders and collecting favors from them.

You will need:
- Leaves and flowers touched by the first rays of the morning sun
- Small stones
- Small stool (optional)

To begin, first collect leaves and flowers from the ground that have been touched by the first rays of sun in the morning. These are leaves and flowers that are not in the shade during dawn but touched by the light directly. Make a small circle with the stones (it does not need to be any bigger than a dinner plate) and gather the flowers inside it.

Once the circle is assembled, sit in front of it, either on the floor or on a small stool. Relax, take a couple of deep breaths, close your eyes, and proceed to chant six times:

OHH AHMM UHMA, UHMA AHMM OHH.

Open your hands, palms toward the circle, and raise your arms to shoulder height, keeping your hands open to the circle of stones full of leaves and flowers.

Keeping your eyes closed, repeat the incantation six more times. Breathe deeply and slowly and recite it another six times; you will have performed the incantation eighteen times in total so far.

Then, open your eyes and place the palms of your hands on the ground to gain control. In this way, we believe that the energy of the sorcerer will nourish the land from which these spirits are manifesting upon hearing that they are called in their own language.

Proceed to observe the seemingly empty space between you and the tiny altar of stones and flowers. Keep your eyes on this space for about five minutes in complete silence, seeking to notice or perceive any change in the air or in the breeze, any slight flashes of light without apparent origin, or any certain sounds that may seem to be of animal origin even if you know there are no animals nearby.

When these spirits are invoked on a large scale, sounds similar to the meowing of a cat can be heard. There may also be a sound similar to the noise made by dogs when they drink water. These are quite peculiar sounds, but they are the closest thing to the sound that you are likely to get. Listen.

Once the five minutes are up, pronounce the following six times (you can keep this book nearby as a guide or write it down on paper):

UUULAUH URAI ANNNUURIIIA.

The closest modern translation of this from the native language would be something similar to "I recognize your presence, thank you" or "Thank you for making yourself present."

Once the five minutes have passed, proceed to stand up and simply recite the first incantation again:

OHH AHMM UHMA, UHMA AHMM OHH.

Then open the circle of rocks and release the spirits that have been present. The essence of the flowers and leaves, which was used to help you manifest in the physical plane, will follow you during the coming days and nights, and the kabis will follow, seeking to interact with it and impregnate its essence.

EXERCISE
Advanced Method of Conjuring

This is a slightly more elaborate version of the previous ritual. Use your fingers to draw the shape of a circle in the dirt on the ground. Then, draw a diamond (the traditional figure of the four-pointed diamond in cards) with its points protruding from the circle and a curved figure similar to a snake inside the diamond as you can see in the image here:

Place the leaves and some of the flowers inside the drawing, then make a second circle out of the remaining flowers around the drawing. The rest of the procedure occurs in exactly the same way as in the previous ritual.

This ritual is performed to conjure back all the kabis that have been conjured in the past. The symbol represents the traces of the native gods. All the kabis spirits that have been invoked before and over the years, which have abandoned us for some reason and we no longer feel their presence or have been neglected and we believe they have left, will heed this call.

Other Exercises and Experiments

1. After you have performed either of these rituals at least five different times on different days (preferably in different places), replace the flowers and leaves with a feather of some bird that you have with you. This will manifest the kabis using the energy of the bird in question.
2. Perform the ritual again with a pot of flowers that you have at home. Notice how the flowers begin to grow and/or deteriorate in the following days.
3. Perform the ritual in different open places, such as in parks or in a nearby field.
4. Perform the ritual at night a few hours before bed. Pay attention to how your sleep cycles act during the following nights.

Simple Dream Spells for Spiritual Alliance

Here is a list of easy and simple spells from magical Venezuelan folklore for your own use. These simple recipes have been passed down orally in my hometown for generations and are part of our magical traditions.

1. A cup of coffee by the door in the morning signals to spirits and ghosts that they are welcome in the home.
2. A crystal ball next to a bedside glass of water helps reveal the faces of our allied spirits and familiar ghosts.
3. A necklace made of red string and blessed coffee beans on a full moon keeps family ghosts close.
4. An infusion of jasmine and cornflower should be drunk nine nights in a row to open the spiritual eyes and the third eye. Drinking this is effective for those who practice astral projection or move between the dream world and otherworlds.
5. Dried jasmine and cornflower flowers can be mixed with chrysanthemum flowers and burned as a votive incense to win the favor of the spirits and ghosts around us.
6. Light some candles in the name of San Cipriano, the famous and very wise witch/sorcerer, and ask him for clarity and clairvoyance every night for eleven nights in a row.

Dream Magic Insight
CHARM BAG TO MEET YOUR FAMILIAR IN YOUR DREAMS
BY ARIANA CARRASCA

Charm bags are one of the most underrated forms of sorcery and, in turn, among the most popular. According to your level of experience, you can create these charms and make them as powerful as you can.

You will need:
- Blue charm bag or blue cloth tied with cord or string (to represent communication)
- Handful of mugwort (as a spirit of dreaming and divination)
- Object tied to your familiar or spirit sigil (to act as a taglock or representation of the spirit)

Take three deep breaths, inhaling for three counts and exhaling for three. This aligns and calms your inner spirit so that you're prepared and in the right headspace to perform the spell.

Grab a handful of mugwort and hold it in your hands. Take a moment to inhale the scent of the herb and feel its energy. As an animist, I usually whisper softly to the mugwort, repeating the following three times:

> **Spirit of mugwort, work with me here in this magic.**
> **Connect me to my familiar, may (name) (or [he/she/they]) appear to me in my dreams.**
> **Let my familiar find (his/her/their) way to me, in this liminal space in my sleep.**

Place the mugwort inside the blue charm bag or fabric. Then, take the object that is tied to your familiar, visualize your familiar spirit in your mind clearly (if possible), and call out to him/her/them. Ask for the spirit's presence and gesture to the object as a token of them.

Place the object inside the blue charm bag or fabric and close it up. Lay it on the table and rub your hands together. As you do so, acknowledge the energy building up and focus on your goal to meet your familiar in your dreams. You can chant this intention repeatedly, whisper it, or say it firmly in your mind. When you're ready, push the energy into the charm bag and hold it in your hands. Seal the spell by kissing the charm bag three times.

Before you sleep, try to avoid consuming any immersive media, such as TV, or scrolling through social media. This allows for the mind to be empty, so to speak, and ensures that your dreams won't be influenced by the information recently absorbed. If you usually struggle to remember your dreams, take some time to practice techniques to aid in this before you cast the spell. Having a consistent sleep cycle can help, along with maintaining a dream journal to write down pieces of what you can remember; over time you'll find you're better able to recall what you dreamed.

To finalize the spell, place the charm bag underneath your pillow or under the bed. Before you head to sleep, repeat the following:

Spirit that which is familiar to me, come find me in my dreams.

Remember to write down what you dreamed and be prepared for this to take time; it might not happen on the first go. Outside of the spell, be sure to give regular offerings to your familiar to strengthen your bond, as this will encourage their presence and communication.

Happy dreaming!

TRIBAL TALES
PACAHUARA PEOPLE

The Pacahuara is one of the most difficult ethnic groups in Bolivia to find, and it is considered to be on the list of uncontacted people from Amazonas. Although for many years it was believed that only four people made up the remnants of this tribe, today we know that another fifty members of this group live on the borders of Brazil, specifically around the Rio Negro.

Although their language does not have a written form, it is similar to the current languages that have come from Arawak as well as the languages spoken by the Wayúu. Little is known about their culture and traditions because they prefer to stay distant. However, we know that they practice a traditional tribal religion; venerate the river and the heavens as deities whose names should not be written, much less pronounced outside the tribe; and believe the animals were created by a divinity of a feminine character, while the plants and trees were a gift from the rivers.

In their traditional religion, the *inauibo*, or "dreams," (at least that is how I suppose it is written because I have only heard it spoken) consist of long conversations that we have with the gods while we sleep. According to this vision, dreams occur in a divine language that we cannot pronounce with our tongues, and that is why dreams are full of secrets and mysteries. Unless an important event (birth, death, earthquake) occurs in the dream, the visions should not be shared with more than parents and chiefs of the tribe, who are the only ones with the divine right to know and interpret it.

CHAPTER 5
LUCID DREAMING & DREAM WALKING

Your dreams are connected with each and every one of your incarnation purposes, with each and every one of your past lives, and with each and every path and decision for your future lives. Dreams are perfectly designed by your subconscious (and by your unconscious in each of your different lives) to be guides and paths, which are full of signs. These signs are discovered step-by-step to help you achieve the alignment that you seek within yourself, with your personal purpose, with your goals of evolution and growth, and with everything you want.

Lucid dreams are more common than we think. They are those visions that occur while we sleep in which we feel or perceive in some way that we have control over the dream—over our presence in it or over the elements that compose it.

While dreams occur practically instantaneously and are presented as visions in which we limit ourselves to following a role (as an assistant to the play or as one of the actors in it), in lucid dreams we feel and perceive that we are aware of our thoughts and our actions. We are perfectly aware of the intentions behind them, and furthermore, we are able to take the dream in a desired direction, such as recapitulating a past memory or going far into the future. In a lucid dream, we are able to break the rules that limit us to being only passing visitors during rest, and we can consciously contact our ancestors and other loved ones who have departed.

Inducing a Lucid Dream

As mentioned in chapter 1, lucid dreaming is a form of active dreaming. This does not mean that we are quite active during this period of sleep, since when we wake up, we can probably only perceive the memory of what happened as just another dream, or perhaps even convince ourselves that nothing that happened was orchestrated by ourselves, but by our subconscious taking control of the entire vision.

Active dreaming implies that we are aware during the process. We are able to perform certain exercises consciously to differentiate the dream from reality, and it does not affect us physically. On the other hand, a lucid dream leads us to take complete control of the dream experience, leaving us with a sensation similar to insomnia during the day as a physical consequence. This is because although the body has been fully rested, the mind has continued to work consciously for hours and hours. The brain is now perceiving twice as much, which leads to a feeling of physical and mental tiredness, as well as irritability.

Magicians have written dozens or perhaps even hundreds of rituals to be performed during the dream journey, from ecstasy magic rites to rituals that unfold in different places while your physical body remains at rest. The way to carry out these rituals consists entirely of mastering or completely controlling the ability to have a lucid dream, which requires a lot of meditation, often years of practice, and discipline to achieve the desired effects.

The obstacle to this magical realization lies mainly in the fact that although we are sleeping, our brain must continue working. This leads us to embrace a state in which although we remain asleep, a part of our brain keeps filing and compiling information from the recent day and that leads us to work twice as hard to master lucid dreams with certainty and clarity.

EXERCISE
Dream Map

Lucid dreams occur mostly spontaneously, although they can also be induced through exercises, rituals, and various sorcerous methods. One of the most common ways is to create a dream map before going to sleep. It consists of a sheet of paper on which you write down in detail what, where, and with whom you want to dream. That same list is written with the same details several times. Then you go to bed and dream of what you wrote.

Try this exercise out anytime. It is easy to do. But it is likely that you will only perceive a small teasing of its effects the first time you do it. With regular discipline, you will achieve the expected results.

You will need:
- Sheet of paper
- Pen or pencil
- Glass of water
- Symbol of what you wish to dream about (optional)

Just before going to bed, write what you wish to dream about on the piece of paper. It can be a few simple lines, such as "I am remembering my most recent trip to Madrid, and I remember it with all certainty, clarity, and detail; nothing gets in the way of my dream," or it can be a more complex list, such as "Tonight, after closing my eyes, I will feel in my hands the cold metal of the handrails of the Eiffel Tower's staircase. I will climb the steps one by one, and I will feel the breeze on my face. I catch the aroma of coffee from tourists around me, and even the noise of people and the music on their phones doesn't disturb my sleep."

Write these same lines several times and in the same order. It can be three times, it can be six times, it can be twelve times—whatever you want. Then, read the words in a firm voice, decreeing them as an order. Drink the glass of water and proceed to rest.

If you wish, you can place the sheet of paper on the night table next to something that symbolizes what you want to dream about, such as a key-chain with the symbol of the Eiffel Tower, some seashells, or a photograph from your most recent vacation. Keep the symbol on the table for several weeks or months, however long you prefer, and repeat this exercise two to three times per month.

Other Lucid Dreaming Spells

Here are a few other quite effective rituals and easy-to-do workings from my personal cabinet to help you achieve a lucid dream.

RECIPE
Herbal Dream Tea for Lucid Dreaming

This spell promotes restful sleep and a profound lucid dream atmosphere. Combine one tablespoon each of tulsi, also called holy basil, and skullcap in two cups of boiling water. Allow the herbs to steep for ten to fifteen minutes. Best results occur if the tea is ingested before bed on an empty stomach.

RECIPE
Charm Bag or Incense to Promote Lucid Dreaming

Blend the dried leaves of ashwagandha, tulsi, and skullcap with rose petals in equal parts during a new moon night. Burn the incense before meditation or sleep, or save the mixture in a blue or indigo charm bag and keep it on the bed or close to the bed two to three nights a week.

RECIPE
Herbal Bath Infusion to Sleep Well and Deep

Craft a blend with six spoons of each of these dried herbs: catnip, valerian, kava kava, passionflower, lavender, and chamomile flower. Keep the blend in a crystal jar or a wooden box to keep it fresh and clean. This mix provides a gentle, calming effect to help you fall asleep faster and maximize the restorative deep sleep cycle. It is also an excellent mix to add to your bath and soak in if you are training yourself to have a lucid dream without waking up suddenly in the night.

RECIPE
Lucid Dreaming Tonic

This calming night tonic was designed to enhance deep dreaming, help soothe the nervous system, and support restful sleep.

You will need:
- 1 teaspoon ashwagandha
- 1 teaspoon passionflower
- 1 teaspoon kava kava
- 1 teaspoon skullcap
- 1 teaspoon cinnamon bark
- 1 teaspoon ginger
- 2 glasses of water
- Small pot
- Mixing spoon
- Strainer
- Small cauldron or bowl

You can also add (in future doses):
- 1 teaspoon rose geranium
- 1 teaspoon rose petals
- 1 teaspoon stevia (just for flavor)

In the small pot, boil all the ingredients with the water from one of the glasses. Stir the infusion continuously, and once it is ready (it should have a uniform color and appearance), strain the mixture and pour it into the small cold cauldron or bowl. Let the mixture stand for fifteen minutes, and then add the second glass of cold water.

Drink a tablespoon of this infusion just one hour before bedtime. Keep the rest of the mixture in a sealed glass container, and drink one tablespoon every two nights.

RECIPE
Intuition Flower Tea

Blue lotus and mugwort flowers are tea flowers known to provoke deep meditation and motivate lucid dreaming. The effects of these plants are euphoric while helping to cool down the nervous system and promote a feeling of relaxation to the whole body. To make the tea, mix the dried flowers together and use about one to two teaspoons of the mix per cup of water. Allow the mix to steep in near-boiling water for about ten minutes.

RECIPE
An Intuition Potion

Blue lotus flowers induce deep dreams and enhance our psychic vision in them. Bring two cups of water or milk to a boil and add the following ingredients one at a time, pausing five minutes between each while mixing. Serve in a cup and let cool for five minutes. Drink this concoction calmly. You can accompany it with a brief meditation or soft background music.

You will need:
- 3 teaspoons blue lotus flowers
- 1 teaspoon mugwort
- 1 teaspoon rose petals
- 1 teaspoon chamomile flowers
- 1 spoon honey (optional)

Dream Walking

Dream walking is an extraordinary and unusual ability that is a manifestation of individual psychic talent. It is considered one of the forms of experimental magic in the realm of dream magic. The travelers, or dream walkers, also known as *caminantes* (walkers) in Latin America, and oneironauts, according to the most modern scholars, are those individuals (humans and animals) who manifest the ability to move outside the usual dream routine. Thus, they are able to move between worlds, either in the world of dreams or in worlds and universes with a different energy vibration, such as the world of spirits or one of those worlds that, according to different myths, can be inhabited by demons, evil spirits, and other entities of a low-energy vibration.

While the lucid dreamer witnesses events in dreams while also conscious, *dream walker* is the term used for individuals who, either by voluntary or involuntary action, can move beyond the created dream. Imagine there is a curtain that separates us from the rest of the realities. The dream walker crosses through it to other planes, and once in them, the walkers in question are able to wander between other minds, other dreams, and other worlds.

Most dream walkers out there acknowledge that these episodes occur mostly involuntarily, and most of the cases occur infrequently, either after several months or with several years between them. However, when the psychic episodes do happen, they usually occur for several nights in a row, the ability often unlocked by cosmic events or stressful situations.

Timing

Dream walkers often discover this ability in early adolescence, though it is not unusual for an adult to begin experiencing these kinds of situations.

As with common dreams, the experiences associated with lucid dreaming and dream walking are easily forgotten upon awakening. In certain cases, some of these experiences could be so traumatic that the individual unconsciously erases them completely from their head or blocks the memory of them.

We can assume that everyone, at some point, has experienced that strange sensation of falling from a large building when going to sleep. There are certainly a dozen different scientific explanations for this, although conveniently most of these scientific explanations do not attribute the problem to night visions that happen prior to the experience. Some examples include dreaming that you are walking between buildings, on clouds, or even on the surface of water and falling.

When this experience occurs with children, and this is something that I have more experience with than I would like because of my multiple nephews, the children always seem to remember all kinds of monstrous phenomena. Unlike adults, who remember falling, children remember weird creatures with hundreds of eyes and horns, winged beasts, or monsters with big mouths and lots of teeth—always in pretty dark places.

This seems to be a dream walking experience in which the traveler (the child in question) falls or descends to lower planes, where these low-energy creatures live, and immediately wakes up. Although many times we limit ourselves to thinking that it was just a nightmare due to the impressionable mind of the child, we could be ignoring a larger problem, possibly the memory of a triggering and traumatic experience. After repeating the experience several more times, the child consciously blocks these problem dreams so they do not seem to remember them anymore. In the process, they unconsciously block these abilities or psychic manifestations, which may or may not manifest again in adulthood.

Dream walking is often considered an inherited talent. In the Caribbean, the art of walking between dreams and nightmares is considered a gift given by the divinity or some superior entity that is passed down from generation to generation. Even so, there are multiple common rituals in Latin American folklore and oral traditions on how to awaken this ability and make use of it.

Spells for the Dream Walker

Here is a collection of easy traditional spells from my land, slightly modified and properly translated for your use. I do not include this list of spells for you to try to put them all into practice, but rather for you to choose those that you feel are most suitable for your practice and within your financial reach.

EXERCISE
The Perfect Charm Bag for a Dream Walker

Prepare a bag of blue or purple cloth smaller than the fist of your hand. Fill the bag with a piece of lapis lazuli and equal parts mugwort and Saint John's wort. Seal the bag with gold thread or blue or purple fabric ribbon and enshrine it in a circle of salt. Keep this talisman with you, either under your pillow or in a saucer by your bed, to clear your spiritual vision and give yourself protection when you are going to perform this sort of magical work between worlds.

EXERCISE
Incense Bottled for the Altar of Dream Walkers

If you already have an altar and are a regular magic worker who is trying to deepen its power related to the world of dreams, this exercise will help you a lot.

To make the incense, you will need:
- Mortar and pestle
- 1 part acacia leaves
- 1 part laurel leaves
- 1 part cedarwood chips
- 1 part copal
- 1 part myrrh
- 1 part mugwort
- 1 part star anise
- 1 part red rose petals
- 1 part lavender flowers

Mix the dried herbs in the mortar with the pestle. Seal the mixture in a tall glass bottle and keep it in a cool place with regular lighting. Extract two tablespoons of the mixture every one to two weeks to burn with charcoal in a censer.

This supercharged incense has the properties to protect you mentally and emotionally while doing astral travel or living a lucid dream. It also relaxes and softens your energy, allowing you to move more easily or with more conscious actions between dreams.

EXERCISE
Scrying Spell with Fire and Water
(to Perform after Dream Walking)

If you have recently woken up from an experience linked to dream walking, so recent that you still carry some images and sensations in your mind and body, I advise you to perform this spell in the following hours. That is because the images and memories of the dream that remain in your consciousness can easily be forgotten or modified throughout the day.

You will need:
- Lighter or matches
- White candle in candleholder
- Fabric ribbon or thick string
- Handful of yerba santa (tarweed)
- Handful of rosemary
- Glass of water
- Dark bowl, preferably made of wood or some kind of mineral
- Heatproof container or plate

In a comfortable and distraction-free space, preferably outside where you can sit in broad daylight, place all of your supplies in front of you. Light the candle and use the ribbon or thread to tie the plants together, making a small bouquet of herbs. Slowly pour the water into the bowl and, as you watch the water occupy the bowl, say out loud:

> With my guides, I walk back into the night.
> In the sweetest shadow, I immerse myself.
> I let you spirits show me right.
> Guide me to see beyond the lies.
> I look back with my inner eyes.

The darkest deep I saw last night.
To take the truth I seek to arise.

Once you have filled the bowl a little more than halfway, hold your handful of herbs with one hand and light one end of it with the candle flame. Move the herbs around the bowl, creating a thin smoke curtain, while reciting the incantation two more times.

Set the herbs aside on the heatproof container and focus on observing the surface of the water in the bowl. Observe the shapes the smoke forms on the surface.

At the end, once the smoke clears, dispose of the water outside and extinguish the candle. Let the herbs burn all the way down, using the smoke as natural incense to cleanse the air after the ritual.

Dream Magic Insight
PARA AYUDAR A CONCILIAR EL SUEÑO (REST DREAM SPELL)
BY MARIA ELENA U.

These magical Venezuelan folklore recipes have remained in my family's diaries and cookbooks for at least four generations. These recipes are carried out to prevent night visions from turning into nightmares and from causing you to wake up, allowing you to deepen the dream experience and stay asleep a little longer.

Recipe I
You will need:
- 5 leaves of *prodigiosa* (*Brickellia cavanillesii*)
- 5 leaves of *pronto alivio* (*Lippia alba*)
- Cascarilla powder
- 2 pieces of cotton
- Small sprig of rosemary (optional)
- White cord

After a cold and refreshing shower, place the leaves of both plants and the powder on one of the pieces of cotton, and if you wish, add the small sprig of rosemary. Cover with a second piece of cotton and tie with the white cord. Place this herbal charm inside the pillow to improve sleep and deep rest.

Recipe II
You will need:
- 4 lengths of yellow or white thread
- 8 sprigs of fresh rue
- Glass of water with a bit of salt

Using a length of thread, tie two sprigs together at their centers, forming a small cross. Repeat this step with the other branches.

Place one cross of rue under your pillow, another under the sheet at waist height, another under the sheet at the height the feet go, and the fourth cross of rue under the bed on the glass of water and salt.

Keep the crosses there for four nights in a row, and then throw them in the trash.

TRIBAL TALES
ONA PEOPLE / ONAWO OR
SELK'NAM / THE SHAMANS

The Selk'nam, or Ona, were an Amerindian people
who lived until the beginning of the twentieth century in the north and
center of the Big Island of Tierra del Fuego (Kárwkènká in the Selk'nam
language) at the southern end of the South American continent in Argentina and Chile. Originally these peoples were terrestrial nomads, hunters,
and gatherers. After a genocide at the beginning of the twentieth century
and a process of transculturation that operated for more than a century, the
Selk'nam were dispersed throughout the continent, and a number of children were sold in mainland ports. The language has been extinct for decades.
However, there are currently efforts by Selk'nam descendants to recover the
culture and revitalize the language.

During the Selk'nam's male initiation rites, the elders revealed tribal
secrets to the young men, or *klóketen*. These initiation rites, called H'ain,
were carried out around the age of eighteen, and it gave young men the category of adults. The rites were based on a myth that narrated how, in a myth-
ical time, the women kept the men dominated by disguising themselves as
spirits. In the myth, a man called Sol discovered the impostor, and all the
women, except his wife, Luna, were murdered. Since then, the men appropriated the deception and continued to represent it in order to dominate
women in turn. The women never learned that the masked males were not
truly spirits, but the males found out at the initiation rite.

Temáukel was the denomination of a great supernatural entity that they
believed kept the world in order. The creator deity of the world was called
Kénos, or Quénos. The sun and the moon, which they called Krenn and
Kreen, had great importance for them. The sun was the husband of the
moon, and he ran after her to punish her without ever reaching her.

The shamans, called *xo'on*, helped hunters and cured illnesses. They
received their power from the spirits of the dead shamans, who appeared to
them only in dreams. These dreams should never be interrupted, which is
why the rest of the xo'on was so valuable and important. It was protected to

the point of preparing various brews of herbs and wildflowers to appease the medium and allow him more hours of sleep.

The visions and dreams of the xo'on were of considerable importance for their religion and their culture. The dreams were narrated in public and interpreted over and over again until they mixed with their oral folklore. The xo'on were considered as respectable as they were dangerous because they possessed the secrets of dreams and could cause the death of the enemy from within them.

Dreams were considered their sacred means to communicate not only with the afterlife (made up of the souls of deceased relatives) but with other shamans of the past, with divine and protective spirits, and with other superior entities. Through dreams, they could invoke the animal spirits that protected them from warriors, as well as possess the consciousness and will of wild animals and use them as their night vehicle, an esoteric belief that they shared with many other South American tribes.

The Spiritist Hierarchy

According to anthropologists and ethnologists Anne Chapman and Martín Gusinde, the priests and sorcerers of the Ona people was made up of a spiritist hierarchy with three categories: *xo'on*, *lailuka*, and *cha-ain*.[25]

Xo'on (Shamans)

Xo'on were those priests who enjoyed high prestige. They were dedicated to solving all kinds of worldly affairs through sorcery and by means considered supernatural. Each shaman had an apprentice who acted as a novice and assistant to the shaman for many years. They were elevated to the rank of xo'on once the master shaman died and visited the novice through a dream to reveal the secrets they must know.

They were the officiants of all religious ceremonies, funeral rites, and celebrations. They were considered the makers of the weather, as it was believed they were capable of altering the natural movement of clouds and conjuring rain and other elements. For all these functions, they made use of various herbal methods to enter a trance or fall into a state of deep sleep because their

....

25. Chapman, *End of a World.*
   Chapman, *Hain.*

power was limited by the physical body. They had to project themselves outside the body (either while sleeping or in a trance) in order to free their spirit
and use their magical and spiritual power to its full potential.

From the world of dreams and spirits, they were able to move between
other worlds, enter dreams to cure or manifest nightmares, or learn secrets.

Lailuka (Sages)

The lailuka were considered the wise elders of the tribe. They did not sing
any kind of songs, prayers, or spells, nor were they given magical powers or
trained to enter a trance.

The wise people in the tribe had three main functions: to know and teach
the mythology, traditions, and history of the tribe; to study and protect their
language as well as the secret language of the spirits so that it is not lost; and
to assign the names of each member of the tribe (a task that is considered
sacred).When assigning names, the sages gave two different kinds: common
names and names of high rank.

Common names were assigned to the people of the tribe according to
their physical characteristics or character traits. They were also assigned to
foreigners and visitors who had earned the respect of the tribe.

The names of high rank, or names of prestige, were later assigned to replace
the common names of children and adults who demonstrated superior wisdom
and character or to members of the tribe who had achieved some incredible feat,
as they were then considered human beings of divine nature.

Cha-Ain (Prophets)

Cha-ain were the highest in the hierarchy. They were considered superior to
shamans and sages. In mythology, each person was born under the shelter
of a star in the firmament, each individual being the incarnate soul of that
star. The work of the cha-ain was to study the names and histories of all the
stars in the firmament; guess which stars corresponded to each person; and
through reading the movement of the stars, read the events of the past and
predict the future.

Although in the first two categories there were men and women equally,
it was quite rare, and perhaps even unusual, when a woman was assigned to
the level of the prophets.

CHAPTER 6

DREAM COMMUNICATION

When I was a child, I used to meet all kinds of strange creatures in my dreams. My parents did not have the same dreams as me, so it was easy for me to assume that it was from watching television. I began to draw the creatures in my notebooks, and it was only a matter of time before my parents found these notebooks and threw them away. They didn't understand what I was looking for by drawing them, but I was searching for a connection, an explanation. Something as simple as that.

I drew the Blue Queen—that's how I referred to this entity—who was a fairly robust woman with a huge chest. Her skin looked like blue rock with small cracks on all sides, and her head floated, detached from her body. It looked like an even bluer rock, much like lapis lazuli, with deep cracks forming the eyes. The Blue Queen's long arms never failed to point to the sky, and as she danced around, she seemed to change her size between each round, becoming, at times, as small as a tiny fish and, at other times, as big as a tower.

After a long period of time, I stopped dreaming about her and any other creatures. I guess I unconsciously said goodbye to them and kept away from all these interesting beings that only appeared while I was sleeping. Then, years later, my twin nephews, who were diagnosed with a high degree of autism, began drawing similar creatures. One day, Yogelis, at age 11, told me, "Uncle, the Blue Lady sends you her regards." This was the trigger, and I just had to sit down to bring back all my memories. After a long afternoon, I realized that everything I had experienced had been as real as the cup of chamomile tea that I was drinking while watching my nephew draw those strange friends from the past.

Years ago, Master Serapis appeared to me in a meditation. Master Serapis, also called Sar Apis or Serapis Bey, is one of the Masters of the Ancient Wisdom on Theosophy, a spiritual ascended master, and a member of the Great White Brotherhood. He is lord of the fourth ray, which represents the purity of God. In that meditation, he said:

What we see in our dreams, most of the time, has nothing to do with the reality that we live but with the reality that we are destined to manifest with memories of our past lives that are fleeing to remain sealed and with profound wisdom that only our immortal spirit can understand.

I did not understand this when I was young and having visits from the Blue Lady and others.

The key to connecting with this wisdom is dialogue, which is an important part of this type of magic and sorcery. Pop culture and some esoteric books have made an effort to make it look "easy and fast" to work with spirits, suggesting that readers make pacts with spirits from other cultures and other lands without any relation to the reader, focusing most of these unpracticed spells on collecting herbs and elements, and getting wrapped up in making pacts just because—completely forgetting the importance of working on our relationship with these entities from other planes and how important the dialogue with them is.

Dialogue is the negotiation in magic. It is the conversation that a sorcerer and a witch have with spiritual entities and astral beings from other planes. Examples of this can be found in the practices of the cacao ceremony and the ingestion of ayahuasca, which lead us to enter our own inner world and, from there, to dialogue with our inner self, with our traumas and fears, as well as with our conscious spirit.

Once we understand the power of dialogue in magic, we are able to open ourselves to a higher understanding overall and to a higher understanding of our dreams. From there, we can better understand the results of our magical work (our actions) and the causes that lead us to do it (our intentions).

Rules of the Game

The world of dreams is not governed by the same rules as the physical world, and that is something that we must take into account when we try to decipher hidden meaning in the world of dreams and when we try to use dreams as a means of communication with the spirit world and other planes of existence.

There are four rules that govern the physical universe in which we move. These concepts are important to take into account because they do not appear in the world of dreams. They are the following: gravity, time, space, and shape.

Gravity

Gravity, in scientific terms, is the force that attracts various bodies to one another. Examples would be bodies on Earth being attracted to it or the planets being attracted to each other by their own magnetic fields.

Gravity leads us to the study and understanding of the magnetic fields of Earth and other planets. The study of gravity leads to the existence of our own solar system and to the understanding that all living creatures in the universe have a dense gravitational field of their own. Our personal grav-itational field works and connects in perfect harmony with the rest of the things, places, and people that surround us. Without it, we would be floating adrift in the universe.

In the dream world, gravity is as relative as colors, which are very change-able. Gravity is only reflected in dreams when the important thing to notice is a specific place. If you close your eyes for a moment and try to remember the most recent dream you had, I bet you don't remember the floor in much detail. Perhaps you remember the faces of the people, the situations, or cer-tain colors in some garments instead. When it comes to the floor, you only see it if it has a singular and unusual color (a yellow floor or purple soil, for example). If the floor or ground has very specific patterns and shapes, it is because there is a message in them.

Only in these very specific scenarios will the floor be remembered. Nor-mally, in dreams, the ground is not glimpsed since it is not necessary for the interpretation of the dream or the message trying to manifest at the moment.

Time

Time is relative—both in the physical world and in the spiritual world. In the dream world, time is practically nonexistent.

This lack of time seems to be a problem for the spirits and deities that inhabit this kingdom because they are not able to differentiate between the past and the future. The same happens to us. In the world of dreams, it is easy to connect with multiple characters that we do not know (mostly ancestors), and they can appear in different forms than ones they had in life and at dif-ferent ages.

You can connect well in the world of dreams with your grandparents or parents and not recognize them because they look much younger than you remember. But it is also possible to meet spirits who choose to wear their older appearances, an aspect that, at first glance, denotes their wisdom and experience.

Time in the world of dreams passes in very different ways than the phys-ical plane. You can easily fall asleep for only a few minutes and wake up remembering a long dream full of details, just as you can sleep a whole night and wake up only remembering minute fragments of a rather short dream.

There seems to be no direct connection between your hours of rest and your time in the dream world.

Space

Our understanding of space is an entirely physical understanding, linked to territories and borders, barriers, walls, roofs, and roads.

Visualize, for an instant, a world where the laws of physical space do not apply, where you are surrounded by an infinite sea of golden sands, then you can see certain objects and people at a far distance. They are almost like tiny points on the border.

How many steps are you already in front of them?

In the world of dreams, you keep moving at the same speed, or at least that is what this human sensation makes us believe. The truth is that it does not depend on the speed at which you move but on the space between you and the things you want to be close to. Everything that you want to keep away from you, or that for some reason you feel is moving away from you emotionally, is reflected in the world of dreams as something distant and far away, almost impossible to look at and reach. On the other hand, everything you want or are destined to obtain, even without knowing what it is, does not seem to take much time to reach you in this astral world. After all, time is just an illusion in the physical universe, and we perceive it with our physical body. But again—and as was mentioned before—timing in dreams is an odd concept.

Shape

Have you met the little man who has legs on his head and feet instead of hands in your dreams? Shapes change in these astral worlds, as do sizes, textures, sensations, and colors.

The physical form is tied to innumerable laws of physics that are capable of filling entire books, and the fact is that the human body is perfectly developed, either due to evolution or intelligent design (that depends on the personal belief of each individual), for the performance of various tasks and psychomotor functionality. Each limb, each organ, each finger, and each part of the body has different functions according to its shape and mobility.

Once you are in the astral worlds, only human beings maintain physical form because it is the only form that we remember. It is the only thing we know how to be, and that is why we are easily surprised or scared when we find something or someone that looks entirely different to us, such as a purple cow with long horns, a lizard made of copper-colored fire, or a school of long, silver fish that seem to swim in the wind above us.

In the physical world, forms are entirely tied to the laws of physics. These are laws that do not apply in the same way (and perhaps not at all) in the astral worlds, where everything is made of consciousness, memories, spirit, and energy in a constant process of transformation. In the astral plane, even your own form has more to do with the image you have of yourself than with your physical body.

Mediumship & Clairvoyance

When we deal with the subject of dreams, it is of the utmost importance not to underestimate the use of our senses. Our own clairvoyance and mediumship serve as natural tools to help us decipher dreams. I dare say that the more advanced your medium-mystical abilities are, the more advanced, clear, and profound your visions of the spiritual world and your dreams can become, which translates into better and clearer interpretations.

Often people outside of magical communities assume that all witches are seers or clairvoyant in some way. However, that is not true. Not all witches perform divination, scry, or communicate with spirits. It is not an interest for some, nor a requirement to be a witch. However, becoming proficient in a form of seership is a great way to communicate with spirits in the dream world. I will briefly guide you through a series of magical thoughts, exercises, infusions, and rituals. They will lead you to discover your potential, your own clairvoyance, and your ability to recognize the world that surrounds you or, rather, the world that is hidden behind the world around you. But first, let's talk about mediumship and clairvoyance.

Mediumship

A medium is, in practical terms, any individual who is capable of serving as an intermediary between the spirit world and the physical world. It is a term that has been used to refer regularly (and perhaps wrongly) to shamans, seers, and witches for several centuries.

We can interpret mediumship in two ways: either as the innate talent of certain individuals to act as an anchor for the connection between both worlds or as ritual practice through the use of various means (spells, potions, etc.) to make contact with the afterlife.

Mediums can work, in many cases, through the use of glass balls and mirrors or a Ouija board. In other cases, a medium is a channeler, which is a person trained for years to act as a bridge between both worlds, allowing one or more spiritual entities to communicate with the living through them. This bridge works both ways, as the medium can also carry a message from the world of the living to other spiritual realms.

For the native and Indigenous cultures of the Americas, the concept of a world or spiritual plane that connects our world with the world of spirits was not new. For them, the spirits and souls of the ancestors remained among us for a long period of time, as is the case, for example, in the celebration of el Día de los Muertos (Day of the Dead). It is of great importance in Mexican culture, where those who have departed but are still among us are celebrated.[26] However, for more modern witches, the similar idea of this—the limbo—seems to be a more recent concept and linked to a Christian origin, as suggested by the first uses of this term in Latin around 1300.[27]

In a few words, modern-age spiritualists have only recently begun to discover the idea of limbo. Just as most of the living do not have the ability to communicate with the deceased, neither do the spirits, because once they are in limbo, as well as in most mystical and spiritual realms, seeing the living is difficult. It's similar to how difficult it is to identify a grain of sand as different from the rest in the middle of the ocean.

For this and many other reasons, it is extremely important to understand the mystical art of mediumship. Through mediumship, we can understand the messages that we are receiving from other worlds, and we can learn to carry our messages or messages from our loved ones to other realms. In

....

26. Gironés, *Llewellyn's Little Book of the Day of the Dead*.
27. Beekes, *Etymological Dictionary of Greek*.
    Vaan, *Etymological Dictionary of Latin and the other Italic Languages*.

addition to all this, mediumship will allow you to have a greater understanding of what you see, perceive, and hear in the hereafter.

Mediumship and its practice are the key to understanding what you find in the dreamworld and other spiritual or astral planes. Furthermore, big scenes and visuals from the dreamworld are often a reflection of something else happening in the physical or spiritual world, and it will require all of your understanding and vision to manifest.

Clairvoyance

The English term *clairvoyance* comes from French *clair* (clear) and *voyance* (vision). The translation we use in Spanish is *clarividencia*, which combines two different but related terms, *claro* (clearer) and *videncia* (clairvoyance).

The term *videncia* refers to the extrasensory vision that some people develop, learn, or inherit. This sense is used to see spirits and the souls of the dead, to visualize the future through unexpected visions, or to find future events in dreams. The word *clarividencia*, on the other hand, refers to a professional clairvoyant, or someone who is trained for an extended period of time to become a professional capable of delving into the world of spirits and dreams voluntarily and instantly—whenever required or needed.

In Latin American culture, to be a medium or a spiritual worker, it is often necessary to be considered a clairvoyant. One cannot be a clairvoyant if one is not first a person with the gift of the vision.

Clairvoyance is the term we use to put together all those psychic or spiritual experiences that allow us to gain certain extra information (that is often inaccessible through other methods) of some person, object, situation, place, or even emotion.

Clairvoyance is perhaps one of the most sought-after gifts, and at the same time it is underestimated by witches. It is that gift that once we get, we can use to see the truth, see the future and the past, or to prevent spiritual and astral dangers, as well as to advance in our own individual and spiritual process.

Visualizing

We have talked about how important clairvoyance is in relation to the spiritual world and the interpretation of dreams, as well as the relevance of mediumship for those who seek to enter the world of spirits and work with them. Mediumship and clairvoyance must go hand in hand for the interpretation of dreams and other forms of divination; they are both advanced forms of our senses that allow us to touch and enter the various spiritual planes.

Dream work as a form of communication is—and has always been—a practice of vital importance among Indigenous communities, the world of dreams being an extension or intermediate corridor between the living and the world of the ancestors. For this reason, I am including a couple of exercises for you to carry out in your free time to develop your vision and psychic experience.

EXERCISE
Visualization, Part I

Use this exercise to clear your mind of obstacles that do not allow you to visualize, channel, and remember your own dreams. I have put this spell into practice in the company of a small group, and the number used to vary between three and six participants. I recommend you try it alone at least a couple of times first, though, so you will have a clearer and more precise result. Later, you can put it into practice in the company of others, performing it as many times as you see necessary.

You will need:
- Incense (A camphor incense cone is recommended.)
- Censer or heat-resistant plate
- Lighter or matches
- Chair or blanket to sit on
- Notebook and pen

Recommended moon phase: New moon for first use; you can later do it with other moon phases.

Early in the morning, go to a place where you can see or feel the fluidity and movement of abundant water. It can be a lake, a natural spring, a river, a waterfall, or even a small park pond close to you. Once there, light the incense on the censer or heat-resistant plate. Sit in front of the water in whichever way is most comfortable for you, either on the blanket on the ground in the lotus position or on a chair or rock.

Close your eyes for three to ten minutes. Avoid all possible distractions, and focus on the sound of the water, focus on the flow of the wind, focus on the aroma of the incense, and focus on channeling and synchronizing with the water in front of you and with all the nature that surrounds you.

While keeping your eyes closed, visualize that darkness taking shape and rhythm. Give it the movement and cadence of the water waves. Visualize the waves that are formed, and visualize slight flashes of light appearing on this dark surface.

As you perform this exercise, the spirit of the water itself will feel more receptive, and it will feel that you are trying to channel with its movement and its energy. During this process, just as you are more open to a new experience, the water will seek to give you the experience that you are looking for.

When you feel that you are more receptive, it is the right time to open your eyes. Open them, look at the water in front of you, and notice the shapes and flashes of light that form on the surface of the water. When you see waves forming on the surface of the water, do not seek to understand their origin. Instead, seek to observe what these waves are showing you. Look in full detail at the shapes, figures, colors, and even sounds and sensations that you can perceive.

The waters have always acted as direct messengers from beyond and many other worlds. Great magicians make use of water mirrors to enter other worlds during their long meditations, and during this exercise, you will visualize the messages and omens hidden in your most recent dreams on the surface of the water. You will be able to receive them more clearly. The waters act as portals to other worlds for the magician who is open to understanding.

Once you have captured enough images and feelings, write them down in your notebook. When you feel ready, that there are no more signs to pick up, you can retire home and meditate on what you have seen and written. Read your notes and dedicate yourself to understanding what these visions seek to indicate.

When you want to advance with the practice of this exercise, you can carry it out with the waxing moon and later with the full moon. You should notice a difference in the results, such as small signs that appear in your environment, visions, or dreams. Maybe you even start to catch certain signs and visions without performing this exercise so often or without carrying out all of the exercise completely. These are results of practice.

EXERCISE
Visualization, Part II

Once you have advanced with the previous ritual and you have carried it out at least a couple of times, you can move on to this other exercise. It has the same purpose but requires greater concentration, greater visualization skills, and more experience, especially because you will make use of water that is not in free movement with nature.

You will need:
- Table or clear, comfortable spot on the floor
- Cascarilla, coarse salt, or table salt mixed with rosemary
- Large bowl
- Clean water
- Cone of myrrh or camphor frankincense incense
- Censer, small cauldron, or heat-resistant plate
- Three white candles in candleholders
- A shell

Recommended moon phase: Crescent/waxing moon to full moon

Before you begin, a note that the bowl should be made of wood, metal, glass, or any mineral. The bigger the bowl, the more comfortable you are going to feel with the exercise, but you can start with a small one. In esoteric stores, you can find bowls in a variety of sizes and materials. Regardless of the size and material, just make sure they do not contain any type of illustrations or designs in the interior.

On a table or in a comfortable space on the floor of your home, draw a circle slightly larger than the bowl using the cascarilla, coarse salt, or combination of table salt and rosemary.

Place the bowl in the center of the circle and fill it three-quarters full of water. Place the incense on the censer, in the cauldron, or on the heat-resistant plate. Then put the incense and candles around the circle and proceed to light them.

The candlelight is there to give you clarity and activate the energy, and the incense is there to keep away any negative entity that tries to disturb the process. The circle is there for two purposes: the first is to prevent any negative energy or entity below your energy level from disturbing you or manifesting in visions through the water, and the second is to keep your energy focused on the bowl and the water.

Once your environment is prepared, sit back, close your eyes, and repeat the visualization performed in the previous exercise.

Visualize the surface of the water without distractions. Focus on it fully and breathe deeply and slowly during the process. Your energy is connected with the water in front of you and it will project your visions, so focus your attention on the water.

Continue this visualization until you feel that you have received enough information. If you feel exhausted or satisfied with the ritual, you can extinguish the candles, dump the water, and clean the place of the ritual. When you want to repeat the exercise, use the same candles that you previously extinguished or replace them with new ones.

Dream Magic Insight
KNOW YOUR ENEMY'S PLAN IN ADVANCE
BY MISS AIDA

My mother was a witch from Cuba and had always proclaimed that anise produced psychic visions. Whenever I needed a psychic vision in a difficult situation, she would prepare the following tea. The function of this particular spell is to let you know the plan of your enemy before it is executed. It is a perfect form of precaution in case you feel that one of those "very confused fans" is plotting something against you or your loved ones.

You will need:

- ½ teaspoon anise seeds
- 1 cup boiling water
- Anise extract
- Teacup
- Notebook
- Pencil/pen

Note that many Hoodoo practitioners will instead use star anise for the tea, but my preference is the seeds.

First, put the anise seeds in the boiling water and steep for a few minutes. Then, without straining the tea, drink it while applying anise extract to your third eye, as well as your temples.

Immediately before going to bed, repeat the process just described. Then, recite Psalm 42, which will assist you in dreaming true. Always pray aloud because sound is emitted energy that facilitates manifestation of your desires.

> As the hart panteth after the water brooks, so panteth my soul after thee, O God.
> My soul thirsteth for God, for the living God: when shall I come and appear before God?

My tears have been my meat day and night, while they continually
   say unto me, Where is thy God?
When I remember these things, I pour out my soul in me: for I had
   gone with the multitude, I went with them to the house of God,
   with the voice of joy and praise, with a multitude that kept
   holyday.
Why art thou cast down, O my soul? and why art thou disquieted
   in me? hope thou in God: for I shall yet praise him for the help of
   his countenance.
O my God, my soul is cast down within me: therefore will I remember thee from the land of Jordan, and of the Hermonites, from
   the hill Mizar.
Deep calleth unto deep at the noise of thy waterspouts: all thy
   waves and thy billows are gone over me.
Yet the Lord will command his loving kindness in the day time, and
   in the night his song shall be with me, and my prayer unto the
   God of my life.
I will say unto God my rock, Why hast thou forgotten me? why go I
   mourning because of the oppression of the enemy?
As with a sword in my bones, mine enemies reproach me; while
   they say daily unto me, Where is thy God?
Why art thou cast down, O my soul? and why art thou disquieted
   within me? hope thou in God: for I shall yet praise him, who is
   the health of my countenance, and my God.

Next state your petition and close the prayer with the word *amen*.

Keep a notebook and pencil/pen at your bedside, and in the morning, immediately jot down what you have dreamed. Don't depend on your memory to remember because, if you're like me, you might forget the dream after only a few minutes!

Repeat this process every night until you have learned what you need to know.

TRIBAL TALES
THE YANOMAMI PEOPLE

The Yanomami tribe is one of the tribes that we study the most in schools in Venezuela. This Indigenous ethnic group does not exceed 35,000 inhabitants, and they live in the Amazon rainforest on the border between Venezuela and Brazil.

Although many of these people have converted to Catholicism and Protestantism due to social pressure during recent decades, their oral folklore is one of the richest in the Amazon. Their stories span from the beginning of the world and the creation of the sky to the adventures of several native heroes and their search to free the rivers that run through the Amazon, which, according to myth, were trapped in a hidden cave that could only be accessed at night.

Many of the customs of the people have not changed, such as *miyakira* (the art of painting one's face with the family colors); cannibalism as a sacred ritual; ingesting the ashes of the deceased (Yupu Ushi) in a collective ritual to bring back the energy of the eggs to the family circle; and anointing the tips of their arrows and blowpipes (Yoroa) with curare (*Anomospermum grandiflora*) to poison animals without altering their consciousness, as this is part of a sacred rite or magic related to various plants and herbs of the Amazon.

For the Yanomami nation, the Yimika taai (prediction through dreams) is a gift that only two classes of individuals receive: those who have been blessed by heaven with the vision of spirits and those who have lived more than one life and therefore return to the world with access to the *mou*, a bridge formed by trees that connects our rivers with the rivers of the otherworld. From that place, they are able to intercede between dreams and the souls of the deceased, as well as communicate with the elder spirits and ancestors.

The world of the spirits in the Yanomami culture is of vital importance because the balance and health in the world of the living depend on it. Those who do not pay respect to the sacred ceremonies are trapped in the branches of the trees that create the bridge, and they are destined to watch everyone enter the otherworld without being able to move for eternity.

The only one who has managed to escape from the bridge is Hõõ, a mystical being who cannot enter the world of dreams and the deceased. He uses a stick to suck the brains from the skulls of those he kills in order to remain among the living. Hōō confuses his victims by taking the faces of their relatives and throwing himself on the ground in front of them, asking for help.

In this culture, dreams are always loaded with messages and visions that are sent by those in the afterlife. Even the dreams that seem the simplest and easiest to explain can be loaded with powerful messages, as well as terrible predictions of the future.

CHAPTER 7

DREAM PROTECTION

Psychic attack is the term that is popularly given to negative energy that causes immediate damage to an individual. The attack may have been sent consciously or unconsciously to cause damage to the individual, their life, or their family.

The damage caused can affect the emotional, physical, spiritual, or mental state of the person who suffers it. These negative energies can be projected in the form of thought, and they are often motivated by jealousy toward the recipient. That being said, a psychic attack can also be provoked for other reasons.

Psychic Attacks

A psychic attack tends to be an energetic attack—a power struggle between the sender and the victim. Even if the sender is not aware of their actions, the attack will match the level of their mental power, and the consequences of it will depend entirely on the psychic level of the receiver.

Psychic attacks are sometimes unconsciously caused by people in the victim's family environment, including relatives and close friends. Jealousy, envy, anger, and fights in the home can turn into psychic attacks, even if the sender does not consciously wish to cause harm.

If a person feels diminished, ignored, displaced, inferior, or emotionally hurt for some reason and feels emotionally repressed, those emotions can seek a way to express themselves. And sometimes they will find expression in the manifestation of damage toward another person, which is an attack of psychic energy. In the field of sorcery, these assaults are one of the faster forms of magic.

Symptoms of an Attack

There are many symptoms of and ways to recgonize a psychic attack. The victim of the attack tends to have continuous nightmares and see their attacker many times in their dreams and meditations as an evil figure. The affected person may feel psychically attacked and emotionally violated, as well as physically tired and drained of energy for no apparent reason. They often have all kinds of pains and marks (similar to bruises and bites) in various parts of the body, especially in the arms, legs, and neck.

Many of these attacks occur during the night when we are asleep. When we are at rest, we do not pay attention—we are not focused. We remain asleep, and that is when the attack manifests itself in its true form, causing, at first, signs of anxiety, insomnia, a cold sweat, or the sensation of a weight on the back, shoulders, and neck.

According to the Conny Méndez School of Christian Metaphysics in Venezuela, the cause of these attacks can also include complaints, criticism, judgment, resentment, professional envy and jealousy, speaking ill of someone, slandering a person, and even belittling them.[28] All of these are various

....
28. Méndez, *Metafísica 4 en 1.*

forms of psychic attacks that unconsciously drain the energy of the one being talked about. If the person energetically protects themselves, it is possible that these attacks will not go on to cause greater damage than an uncertain sensation of alert that appears suddenly.

Protecting Yourself

As mentioned, psychic attacks occur mostly at night. This can be due to two reasons. First, many witches prefer to work at night, either because of tradition or modernity and work schedules. Second, it is the time after all the stress and daily work that we find ourselves resting and repairing. While sleeping, our energy system is recovering from the daily overload we receive when interacting with other individuals and situations, and it is when we are most vulnerable.

There are hundreds of talismans and natural amulets from our folklore that can be used to prevent, avoid, and send back psychic attacks, including:

- Hanging a small round mirror with a silver frame over the bed.
- Drawing a pentagram with salt and white pepper under it.
- Carrying a bracelet made of red thread and small pieces of coral with you.
- Anointing a silver or gold ring with mugwort oil and myrrh on the night of a full moon while staring at the moon.
- Drying the heart of a white hen in the sun for several days, crushing it with devil's needle weed and asafoetida root, and throwing it around your house and in front of your enemy's house.
- Embroidering the name of the psychic witch (your enemy) six times in reverse in red and blue thread on a piece of the witch's clothing and burying it on the night of a new moon.

Protection against psychic attacks does not have to be complex. Daily exercises visualizing and expanding your aura in front of a mirror are of great help for these occasions too. They lead you to work on your own individual energy and thus strengthen your energy field.

Since psychic attacks often happen while you are asleep, it is advisable to take between five and ten minutes to practice some visualization before going to bed. With the mind's eye, visualize how your aura cleanses and expands and how it takes on different colors, tones, and shapes so that when an external psychic energy arrives trying to disturb, it is not capable of causing harm.

For example, when getting ready to sleep, close your eyes and immediately visualize an energy field that expands from your skin and covers the entire room and the people in it. It is a simple method and daily practice that will protect you psychically—even while you sleep. In a certain way, you are commanding your energy to move in your environment and take care of yourself while you rest.

Sprinkling a little salt water in the corners of the room before sleeping is another form of spiritual care. Both elements are considered powerful symbols of purification, and a pinch of water and salt in the corners will scare any ill-intentioned spirits that were waiting to disturb us at night from the room, whether they came there voluntarily or were sent by someone else.

EXERCISE
Incense to Protect Yourself Against Psychic Attacks

This is an incense to use for protection against any psychic attacks. Burn it whenever you are in need.

You will need:
- Mortar and pestle
- Equal parts dried passionflower, white rose, white sage, frankincense, skullcap, *Calea zacatechichi*, and blue sage
- Charcoal
- Censer or heat-resistant plate
- Lighter or matches
- A fan to help move smoke around the room (optional)

In the mortar, mix all the dried plants together. Two hours before going to sleep, place the charcoal in the censer or on the heat-resistant plate, light it, and put this herbal mix over it.

Are Nightmares a Psychic Attack?

The true and quick answer would be no, nightmares are not the response to a psychic attack or the consequence of it—at least not in most cases.

While this question may be common in the field of witchcraft, where nightmares and dreams seem to be two sides of the same coin, dreams and nightmares represent entirely different aspects of our psyches. Although the former can be interpreted as omens of the future and reminders of the past, the latter are fueled by anxiety, fear, sadness, and other negative emotions or present situations that are not happening as we would like. Some of these fears and anxieties can even be caused by individual traumas and memories of conflicts we have experienced.

Nightmares can be a psychic response to a present situation that we are experiencing but do not perceive instantly or firsthand, similar to a physic attack, but this does not mean that every time we have a nightmare someone is wishing us something bad. It does not mean that we should ignore nightmares completely either. What it means is that although occasionally nightmares can represent an omen of the future or, rather, a warning from it, these should not be taken for granted. Nightmares and dreams should be studied and analyzed with a certain calm and objectivity, and one should not simply assume that every time they cannot sleep it is because someone is lighting black candles with their name written on them.

Just as we interpret dreams, analyzing them in depth, we can—and should— do the same with nightmares. Studying them will help you to understand their origin and purpose. Perhaps it is just a bad dream induced by a recent situation, perhaps it's a hidden memory of a past life, perhaps it really is a true warning of the future, or perhaps it is a vision sent by another witch to interrupt your dream.

EXERCISE
An Incense Formula You Need to Try

You can prepare this blend for yourself or someone else; the only requirement is burning it in the room of the person who is having nightmares. This incense does not dispel the nightmare, but it does provide an atmosphere of adequate protection and clarity so that you can perceive the message or omen that is disguised behind it. In the case of a psychic attack being carried out by some witch, this incense can be used to lessen the effects of the attack.

You will need:
- Equal parts dried lavender flowers, mugwort, and white rose petals
- Mortar and pestle
- Censer or heat-resistant plate
- Lighter or matches
- Charcoal

Mix the herbs for a few minutes using the mortar and pestle. Once they are mixed, place a portion of the incense in the censer or on the heat-resistant plate. Put the censer or plate in a corner of the room and light the piece of charcoal. Place the charcoal in the censer or on the plate with the rest of the mixture and let it spread the smoke. As the incense burns, recite the following incantation:

> **My understanding flows like smoke flows.**
> **My prayers rise along with this.**
> **My prayers reach my guardians and teachers,**
> **and I allow myself to see what is hidden in the dark night.**
> **Nothing escapes our vision.**
> **I find clarity in the night and discover the truth.**

EXERCISE
Venezuelan Old Folk Spell Against a Bad Witch

The following is a traditional spell from Venezuelan folklore, which I have translated and arranged, that has been transmitted orally in my native country for at least five generations. It is one of those traditional recipes that somehow practically everyone involved with witchcraft knows, and more than one grandmother seems to have learned it from her mother, too, so it's quite difficult to get its origin.

There are a few variations of the spell. However, the only difference between the version that you will find here and others out there is that I took the time to translate and linguistically accommodate the Spanish words at the end of the original, also translating some Portuguese phrases into English.

I decided, after sleeping on it many times, to include this spell for two reasons: to show how simple our magical procedures are for the most part and in their most natural form, and because it is one of those rituals that practically every witch knows and loves but no one else seems to have written down. I wanted to be the first to do so—before someone steals it from our culture and "reinterprets" it for their own purposes, probably whitewashing it.

Purpose and Variation

This spell was performed by wives to keep away other women looking to flirt with their husbands, and it has also been used to nullify a witch and all their spells and curses against the individual. It is always done with the assistance of someone else, and it is often two or more people casting the spell together against a shared enemy. The spell is commonly performed with a doll that is kept at home. It can be an old plastic doll or a cloth doll; the important part is that the doll has the same hair color and sex assigned to the person who is going to be bewitched. At home, after some time, my mom began to vary this spell by making her own dolls with wax and occasionally Plasticine.

You will need:

- One or more friends to perform the ritual with
- Scissors
- Spool of red thread
- Spool of white thread
- Black candle in candleholder
- Lighter or matches
- Doll or figure that represents the person to bewitched
- Needle

Time and place: This spell can be done at home—or in any space that you consider suitable for the ritual—in the hours between noon and sunset. Never perform it after dark.

Using the scissors, cut a strand of red thread as long as your arm. Repeat this first step, creating additional lengths of red thread until there are as many strands as participants. Then cut a single strand of white thread roughly half as long as the red.

Once the strands are ready, sit facing one another in a small circle with the elements and ingredients in the center. Take a deep breath and light the candle. Once the candle is lit, have one of the participants take the needle in hand and recite the following incantation while threading the needle. They will then pass the needle to the next person, who will also recite the incantation, and so on until everyone has recited it once.

> **To the spirits present in this place,**
> **this magical day and at this magical hour,**
> **we invite you to unleash your courage**
> **on this magical day and at this magical hour.**
> **We ask for your assistance and support in this ritual**
> **on this magical day and at this magical hour.**
> **Be present and guide our hands in this work**
> **on this magical day and at this magical hour.**

Now, the last witch holding the needle sticks it into the doll or wax figure, preferably into the left leg. One end of each strand of thread must be tied to this needle.

To continue the ritual, each witch must take the doll in their hands, and as they recite the following incantation, they must wrap one of the red threads around the doll from heels to neck. While they wrap and recite, the accompanying witch, or witches, recites "for three times three" in a low voice.

> **For three times three, three times I look at you.**
> **For three times three, three times I measure you.**
> **For three times three, three times I follow you.**
> **For three times three, three times I tie you up.**
> **For three times three, three times I tame you.**
> **For three times three, three times I catch you.**
> **For three times three, three times I blind you.**
> **For three times three, three times I silence you.**
> **For three times three, three times I push you away.**
> **For three times three …**

Three times. Three times. Three times.
I annul all your spells and your influence over me.

Once all the witches in the circle have tied the figure up to the neck, one of the participants must take the remaining white thread and tie it from heels to neck, reciting once more the previous incantation while the other witch(es) say "for three times three." Tie a knot at the end, tying all the ends of the threads together.

After the threads are tied, blow out the candle. This symbolizes the power of the spell's target being definitively extinguished. Bury both items, the figure and the candle, together in a hole in a nearby yard or park or in a pot with soil, making sure they will never see light again.

After the night of the spell, the witch who has been cursed with this spell will begin to lose any magical or psychic influence on the person who performed the ritual. They will also receive a bad omen or vision as a warning in their dreams whenever they try to wish you any damage.

Dream Magic Insight
DREAM PROTECTION SPELL
BY J. ALLEN CROSS

Here is an exercise that will protect you from harmful spells, meddlesome spirits, and nasty energies while sleeping. It uses Spanish moss, which is excellent for entangling all kinds of bad things that may come for you in the night.

You will need:
- Lighter or matches
- White stick candle in candleholder
- Mortar and pestle
- Spanish moss, divided
- Personal item of yours, such as some hair or nail clippings
- Dried rosemary and lavender

Light the candle and place the mortar and pestle on your nightstand. Remove the pestle and fill the mortar with some of the Spanish moss. Make a small depression in the moss and insert your personal item, symbolically surrounding yourself with the energy of the Spanish moss.

Sprinkle the dried rosemary and lavender over the top; these will repel harmful energies and protect you during your sleep. Place a layer of moss on top to make sure everything's covered, then set the pestle across the top horizontally so each end is resting on the rim of the mortar. This not only holds the moss in place, but it also acts as an alarm. If something tries to get through in the night, the pestle will roll off and wake you up. Blow out the candle before going to sleep and relight it the next night as you're getting ready for bed to reactivate the spell. Again, remember to blow it out when you go to sleep.

TRIBAL TALES
YAGÁN PEOPLE / YÁMANA
OR TEQUENICA

The Yagán are an Indigenous people of the Fuegian archipelago in the territory of Chile and Argentina. Their traditional way of life was nomadic, and they moved in canoes, dedicated to hunting, gathering, and fishing. Approximately 6,000 years ago, their ancestors traveled from the islands and channels that are south of the Beagle Channel to Cape Horn.

According to the French American anthropologist Anne MacKaye Chapman:

> It is considered that the ancestors of the Yagáns were among the first Americans, they would have emigrated from Asia to America across the Beringia Bridge and that the ancestors of the Yahgans must have been among these early immigrants. Subsequently, they reached the central zone of Chile at least 16,000 years ago, then followed the route of the Chilote canals and crossed to the south, crossing the Isthmus of Ofqui.[29]

The Yagáns, in religious-spiritual terms, believed in a unique and powerful being, Watauinewa, whose name translates as "the old, the eternal, the invariable," and is also colloquially called Hitapuan (my father) or *abailakin* (the strong or powerful). Watauinewa is the creator and monarch of all things, patron of the spiritual world, dreams, life, and death.

Watauniewa is the counterpart of Curspi (the evil one, the corruptor), who, according to tradition, punished the towns with wind, rain, and snow in order to hinder agriculture, obtaining food, and trade with other towns. In some modern lullabies, Curspi is the malevolent spirit that enters the dreams of children to create nightmares. The rainbow, although beautiful, is the messenger of Curspi and indicates that it is seeking to do evil.

If a person has a nightmare, they say, *"Aiyara auyitapi aiya Curai aisitiparicu yalur agunya,"* which translates as "Curpsi is prowling with his shadow to corrupt the good spirit."

....

29. Chapman, *European Encounters with the Yamana People of Cape Horn, before and after Darwin.*

147

In the tradition of the Yámana peoples, the Yekamush healers and priests, who could heal the sick with the use of herbs and mineral waters, heal emotional and spiritual imbalances through prayers. They also had the power to invoke spirits to offer protection, make grains grow, or bring rain.

Funeral Rites

For protection of the tribe, when a Yámana died, the Yekamush wrapped the body with hides and placed the dead's belongings, some polished stones, and herbal amulets next to it. They covered everything with earth and branches and left the place forever because once the body had been buried, the soul of the deceased would manifest for a long time in nightmares to disturb all those who sleep near their resting place.

TRIBAL TALES
QUECHUA PEOPLE / *LOS AÑU*

Quechua is a language of the Indigenous natives of Peru.[30] This language was spoken throughout Venezuela about 5,500 years ago. Currently, said language is reduced to a very corrupted version spoken by the Añu, who live in the Sinamaica lagoon of Zulia state, and the Arawak groups of the upper Orinoco.

The Quechuas arrived in Venezuela in large groups or "herds" roughly 5,500 years ago. They sailed through the rivers that connect the Panorío Ucayali region with the Amazon River, Negro River, the Casiquiare/Orinoco River, the Delta Rivers, and the Caribbean.

For the natives of the Añu people, the esoteric rites are limited to those who have been initiated in their traditions. The initiation is performed only for the youngest. If an adult did not receive the ritual initiation because they were not chosen in childhood, they are always welcome to attend the ceremonies but not to lead or organize them. The child initiate must learn the language of the ancient *aguero* (their own sacred form of Quechua). This language is taught directly by the priest or shaman of the tribe, and it is the language in which all the rites and ceremonies will be handled.

One of the initiation rites of these peoples involves a passage across the river on a night when the full moon is reflected on its surface. This ceremony consists of literally walking from one side of the river to the other while carrying a *tucacas* (a narrow-mouthed clay jar) filled with *yaraja* (an herbal drink). Usually this ceremony is performed in a river near the Urupagua (a region of the river abundant in snakes), and you must walk from one bank of the river to the other again and again until you see the *tocopero* (a pair of owls) flying over or until *tuy* (the owl's hoot is heard).

Dreams are interpreted in daylight and never at night because if dreams are told at night, they can be heard by the Camoruco (bad spirits). Dreams are considered sacred messages loaded with enormous symbolism.

A Cocuy (a dreamer, a person who constantly dreams) or a Cacuyo (a walker who moves between dreams) are not considered sorcerers for the

....
30. Torero, *Lenguas de los Andes*.

tribe but warriors instead. They have been sent by the high spirits that protect the tribe to interpret all kinds of messages or to disturb the rest of the
enemy.

The interpreters of dreams, the Cocuy and the Cacuyo, are considered
blessed people. Only the priest of the tribe should know who they are because
he is going to prepare for them a Sividigua that consists of a protective amulet
in the form of a necklace. The amulet is made with a small piece of skin cut
from the individual's hand that hangs from a long braid made of palm leaves.
The amulet is permanently guarded in the hut of the elder or priest. There he
can pray and purify the amulet daily to keep the warrior who has been blessed
safe from evil spirits.

A character from abroad (*guaiyo*) who has the gift of dreaming very often
or entering dreams is considered the reincarnation of one of their ancestors.
They are well received by the villages and tribes after a private analysis by the
priest.

CHAPTER 8

DREAMERS & SHAPESHIFTERS (AND THEIR SOUTH AMERICAN FOLKLORE)

The shapeshifter is a witch who, in one way or another, changes shape from within the world of dreams. Their power requires years of training to find a balance point between keeping the body at rest while the mind remains active. Like a trained animal, orders are given to one's own mind before going to sleep so that it fulfills a mission, such as possessing the body of a night owl to cross borders and carry a message or to look for someone who is lost. The mission can also be, as Colombian folk legends say, to possess the body of a wolf, coyote, or dog to guard a place or a family.

In the folklore of the Caribbean islands and Trinidad and Tobago, a male witch can take the form of an owl with unusually long black wings to move through the night sky in search of his enemies. He carries in his claws a talisman charged with a curse, usually a carved bone or a root of some poisonous herb, to deposit on the roof of the enemy in order to curse the entire house. For this to happen, the witch must be completely asleep, allowing him to move his conscious mind from one body to another.

Shapeshifting is a way for a witch to cheat the rules or barriers that keep the physical and metaphysical worlds separated. Their physical body stays in a place, resting, while their mind and soul travel long distances in the form of a wild animal or a nocturnal bird, spying while hidden in the night and making agreements with other witches and spirits from beyond. They make use of the physical senses of the animal but also take into account that this form of mediumship allows them to move between both worlds, meaning they are able to interact with all kinds of animals, witches, fairies, and spirits of the night while in the form of the animal. Sometimes the witch will take the form of a domestic animal.

Shapeshifting occurs when a witch understands that their abilities and powers are not limited to their physical body and physical conditions. They are not even limited to the laws of physics, which govern the physical plane. The witch is able to manifest their conscious self outside their body while they sleep and thus move between bodies that keep them anchored to the physical plane. For this to happen, the witch must fall into a deep state of sleep without interventions or distractions. They can do this through deep meditation and breathing exercises, through herbal infusions and magical tisanes, or through enchantments that allow them to reach a nice rest and thus completely disconnect their mind and their senses (touch, sight, smell, hearing, taste) that are part of their physical body.

After the witch has shed their physical anchors, they are able to move out of their physical anatomy. The body is made and formed. It has even evolved to serve as a perfect and ever-changing temporary vehicle for the spirit or human soul. But what are the soul and the body but a light breeze contained in a fragile vessel, ready to break at any moment?

Once out of the body, the soul can move beyond the laws of physics, a situation to which the energetic body is not completely accustomed. Unlike those who practice astral projection until they are experts in it, the witch requires another vehicle. Transformation occurs either by channeling an animal spirit to copy its form or by possessing the body of the animal in question and doing it so many times that the witch ends up being able to take only the spirit's form.

Transformation is one of the many reasons why the practice of dream magic has gradually become the next step for witches in Latin America.

Forms of Shapeshifters

In Mesoamerican folklore, the Indigenous communities believed in the practice of tonal totheism, a form of sorcery practiced by shapeshifters that allowed them to bond with their tonal spirit animal in the otherworld and, through this bond, change the shape of their bodies.

Traditionally shapeshifters were associated with two themes in folklore. The first was gods, demons, and all kinds of fairy beings with the ability to take the forms of various animals and even copy the human form in order to mix with us to fulfill a specific purpose. The second was humans-beasts, as is the case of the werewolf, or lycanthrope, of European folklore, the Slavic god Veles, or the common cougar-men in the oral traditions of the Caribbean and South America.

Although spirits and deities seem to have this ability to change shape voluntarily, human beings change only under the effects of some curse or enchantment, as in the case of werewolves.

In his work *The Immaterial Book of St. Cyprian*, José Leitão compiles the old story of Joao do Serro the *lobisomem* (Portuguese for *werewolf*), which tells of a sorcerer man who makes use of the book of Saint Cyprian to curse others and gain the ability to become a wolf and thus live longer. This little story about grimoires, sorcerers, curses, and werewolves reminds me a lot of the story of *los hombres condor* (the condor men) of the Andes told to me by my grandpa while visiting the Andes as a child. The men were enchanted by a small crowd of old witches who lived in the oldest caves. The witches fed these men with flesh from their bodies and a fermented drink based on corn and herbs complemented with their menstrual blood. The witches could then enter the men's dreams at night, and if the witch managed to make the man release his semen while he remained asleep, he would fall under her spell permanently. Every time the witch called him at night, the man would abandon his clothes, sleepwalk toward the windows, and become a condor to fly toward the witch, who served the Devil.

A similar shapeshifting legend is found in the folklore of Cumanacoa, Venezuela. There, it is forbidden to bathe in the rivers at night. Many would believe that it is to avoid drowning, but the villagers assure that it is because the witches dance with the Devil in a bonfire next to the river and this grants them the power to change shape at night. To transform, the witches place a cut and dried leg of the animal they want to become next to a magical seal under their pillow and lie down to sleep. While sleeping, they change form and travel to the nearest river to celebrate this kind of sabbat. Only the Devil has the power to return them to human form once they are in his presence. At dawn, the witches reappear lying on their beds, alone and remembering the night before like a deep dream.

To ensure falling asleep, the witches consume a concoction that is an infusion of lemon balm, cayenne, and chamomile flowers with a pinch of coarse salt and six grains of earth from the nearest cemetery to help them "sleep like the dead." The witch walks around the room with the infusion in hand, making six laps before taking the first sip.

In various towns in Colombia and Venezuela, it was sometimes believed that those people who presented some kind of personality disorder or bipolar disorder were shapeshifters. It was also common to find holes in the walls of houses with magical drawings within them for all kinds of purposes. The following figures are examples. The first figure symbolizes serpents with heads on both ends of their bodies, which are commonly confused with arrows. The snakes are shedding their skin between the phases of the moon. The white circles next to each head indicate intuition and guidance. Shapeshifters used the drawing to sense when changes were coming or to have control of them and thus prevent damage. If the person with these symbols at home has nightmares or a strange and sudden change of character, it means the transformation is close to happening.

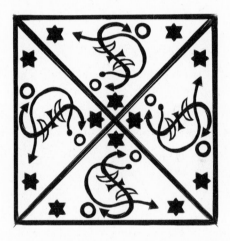

The second symbol is often drawn on the non-visible edge of the doors and entrances of the houses in the city of Merida in Venezuela. The symbol is a part of an old missing magical tradition based on a belief in shapeshifters stemming from local Indigenous cultures. The use of the pentagram demonstrates the European influence in that city. The symbol also depicts the three sexes, the eye of divinity, and the changing spiral of life. A cross is formed by four sickles to cut curses in the four directions of the wind. This talisman is used to detect shapeshifters when they enter the house and to dream with them before their arrival.

Changes During Sleep

There are three types of shapeshifters in general Latin American folklore: those who change their physical form while they sleep after having ingested a series of concoctions and chalks, those whose mind leaves their body while they sleep and their mind possesses the body of a nearby animal in order to move through the world of the living, and those whose mind leaves their body through the mouth and once outside they materialize, taking the form of their animal spirit.

In each of these versions, all individuals make the change during the hours of sleep while the body remains at rest. The visions and memories of the nocturnal experience are reflected the next day as a dream or a nightmare. Spiritual workers commonly explained that dreams looked colorless because they were seen from the senses of animal organs. Our perception of color, as human beings, is notoriously more complex.

On the other hand, in pre-Columbian native folklore, the *bohiques*, Chyquy, Piaches, and Alüjülii, who were the sorcerers, fortune tellers, and spiritual workers of the time, saw the art of shapeshifting in a much more complex way. For these religious-esoteric groups from the south, although they came from different tribal groups, the art of shapeshifting consisted of a form of sorcery that was achieved through dreams. For them, the shapeshifter was more of a spiritual possessor who abandoned their physical body in the night under the form of a dark bird that came out through their mouth or navel. They possessed the bodies of the wild animals that inhabited the environment, and in some darker versions and stories, they possessed the bodies of warriors killed in combat as form of necromancy, which is why these bodies were to always be burned or consumed by the shaman and warriors of the tribe, preventing this kind of prohibited possession.

Among these Mesoamerican religious groups, the shapeshifters literally changed their physical body and became animals, were allies of the dark spirits, and were considered outsiders who worked against the correct balance of things. Their presence was entirely unnatural, not to mention that the shapeshifter suffered an incredibly painful experience as their skin and bones were torn apart as they transformed into the animal form they sought.

It was through dreams that the priests and sorcerers of the time managed to master the art of transmigration and transformation. By remaining conscious during the hours of sleep, they could move to different places and possess all kinds of birds and animals to act as messengers or spies that served the tribe. The practices were transmitted through these dreams from the experienced teacher to the student in order to keep the spells and ritual practices secret.

Today part of these ritual practices is still preserved, such as using the skin of the tapir to create a bag full of herbs previously collected on the edge of the Amazon River to be used as a pillow to sleep. Another option is using the front nails of a *cachicamo*, or giant armadillo, (which measure between 4 and 7.5 inches [10 and 19 centimeters] long) to decorate necklaces and pendant earrings that help anchor the spirit of the sorcerer to the body, preventing their spirit from wandering far away and getting lost in the dark woods.

Birds and Shapeshifters

Growing up I found at least a dozen similar stories related to relatives living in the cities of Guarenas and Guatire in Venezuela or in the city of Ankara in Turkey. There are multiple local legends in these places in relation to witches and sorcerers who change shape during the night while they sleep and seers who receive night visions while they are birds.

There is a saying in Carupano, Venezuela that goes: *Si tienes pesadillas continuas lanza una piedra al pájaro que se para a verte por las mañanas desde la ventana.* (If you have continuous nightmares, throw a stone at the bird that stops to see you in the morning from the window.) Yes, obviously it sounds like a cruel and immoral practice, but it represents a little more of our folklore. According to popular belief in the city, witches move in the form of a bird and hang from the ceilings or windows to spy on others and throw curses and love spells while they sleep. If the person is cursed, they will have nightmares.

Another similar legend comes from the Guacharo caves, a peculiar tourist site in Monagas, Venezuela, where the uncommon guacharo (oilbird) lives. It is the only bird of the *Steatornis* genus, and it inhabits various parts of South America and is common on the Caribbean island of Trinidad (part of Trinidad and Tobago). These nocturnal birds live in caves and feed on the fruits of the oil palm.

There are multiple local legends about the strangeness of these peculiar birds. Apparently, the guacharo are the only nocturnal, flying, fruit-eating birds in the world, and this further fuels the legends. For many local folklorists, these birds are witches who took that form through astral projection and never returned to their human form, forever trapped in the figure either because someone tried to awaken them while they were sleeping or because someone buried their sleeping body in consecrated ground (a church or graveyard) and the witch can no longer return to it.

According to another legend, which was repeated a lot in the local news, these birds are the souls of children who were kidnapped by fairies from the nearby forests and caves. The full version tells us that the souls of individuals from native tribes who died without receiving baptism are destined to wander as fairies, as beings in animal-humanoid forms that walk between the world of the living and the dead. They can return temporarily to the world of the living if they devour virgin human flesh, and that is where the Devil comes in. As an intermediary between fairies and witches, the Devil promises fairies a short but happy life among humans in exchange for their subsequent service. He himself offers the witches the service of the fairies in exchange for a virgin child.

The witch oils their body with a mixture of palm oil, rose petals, and a homemade tincture made from laurel. They lie down to sleep on the ground near the entrance of the cave, and when they fall asleep, they take the form of a guacharo. The witch then finds a child and kidnaps them, attracting them with the form of this curious bird, usually presenting with a bunch of fruit in its beak.

Once the witch has brought the virgin child to the cave, the fairies take them and put them to sleep with a potion based on hibiscus, caladium (heart of Jesus), and laurel tincture. Once the child falls asleep, the fairies extract the consciousness of the child and deposit it in a bowl filled with brown feathers, oil, and blood. The fairies devour the child's flesh in order to take the child's form and return to the world of the living at dawn. As they do so, the mixture of feathers in the bowl begins to breathe. From there, a small guacharo chick is born and flies away. This chick has the soul of the child, who believes they are asleep and living a dream like a bird.

A Short Family Anecdote

My mother never had a good relationship with her mother-in-law, my grandmother, who, after suffering some form of stroke, had lost the ability to walk and move around the house without help. Mom used to tell us when we were little that the "witch who is your grandma" often visited her at night disguised as a black hen and clucked in her sleep to keep her awake. When we visited Grandma, the two of them hardly greeted each other. Although Grandma never moved from her chair to the back of the patio without help, on multiple occasions my older sisters mentioned finding some visiting bird in the rooms even when the windows had been closed.

Similarly, Grandpa forbade frightening birds around the house because he said (we never knew if he was joking or serious) that these were Grandmother's pets. Although I never came across these birds, on a certain occasion I found Grandma asleep on the patio while a huge black bird with a long white crest was resting just a few meters from her. It circled over her several times and then was gone.

Adding even more fire to the legend of Grandma, even today, years after she died, Mom continues to say that our grandma moved among the dead and dreams, flying like a bird. She also claimed that when Grandma fell asleep, she spied on others through the birds, which is why Mom tried not to have pets. The few we did have were brought in by Dad against her will, and they always died mysteriously after a few months, most of the time related to something esoteric. She simply did not trust any animal at home because of this.

Dogs, Goats, Wolves, and Deer

In some stories, when the sorcerer changes their form, half of their body remains human looking while the other half is part goat, dog, wolf, or deer. During these transformations, the sorcerer has glowing red eyes and a long tongue that extends either to (according to some legends) absorb the spirits of dead animals and people by sliding into the mouths of the corpses or to (according to most recent interpretations) absorb their fluids.

This is the case with the Huay Chivo, or Waay-Chivo, legend, which, in recent times, has been culturally associated with the chupacabra. The Huay Chivo is basically a sorcerer and oath breaker of the forces of evil who, having broken his promise of silence and secrecy, is condemned to never be able to transform completely again.

El Cadejo, a very popular spirit in El Salvador, Costa Rica, Panama, Guatemala, and Honduras, is a shapeshifting demon or witch whose soul is projected while sleeping. It appears as a guardian of the roads, taking the form of a long, thin dog. It is hairy with goat's hooves and red eyes.

There are two popular interpretations of the Cadejo: either it is a good witch who appears in this form at night to protect those who come by the crossroads or that the entity is really two demons, one good and one bad, who appear to bless and protect or to curse and kill at the crossroads.

Regardless of the interpretations, dreaming of a white Cadejo is interpreted as a sign that the person should visit a fortune teller or a witch to receive a message. Dreaming of a black Cadejo is considered the most fearsome of omens and indicates that death is behind the person, just as the Cadejo is ready to kill them.

Dreamers and Shapeshifters in Colombia and Venezuela

Jumbie, Mendo, and Chongo are the names given to a wide variety of mischievous spirits in the Caribbean countries. Their greatest popularity and appearance are in the oral traditions of Colombia and Venezuela.

These mischievous spirits, very commonly confused with demons, are the souls of children who have not received baptism. They wander about, doing pranks, causing ill, or crafting nightmares. In the esoteric traditions of the Court of the Fairies of Lionza in Venezuela or Los Encantados in Peru and Colombia, these mischievous spirits are seen and portrayed as allied spirits and intermediaries between people and the fairies of the woods.

These spirits can also be the souls of children who have died from *Mal de Ojo*, or "evil eye," or from some other curse performed by an evil witch. The Jumbie can only be contacted through dreams, and when disturbed, they can cause nightmares. These mischievous spirits also teach witches the art of shapeshifting. To learn from one of these spirits, a witch must go to sleep in the woods the first night of the month and remain there until the spirit makes its appearance in a dream, which commonly occurs after the first seven nights, as this is when the mischievous spirit feels that the witch is in complete comfort and confidence in the space.

The Igneri Shapeshifter Ritual

Today the culture of the Igneri Indigenous people has been mostly lost; their language has been absorbed by the Arawak Indigenous people, and the only thing that is remembered of their culture, according to a few history books and encyclopedias on South American Aboriginal cultures, is their ways of planting, their harvesting techniques, and some of their esoteric beliefs and traditions.

The Igneri saw the seer of the tribe as a divinely anointed being, someone with a kind of divine gift that had to be trained and pushed to the limits to reach closeness to the spirit, who is prepared by the priest of the tribe. The priest was, in turn, a shapeshifter, a medium, and a sorcerer. This individual would be able to take the rank of priest and thus be able to act as a medium between the divinity and the tribe.

Like other Indigenous cultures, they saw a link between the way we see dreams and the way we see the world underwater. For them, dreams were an extension of the spirit world, an aquatic world, and vice versa. Just as water is capable of moving in great waves and entering everywhere, moving between rivers and waterfalls, traveling through mountains, and even entering and leaving our bodies, so could the spirit of all things. For this reason, they saw vital and almost religious importance in the fact that their priest was the shapeshifter and seer of the tribe, that they were an individual who, like water, would be able to move between worlds, between heaven and earth, between dreams and reality, between the world of spirits and the physical world. Their priest was a sorcerer who knew no limits.

The Igneri initiation and transformation rituals were mainly performed in caves to represent their secrecy and exclusivity. This practice remains today in many Afro-Caribbean religious paths where initiations, as in particular paths of Candomblé and Lucumi, are carried out in closed rooms without windows that only those who have been initiated or are in the initiation process can enter.

Today we live in modernity and big cities. Caves are found mainly in public parks, and access to them is highly restricted for many reasons. For this reason, it is essential that, even if rites such as this are performed today, they are performed in a private space without much noise or distractions and with the minimum necessary lighting. Cell phones should be out of the room so you can immerse yourself entirely in the ritual experience and in the disconnection from the outside world. Your senses should be wholly focused on perceiving the world of spirits and not on perceiving "small glimpses" of these in the physical world.

EXERCISE
Shapeshifter Ritual

The following ritual comes from the Iñeri, or Igneri, culture, and from modern reconstructions carried out and translated following the traditions closest to the culture (the mystical traditions of the Arawak and the Cari). The steps of this ritual are arranged in order of difficulty with the idea that you can—and should—start with the easiest part to gain some experience before moving on to the next one.

The goal of this work is to enter the spirit world and interact with it. To be honest, putting this exercise into words was not easy; however, learning it, doing it, and living it has always been a pleasant individual experience. It is just one of those things that we know and rarely write about, except for the ingredients added to the shopping list, and writing this ritual for the book took me several days. While the list of tools and ingredients is quite extensive, the materials are relatively inexpensive and easy to find. They are the primary elements needed to create a modern version of our ritual from the Amazon in your own home.

Each of the following lists is for a separate element to create and use in the ritual. These elements include a necklace, incense, and oil.

For the necklace or ritual anchor, you will need:

- 200 red beads
- Red or white thread
- Bowl of water
- Handful of a variety of dried local flowers

For the ritual oil, you will need:

- Small wooden bowl
- Small spoon
- Virgin olive oil
- Almond oil
- 6 tablespoons mixed grains (rice, lentils, etc.)
- 3 tablespoons brown sugar

For the ritual incense, you will need:

- 1 teaspoon dried local flowers
- 1 teaspoon dried oregano root
- 1 teaspoon dried Sempervivum
- Mortar and pestle

Before the ritual, you will need:

- Glass of water
- Essential oils of your choice
- White candle
- Lighter or matches
- 4½ pounds (2 kilograms) of salt

For the ritual, you will need:

- Censer or a heat-resistant plate
- Charcoal
- Lighter or matches
- Small spoon or dagger

- Ritual incense
- Necklace or anchor
- Brush
- Ritual oil
- Handful of real feathers (So as not to hurt an animal, you can buy these online or pick them up from a pet bird's cage.)
- Wooden bowl with fourteen stones collected by you from four different places around your home
- Long black or red cloth headband to cover your eyes
- Black veil or a long black cloth that will cover your head completely
- Maraca or instrument to make noise
- Notebook and pen
- Dark cloth bag large enough to store all materials above (optional)

Preparing for the Ritual

Choose a time when you can carry out the ritual in your private space and without interruptions, and begin by making the necklace or anchor with the beads and thread. Make a knot at the end of it and place it in the bowl of water. Add the flowers to the bowl, and leave the necklace there until the time of the ritual.

After you've made the necklace, use the spoon to mix the oil ingredients in the bowl, and let it rest until the time of the ritual.

Make the ritual incense by mixing the dried herbs in the mortar with the pestle. Set the mixture aside until the time of the ritual.

About twenty to thirty minutes before the ritual, drink the glass of water, take a hot shower with the essential oils of your choice, and light a white candle to give thanks to the spirits present.

With the salt, draw a large circle on the ground, just as Indigenous peoples did with other natural elements. The size of the circle must be large enough for you to sit inside it with your legs crossed but not too big to occupy your entire room, nor too small to make you feel uncomfortable. It is your ritual space, and it is essential that you feel comfortable inside it.

Place all the implements needed for the ritual around the circle, not inside it.

Important Note:

Your feet should not leave the circle during the ritual, as it becomes your symbolic cave. It is your connection with Mother Earth and the spiritual world. However, your hands can go in the circle or leave it to interact with the elements outside of the same.

Performing the Ritual

Stark naked and very carefully at each step, place the charcoal in the censer or on the heat-resistant plate, light it, and let it burn for five minutes to reach maximum temperature. Once the time has passed, use the dagger or spoon to place a little of the incense on the charcoal. Sit on the ground in the space of the circle.

Pick up the necklace from out of the water with both hands, untangle it, and put it on. Then take the brush and use the oil to draw the following lines on the top of your feet, hands, and wrists. Once these lines are drawn, they will connect with your heart on the chest. Continue to draw symbols on your body in oil, as shown in the following illustration.

Upon completing the symbols, proceed to take the feathers and blow them all around you, letting them fall into the circle. Pick up the stones and place them around you inside the circle, forming your little ritual space.

Take three deep, slow breaths; add more incense to the charcoal; and then recite the following incantation three times:

> Fourteen moons wove the night,
> and we were all water and mud.
> Fourteen dark nights there was no moon,
> and we were all fire and air.
> Fourteen days of light arrived,
> and we were all flesh and blood.
> Fourteen blind walking spirits embodied the bodies we possess,
> and then we are all part of them.
> Fourteen claps were given to make the first of all breathe.
> My feet could be claws, and my arms could be wings.
> My skin could be scales, and my hair could be feathers.
> My claws and all my forms I claim.
> This skin that is my human pride does not serve me tonight.
> I hear the legs of the goat that calls me.
> I hear the wings of the raven that waits for me.
> I hear the hooting of the owl that calls me.
> I hear the breathing of the coyote and the fox that don't sleep.
> My new form I claim until dawn.
> Nameless old spirits guide my flight tonight.

Once you have recited, proceed to blindfold yourself carefully using the headband and cover your head with the veil, keeping the maraca or instrument at hand.

Take six deep and slow breaths, notice and listen to how your breathing changes, and move your head slowly in all directions while taking a deep breath.

Begin to move your arms around and in all directions, keeping your breath slow and as deep as you can. Feel the sweat drip down your forehead and back from your changing body. Visualize how your being comes out through your skin. Visualize the path in front of you that you want to travel. Touch the ground with your claws and feel the feathers on it; these are similar to the feathers that cover you when flying at night.

Get up and crouch several times, stretching your wings and feeling your hooves push against the ground. Sit down again and start making sounds with the maraca or other instrument. Make sounds to the rhythm of your heartbeat; the sound of the maraca is what scares away all the animals that perceive your proximity. Keep moving and stretching within the circle and catch all the sights and sounds that are present in your environment.

End of the Ritual

This exercise does not have a time limit. Continue doing it as long as you consider it necessary; it can be twenty minutes or forty minutes. When you feel it is time to finish, recite the following short incantation:

Thanks for the flight; it's time to rest and return to my skin.

Take six deep breaths in your place without moving. Connect with your body, with your arms, with your hips, with your neck and your spine, with your legs and with your head. Connect back with your organs, feel your pulse and your breath, feel your fingers move like fingers again.

Slowly remove the blindfold, get up, walk outside the circle, and quickly write or draw in a notebook any visions, images, and sounds you perceived.

Collect all the implements, get rid of the ashes of the incense and the water, and keep everything together in a dark cloth bag or a separate cabinet since these same implements will be used every time you want to repeat the ritual.

EXERCISE
Kalinago Night Vision Magic

A second ritual of Indigenous origin carried out by modern Indigenous witches consists of combining the following dried plants in equal amounts in a mortar with nuts and salt, grinding them together, and burning them as incense in the room to generate a night vision. According to the lore, when a medium or a witch makes use of this spell, their consciousness drifts out of their body in the guise of a brown and black bird of prey that moves quickly between dark and gloomy places.

You will need:
- Pinch of soil from the place you wish to visit
- Root or leaves of opium poppy (*Papaver somniferum*)
- Root or leaves of chaconia (*Warszewiczia coccinea*)

- 1 tablespoon almonds or walnuts
- Pinch of salt
- Mortar and pestle
- Lighter or matches
- Two candles in candleholders
- Charcoal
- Censer or heat-resistant plate

At nightfall and in your bedroom, mix the soil, herbs, nuts, and salt together in the mortar and grind with the pestle for several minutes until the ingredients are reduced to the appearance of a dark reddish mass. Light the candles. Place charcoal in the censer or on the plate and light it. Let it sit for several minutes before adding a pinch of the incense.

As the incense burns and the smoke rises, sit in front of it at a distance of at least 4 to 6 feet (1.2 to 1.8 meters), take a deep breath, and recite the following incantation five times:

> One, the sun goes down and the shadow grows.
> Two, dusk rises and dusk approaches.
> Three, the night rushes over us and gives us its cloak.
> Four, feathered and clawed, beaked and winged, I break free.
> One, two, three, four, the night covers me in its cloak.
> One, two, three, four, my wings carry me without fear.
> One, two, three, four, the wind and the night are my allies.

Once you have finished reciting the incantation, lie down on your bed and take a deep breath. See the visions that manifest in and through the smoke.

Keep this exercise in practice for a period of twenty-nine to forty minutes or until the incense runs out.

Once the ritual is over, blow out the candles and store the unused incense in a jar or cloth bag until the next time you wish to use it.

Dream Magic Insight
SLEEP PROTECTION SPELL
BY REV. LAURA GONZÁLEZ

The intention of this spell is to help you feel protected, rested, transformed, and renewed.

We oftentimes carry in our subconscious mind the issues and troubles of the day, and in folk magic, we believe that within our dreams we are able to find relief and solutions. Let's make sure we set ourselves to be protected as we intentionally or intuitively travel to the resting place. This is the realm of the ancestors and their wisdom. It is a place to find answers in the form of messages from our ancestors, our higher self, and the Divine.

It's also important to state in our intentions that we will receive our needed rest and that we will come back to our conscious state feeling transformed and renewed.

You will need:
- The tools of your trade and/or tradition to connect with the Divine and create a sacred space
- Altar or table
- The following cards from a tarot deck:
  - All four aces (wands, swords, cups, and pentacles) to represent the four traditional elements of magic
  - The Sun and the Moon (or the World) to represent the Divine and their protection
  - Death to signify the resting place, renewal, and transformation

Set up a sacred space according to your tradition and belief system. On the altar or table, set up the four aces on the four cardinal points, coinciding with the element you traditionally call on that point. For example, air on the east (swords), fire on the south (wands), water on the west (cups), and earth on the north (pentacles).

At the center of the altar, set up the Sun and the Moon cards (or the World) to evoke the presence of the divine source and their protection.

Place the Death card at the center as well to represent the ability to transform and the wisdom and presence of the ancestors. Facing the east, hold up high the Ace of Swords and speak these words out loud:

> **Element of air, bless me, protect me, transform and renew me with insight, awareness, and wisdom.**

Facing the south, hold up high the Ace of Wands and speak these words out loud:

> **Element of fire, bless me, protect me, transform and renew me with courage, enthusiasm, and healing.**

Facing the west, hold up high the Ace of Cups and speak these words out loud:

> **Element of water, bless me, protect me, transform and renew me with intuition, depth, and love.**

Facing the north, hold up high the Ace of Pentacles and speak these words out loud:

> **Element of earth, bless me, protect me, transform and renew me with stability, growth, and ancestral memories.**

Now, before your altar, acknowledge the presence of the Divine while holding the Sun and the Moon (or the World) cards and speaking these words out loud:

> **Divine as one, Divine as many, celestial bodies of time and wisdom, I am with you as you are within me, from the eons of time now and forever dancing on the liminal spaces of dreams, vision, and wisdom, carrying me through with protection and power.**

Now sit (or lay, if possible) before your altar and hold the card of Death to your heart while speaking these words out loud:

> **As I travel to the resting place, the realm of the ancestors, their divine wisdom is with me, guiding my dreams, answering my questions, sharing messages and solutions.**

I am protected, I am rested, I am transformed, I am renewed.
I am protected, I am rested, I am transformed, I am renewed.
I am protected, I am rested, I am transformed, I am renewed.
When I come back to my awake realm, I'll remember what I've
learned, and that information will be used for the greater good.

Put the Death card back on the altar and sit in contemplation for a few minutes. After you feel the energies of protection and security permeating all your being, proceed to give thanks accordingly to your tradition and belief system and open your sacred space. The work is finished.

Note: Please feel free to adjust any part of this spell to resonate more personally with you and, if you wish to, utilize the three repeating sentences as a nightly meditation.

TRIBAL TALES
THE HAG & THE DREAMING
WITCHES OF TRINIDAD & TOBAGO

The Indigenous culture of Trinidad and Tobago has enormous cultural, esoteric, and linguistic influence from the Arawaks, the Caribs, and the Saladoid people (descendants of the Arawaks).[31] Despite colonization, much of their culture and myths remain, even though they have evolved to adapt.[32]

Bainui, the Dreams, and the Moon

The first human settlements in Trinidad and Tobago date back 7,000 years. This was a time when its first Indigenous inhabitants took refuge in caves; venerated the sun, the moon, and the sea as a trinity of divine unknown spirits; and hid from Bainui, the evil spirit of rain, plague, and death. Bainui was a shapeshifter who only came out at night. He was a sorcerer who had cursed the moon, and it cursed him back so that he did not speak human language. Therefore, Bainui walked between nightmares and dreams, taking the form of the dead in order to communicate with the living.

The Hag of Trinidad

The Soucriant is a type of Machiavellian spirit associated with witches and shapeshifters in Caribbean folklore, specifically in the islands of Dominica, Saint Lucia, Trinidad and Tobago, Guadeloupe, Haiti, Bahamas, Barbados, and Grenada, responding to the name of Ole-Haig in Guyana, Belize, and Jamaica.

This spirit is a blood-sucking, shapeshifting old witch. She maintains the form of an ugly, disheveled old woman during the day when her power is limited by the sun. Once night comes, the old woman sheds her wrinkled skin in a mortar and travels through the skies, taking the form of a woman with large wings, a ball of incandescent fire, or a serpent with wings instead of eyes.

....
31. Wilson, *The Archaeology of the Caribbean.*
32. Wilson, "The Caribbean before European Conquest."

The old witch drinks the blood of her victims while they sleep and that prolongs the hag's life even more. The witch curses those who interrupt her feeding, giving them nightmares from which they can never wake up, blindness, or madness. If the hag drinks a lot of blood from a single victim, the victim can die or become another witch at the service of Gabil or Bazil. This is the demon that appears in the form of a black goat or rooster and hides under the roots of the *Ceiba pentandra*, or the silk cotton tree. It is from this demon that witches receive powers and secrets of black magic in exchange for bags of their victims' blood.

If a man wakes up with bite marks and hickeys around his neck and legs for several days in a row, it is believed that he is being visited by the hag while he sleeps. The way to break this curse is to prepare a piece of raw meat, stuffing it with pepper and mustard seeds and covering it with brown sugar. This magic trap is believed to attract the witch who, upon tasting it, will bite her tongue and wake from her enchanted sleep with a massive migraine.

The witches of Trinidad, also called *sorcières* and *rêveurs vierges,* act as good witches who serve the light. They fight the Soucriant by going into the hag's dreams to prevent her from waking up and changing shape or by making her remain asleep so she cannot search for new victims.

Although the demon Gabil grants powers to the witches and gives them books that he buries under the trees near their houses, he contacts them through dreams. This is why the good witches make amulets and pieces of jewelry with oysters and pearls that they bless to protect dreams. Thanks to these charms, the Devil cannot enter dreams and corrupt others to turn them into his slaves.

PART 2
ENHANCING AND WORKING WITH THE DREAM

CHAPTER 9

DREAM JOURNAL

For various reasons, not all people are capable of remembering their dreams. Although we all dream, it is quite difficult for many to remember what they experienced. I bet that more than once you have heard someone say, "I dreamed something, but I don't remember what it was exactly." This happens more often than you think.

The dream diary, or dream book, as I also like to call it, is one of the best ways to study your dreams in detail and realize what messages they are sending you and what parts of those messages you understand. Writing in the journal will ground you, and using words to describe your dreams will help you remember them. Ideally, one's dream book should be a small notebook that can always be kept close to the bed. That way, the first thing you do when waking up is to write any vision you remember from the night in it.

It is very important that you get into the habit of taking notes, just as you do in a work meeting or at school or university, and it is crucial that you write in your dream journal regularly. This way, you will keep a complete, detailed record of all your impressions, visions, omens, memories, and any fleeting images that remain in your mind when you wake up.

Take into account that your dreams are there to guide you; to show you the future and the past; and to heal you, even from some emotional damage or abuse. That is why it is vitally important to study them. And for this, it is best to keep them in writing.

When I was an uncle for the first time, I noticed that my niece made a strange movement with her eyes while she was sleeping. I asked my sister, and she told me that the baby was dreaming. At that time, I was about twelve years old, so my immediate reaction was one of amazement. The next question was obviously "And do babies dream?" My sister answered "Yes, they always dream." So, I asked the following obvious question: "What do babies dream about?" Then my mother, entering the room, replied with, "Good Ello, babies dream that they are still in the world of dreams, surely with other babies. Now let the baby sleep."

After that short but interesting conversation, I obviously couldn't sit still, so I proceeded to find my crayons and draw what was, for me at that time, the world of dreams. I illustrated a huge field of yellow and purple flowers, white clouds like cotton, and all kind of spirits jumping over the place with some fairies and a pretty rainbow—nothing really funny or different from what you might see in a park.

My dad approached the table and looked at the drawing. He immediately asked me, "Is that the park?" I answered, "No, Dad, it's the world of dreams where the baby is while sleeping." He laughed and responded, "And in the world of dreams there is gravity, and there is a sun, and there are white clouds? More importantly, do the babies see themselves as babies?"

My head practically flew. I was only twelve years old during that conversation, and it was, perhaps, a very deep one for me. My brain filed the conversation away in a drawer, though, and kept it in perfect condition there for years. It wasn't until my dad mentioned the conversation years later that his questions, the ones that left my drawing practically dying due to lack of creativity on the table, came rushing back.

We were talking about certain dreams that Dad had. I remember the dream he was talking about, but he always takes note of these "irregularities" in his schedule, not in a dream diary duly made for it but in his daily work schedule.

For Dad, dreams were an inner reflection of day-to-day. He always saw dreams as a subtle memory of the subconscious. To paraphrase what he's said:

Dreams are a glimpse, not to the memories in your brain but to the facts and events that your energy remembers, as an extra memory that only remembers recent events as an energetic imprint.

From his perspective, dreams reflect not what we see with our eyes but what our energy remembers. Therefore, in dreams we see faces and scenarios that we vaguely remember because we are seeing the forms and appearances of such things in other times—perhaps in other worlds.

In this perspective, which he also learned from his father, dreams, contrary to popular belief, would not show visions of the future but reflections of other lives and moments in other worlds once again. And as we have already mentioned in previous chapters, dreams would not be tied to the laws of the physical world.

Dream Journal Creation

When I started high school, personalized agendas with astrological information, motivational phrases, and covers available in all colors had already become fashionable. These journals, which were a luxury that cost practically an arm and a leg, were called dream agendas. The publishers did an edition every year, and you were supposed to write down the dreams you had there. But unless you were able to remember a dream for all 365 days of the year, you were just carrying around a nice, expensive notebook to fill a few pages with the dates of university exams and some phone numbers.

I did not have the money to buy one of these agendas every year, so I only bought it once. I kept it under my pillow, not on the nightstand as many recommend. The journal was quite useful, but in the end, it was practically just a well-decorated notebook. So, the following years, wanting to follow in the footsteps of my father, who has always seen dreams as something of great depth that deserves to be studied and understood, I began to buy notebooks and diaries to keep with me. To this day, I carry many of my dream diaries, which have evolved into interesting books of enchantments and personal prophecies.

My first diaries were notebooks that I personalized with some dark adhesive paper. Inside the notebooks, I wrote down the few visions that I had in the morning, along with the corresponding date, and included a brief explanation of the dream I had had. On the first page, next to my name, I drew a star. On the next page, I wrote a list of questions that I had to answer after each dream in order to understand it better. The list was:

- Who else was in the dream?
- Did I know these people?
- Where did the dream occur?
- When the dream occurred, was it day or night?
- Did I see myself in the dream, or do I just assume that I was the one who saw everything?
- Did I move from one place to another, or do all the dreams happen in one place?
- How many colors can you distinguish in the dream? *This is more important than you imagine.*
- What were they saying to me in the dream?
- What messages did I perceive?
- Can you see a symbol in the dream?
- *And extremely important:* Could I see my hands in the dream?

Every time I managed to remember a dream, I took notes of every detail, sign, color, and element that I could remember. Then I would answer the questions. After some time, I would not even read the questions. I already knew them, so I responded directly.

Keeping this agenda helped me understand that at first I was only experiencing a memorable dream every four to five days. Having two such dreams in the same week was quite unusual. After the first fourteen dreams I wrote down, I began to notice the dreams becoming more precise, more exact in details. I remembered a greater number of specifics and saw people's faces more clearly.

After two years of this journaling practice, the dreams began to become more frequent. I went from filling one annual diary to filling two and three diaries. Around 2005 to 2007, I also began to keep a different diary. This was where I took notes of my nightmares when I had them. I wanted to keep the visions with messages separate from what would be warnings.

In 2009, precisely in March of 2009, I began to write a dream book. This was where I only took notes of the spells I was performing that related to dreams. I could find hundreds of spells in books, but I did not take notes of these. I just executed them. And yes, I could create dozens of spells, but this dream book was only to write down those spells, rituals, and amulets that I used to enter dreams. What day did I do the spell or ritual? What reactions did it have? How did I sleep that night? What did I dream about that night? What did I dream about during the following nights?

Reviewing these notes constantly, I realized something particular had been happening for years that I had not noticed until this stage. On the nights around the new moon, the dreams became darker—"fuzzier." The details that I wrote down the next morning did not exceed half a page, but on the nights of the full moon (from two days before to one day after), the dreams enjoyed greater clarity. The details that I put in writing those nights easily filled two pages of my agenda and were usually accompanied by conversations with a family member, messages, or some omen that sometimes could be fulfilled in just a matter of days if not in weeks.

On eclipse days, my dreams were practically impossible to describe. On one such occasion, I spent hours trying to describe what had seemed to be a kind of creature with a huge mouth that had more mouths inside it. Suddenly, something came out of all the mouths. Those somethings looked like hands with multiple fingers and blue skin. And at the end of the large mouth, instead of the throat, there was a huge eye with three pupils in it. I could not see the rest of the creature because it remained covered in a cloud. When detailing the dark cloud, I noticed that it was like wet sand. At some point, this weird animal (or spirit) was trying to swallow my feet, but the world seemed to be upside down, and it was devouring me from above.

It had been a dream that was perhaps somewhat disturbing at the time. It was the first time I saw this creature, but not the last. The morning after this dream, I read in the newspapers that there had been a lunar eclipse with a huge range of visibility in Venezuela the night before. Obviously, I made a note of it.

Although the lunar phases have a great influence on the hours of sleep and on the way in which sleep manifests itself, solar eclipses and the changing of the seasons do not seem to have the same effect.

All these little discoveries I made were thanks to the fact that I carried a small agenda to write down observations.

Once you have your dream journal, you can personalize it and create an intimate connection with it. You can buy paper to cover it and draw the symbols and stars that make you feel more comfortable and relaxed on it. You can, as in my case, place some dried herbs and aromatic flowers between the pages to develop a good vibe and remind you that nature is everywhere. Try dried roses, chamomile flowers, linden, and jasmine; the relaxing aromas will also help you sleep.

Look at your dream journal not as a diary to record only your night visions but as a detailed record of your experiences as a medium, your psychic reach, and your adventures between worlds. The dream planner is a powerful instrument of witches. Once you have filled out a planner and read it in detail, you will end up finding all kinds of omens, advice, and even powerful high-magic spells disguised as simple dreams.

Many times the journal ends up becoming a spell journal, a small grimoire written spontaneously by witches, for it is important to write down not only your dreams but also their interpretations, your recipes for tisanes and teas to sleep and induce sleep, the results you had using these, and drawing those symbols that are present in said visions, as well as your own versions of those spells and mystical formulas to induce lucid dreams and travel between dreams.

EXERCISE
A Little Dream Journal Ritual

Use this exercise to manifest dreams with clarity and an abundance of details and put them in writing in your journal.

You will need:

- Cup of chamomile tea
- Censer or heat-resistant plate
- Myrrh or palo santo incense
- Lighter or matches
- Dream journal and pen

On a Monday night, preferably a Monday after a new moon, drink the chamomile tea with your body totally calm. Relax your mind and your body, then light your incense. Move your dream journal through the smoke of the incense several times. As you do so, pray the following several times in a low and clear voice:

My dreams are clear, and their omens are accurate.

Go to sleep with a sense of calm and rest well. Take notes the next day of any details you saw in the dream.

Enhancing Your Dream Journal

There are many things you can do to give your dream journal more power. Alongside simply writing down what you experience, draw images you remember from your dreams; add some poems and spells inspired by your dreams; or try what I particularly like to do and include some dried herbs in between the pages. This will charge the diary. You can also add oils to make dreams and visions abound at night.

Dried Plants

I learned how to use certain herbs from my mom, who worked in her own natural temple near a river on the outskirts of the city. She always collected herbs and flowers from the river. She researched what plants they were and added them to her personal herbal journal with a stapler or sometimes tape—whatever tool was at hand. She adhered the fresh plants to the pages and wrote the various names, descriptions, and uses of each one. With the passing of days, the plants ended up completely drying out, and the book now looks increasingly chubby and loaded.

Taking on this exercise will allow you to learn day after day from the plants that surround you, from the herbs, flowers, and trees growing in your environment that are nourished daily by your own energy and magical presence. The plants in traditional Indigenous witchcraft are often used dried for incense and spells or fresh for healing rituals and spiritual offerings.

In your dream journal, you can include herbs that will help you to have abundant dreams or to have dreams focused on a special topic. For example:

- *Adam and Eve roots:* To attract romantic and seductive dreams
- *Carnations:* To be lucky in dreaming what you want, and to make dreams come true
- *White and yellow chrysanthemums:* To gain psychic strength and perseverance
- *Dahlias:* For good fortune and good luck
- *Forget-me-nots:* Not only to better remember dreams but also to clarify and define your intuition
- *High John the conqueror:* For you to conquer dreams and all your obstacles
- *Five bay leaves:* For dreams to manifest and lead you to fame and good fortune
- *Roses:* Red roses to focus this dream energy on the path of love; yellow roses to focus on money, good fortune, and joy; or white roses for purity, calm, good rest, and protection

RECIPE
Journal Herbal Mix

I am a bit obsessed with creating mojo bags (also called sachets) for all kinds of magical purposes. Here is one I created to hang from my dream journal. Although it looks like simple decoration, it is used to enhance the magic of the journal, turning it into a powerful dream talisman.

You will need:
- Blue or white candle
- Lighter or matches
- Small blue mojo bag or two squares of blue cloth sewn into a bag with blue or golden thread
- 1 tablespoon valerian (recommended plant for sleeping)
- 1 tablespoon lavender (protection and enthusiasm)
- 1 tablespoon white rose petals (purity and protection)
- Small piece of crystal quartz (optional)
- Golden or blue tread
- Scissors (to cut the thread)

Light the candle and put all the herbs and the crystal in the bag one by one. Close the bag and tie it with the thread. Attach a long end of the thread to the journal; you can use glue, tape, or stickers to do so.

Dream Oils

Fragrances have enormous power over our senses, especially when sleeping. A sweet, fresh, and subtle fragrance, such as cinnamon or eucalyptus, in your room can help you sleep better, while asafoetida or valerian can have a fragrance that is far from exquisite. They can thus ruin your rest.

You can add a few drops of essential oil between the pages and corners of your journal, which will stay close to you while you sleep. Like the talisman, it will also provide a feeling of full rest.

I advise you to sprinkle three to six drops of essential oil for sleep on the cover or between the pages of your dream journal. You will turn your dream journal into a powerful protective talisman.

Here are some other essential oils that can be used:

- *Lavender oil:* To provide a good and full rest
- *Rose oil:* To provide protection and attract good fortune, beauty, and love
- *Orange oil:* To attract financial joy and abundance or dreams of abundance and fulfillment
- *Eucalyptus oil:* To provide protection, calm, and insight
- *Sage oil:* To attract divine protection, especially psychic protection

Dream Magic Insight
GUARDIAN OF DREAMS:
A JOURNAL CONSECRATION RITUAL
BY ELLA HARRISON

Reading through our dream journal can be like looking through a window into our unconscious. While in a dream state, we are immersed and usually do not concern ourselves with the deeper symbolisms and patterns that continually emerge with dreams. Yet dreams have held human fascination for decades, and psychologists such as Freud have dedicated whole books to unraveling the meanings of dreams. Keeping a journal can allow you to process and analyze dreams with a clear mind—using the conscious to discover the unconscious. Even if you do not feel that you have any dreams right now, keeping a journal can signal to your brain that this subject is important to you, and with time you may find yourself experiencing more dreams. It is like shining a light on a dark corner of your mind for the first time. You may be surprised at what you'll find.

In animism, one believes in the animated spirit in everything, and to apply this concept to a journal would be to view the journal as a guardian of dreams. This is not just a soulless journal but a working companion that keeps your dreams and, in turn, part of your mind safe.

Use this spell to consecrate and awaken your journal so it may tuck away these pieces of you safely.

You will need:
- Dream journal
- Red or black cotton thread at least 10 inches (25 centimeters) long
- Personal taglock, such as hair, spit, or even blood if you're comfortable
- Glue or tape
- Pen with red or black ink

Recommended time and moon phase: On a Monday or Wednesday of a new or full moon.

Prepare yourself and your space depending on your path or tradition. For example, you could begin by taking a cleansing bath/shower, opening a circle or hollowing a compass, grounding and centering, etc. Take your thread and open your journal to the middle. Place the thread down the center and around the back binding, then tie it together so it creates a sort of bookmark.

Next, flip to the first page of the journal. Take your taglock and attach or otherwise transfer it onto that first page. If you are using spit or blood, smudge it on the corner of the page. If you are using hair or some another tangible object, use glue or tape.

Now take your pen and introduce yourself to the journal. Write about yourself as if you were writing a pen pal letter. Then, once you have introduced yourself, focus on your energy and the intention you have for this journal. Allow yourself to write freely about what this journal will become to you, how you see yourself working with it, and your hopes to connect and discover more about yourself and your unconscious. Write this in the form of addressing the journal. For example, *Dear journal, my intentions are…*

Some helpful prompts may be:

- May my dreams be safely contained by you to be unraveled by myself with your assistance.
- May you, dear journal, offer clarity and lift the veil to the dream world and what lies hidden within.
- May you, dear journal, assist me in understanding myself and connect with those who wish to present themselves in the dreams' liminal space.

Once you have written all these things down and you are content with your words, use your breath to breathe life into your journal. From now on, try to write down every dream (or lack thereof) in your journal, as well as your thoughts on these dreams. Don't forget the dates too. When opening the diary, knock or breathe on it to awaken it from its sleep. When closing it, wrap the thread around it to keep it protected.

TRIBAL TALES
HOTÏ PEOPLE

The Hotï, Jodï, or Joti are an Amerindian people who live in the Sierra de Maigualida in the Venezuelan Amazon. Also known as Chicano, Shicana, Yuana, Yuwana, and Waruwaru, they call themselves Hodï, or Hotï, which means "people" or "town." In the year 2011, there were only 982 members.

For the descendants of the Hotï people, the tribal shaman is not only a spiritual leader but also a storyteller, a language healer, and a social adviser. Waunau (dreams) represent the means used by the native spirits of their ancestors to communicate with them. From their religious tradition, people who do not have dreams are seen as Abujres, or "people with an uncertain path and destiny." The more dreams people have, the more they are in contact with the world of spirits and ancestors.

For the Hotï people, dreams are interpreted in two ways: as memories of ancestors who were unable to conclude or tell their own story or as messages from the afterlife sent by the deceased and ancestors. The Hotï share a vision in which all are born to become ancestors, except those who have an uncertain path or destiny. Those with an uncertain path are destined to be born, grow up, die, and return to earth, while everyone else becomes ancestors. The ancestors subsequently integrate into the greater spirits, forming a single collective consciousness. But they must first come to the world to learn and heal the following generations. In this way, the collective consciousness will be more beautiful, wiser, and bigger.

CHAPTER 10

DREAM ALTAR

The altar is a sacred and intimate space of connection between the mystic and our gods and spiritual guides. For those more adept at meditation and internal work, it is a space for understanding and re-evaluation and a space for study and craft.

The altar is more than a modern, decorative space full of books, candles, and divine imagery that leads us to connect with our divinities. It is like our temple at home. It can be formed on a table, on the edge of a window, or in a small corner of the bedroom. It is the place where we focus our magical work, create all kinds of spells, store knowledge, and keep various amulets and talismans until it is time to use them.

An altar can be as small or as wide as the space chosen allows. It can also be left uncovered or covered with long curtains that hang from the ceiling. All these factors are variables that will depend entirely on the practitioner, not the teacher, not the guide, and many times not even the magical tradition that they practice.

In Wiccan traditions, the altar serves not only as a connection space with the oldest gods to carry out all kinds of celebrations and sabbats but also as a space for spellcasting, creation, and creativity. The initiate can put all their knowledge into practice there and perform a wide variety of spells and rituals.

In Afro-Caribbean traditions (Candomblé, Quimbanda, Lucumi), the altar is often a large, functional space to store spiritual items and all kinds of ritual objects. In these traditions, the altar is seen more as a magical space that occupies a corner of the house or even a complete wall, allowing rituals, ceremonial dances, and sacred songs to be performed in a much larger space (compared to Wiccan traditions, for example) as long as said esoteric works are performed from a visible point of the altar.

For the spiritist traditions of Portugal, which are well rooted in the Caribbean, the altar consists of a small space where elements of the esoteric tradition merge, such as personal items and photographs of the ancestors, saint imagery, and small books about praying. Thus, it is functioning more as a portal or medium for the oracle or the witch.

An altar of dreams is a workspace made and decorated with a focus on dreams. It is a space entirely dedicated to individual magic and the analysis of our night visions and astral journeys. It is a space devoted to us and our individual connection with the spiritual. It is not another altar with images of gods and saints because it is not a space to work with them. It is a magical work area to practice divination related to dreams, burn incense, prepare potions, hang our talismans, and place our cup of tea before bed.

Now, here we are going to first discuss how to build a general altar before moving on to create our own dream altar.

A General Altar

There is a wide variety of books available that give options on how to create a magical altar. In these modern days, we have modern authors writing to teach you the way to create a very functional altar space at home, including *Witchful Thinking* by Zoë Howe and *Witch Life* by Emma Kathryn.

There are several elements most altars have in common: candles; censers; statues; representations of the elements; and glasses with water, glasses with wine, or glasses of both. There are also some common altar restrictions, and according to each tradition, some can be quite specific. In Lucumi, for example, you would never stand naked in front of the altar. On the other hand, some restrictions are simpler and certainly logical, such as not placing anything in the space of the altar that does not correspond to it. This might include combs, cell phones, car keys, etc.

As you begin to craft your altar, do not worry about filling the space and buying everything you think you need. Most sorcerers acquire their items over time, and this often takes years, so don't feel obligated to run to the nearest botanical to find everything that appears in this book.

Choose Your Space

To create a general altar, you can start simply by selecting the space that is going to become your sacred place of connection and spiritual evolution. First, choose which room you are going to have the altar in and pick an appropriate wall or corner. Then, find a table or flat surface to use as the altar. For some time while I lived alone, my altar consisted of an old plastic chair covered with a thick orange towel on which I placed a round wooden base with a small censer (to represent the air element), a hand mirror (for my protection and visualization rituals), a cup with water (to symbolize the presence of the water spirits), a saucer with salt (for purification and to symbolize the earth and its gnomes), a fan (to move the incense smoke around the room), and some candles (to symbolize fire). Once you've chosen a table, you need a good cleaning of the site. This can be done by simply sprinkling a little salt on the floor and sweeping it later to cancel negative energies.

In Venezuelan and Colombian Indigenous practices, altars are made of rock from a park or a river, while specifically in the South American magical tradition of *Los Encantados* (The Enchanted Ones), the altars are

194 * Chapter 10

recommended to be made of rock or marble. These are quite resistant elements that will also be constantly anointed with the ritual magic of the sorcerer who works on them. However, a wooden board is also fine.

In various ritual sites of the cities of Caracas in Venezuela and Cartagena in Colombia, it is common to find makeshift rural altars that consist of a wooden board placed on four bricks with ritual symbols drawn with chalk or with husks painted with tempera. Although the material is perhaps not the most resistant, it does not detract from the magic of the sorcerer or practitioner in question.

Altar Items

Once you have found your location and a table, cover the table or flat surface with a dark tablecloth. This will be used for the altar and nothing else. Then, place any items collected on the altar.

As a personal recommendation, look for items that have the precise size for your space, and try to acquire elements resistant to heat and fire, such as those made from bronze or steel. Ceramic or metal censers are ideal, even when those made of wood provide a more ecological and traditional look. Get glass bottles for storing oils and herbs, as they are more suitable than plastic bottles.

It is recommended to put items on the altar clockwise starting from the east and continuing to the south, west, and north. According to your magical tradition, there may be differences in this order. If you do not belong or have not been initiated to any magical tradition, start with the most basic and begin in the east, placing items associated with the air/wind element. This might include fans, censers, or a hanging bell. Then, toward the south, place items associated with the element fire, such as candles, matches, a candelabra, or candleholders. Next, toward the west, place items associated with the element of water. These might include a bowl or a glass of water, a glass of wine, or seashells. Finally, toward the north, position items that represent and connect with earth, including salt, sand, rocks and minerals, or plants.

Statuettes and all kinds of images associated with your religious tradition are welcome to this space. They can be figures or representations of orishas, goddesses, angels, spirits, demons, fairies, etc. Although it is ideal to keep separate altars if you belong to more than one tradition, I will not deny that, on more than one occasion between one move and another, I have learned to improvise with all my gods and spiritual guides confined in a tiny space. When I arrived in the United States and did not have the money to create a completely new altar, I bought a small wooden shoe rack and plastic cylinders for twelve dollars at a local store. I covered the rack with a long purple scarf and placed some aluminum trays on it—the type restaurants use to serve takeout food. On these trays, I lit candles and burned incense daily.

It was not ideal, but it is proof that you can adapt to any situation. I suppose that all my magical work paid off or simply my guides required more space, because a few months later, I had two separate, much wider altar tables placed one in front of the other, creating a large ritual space in the center.

The Altar of Dreams

Since I have taught you the most basic things you should know about the creation and use of a general magical altar, I will now offer you two dream altar options here. Both are perfect for a Dream Witch and both are derived from Latin American witchcraft. The first option is my version, and it borrows elements from two of my different but very similar traditions: the popular South American magical tradition Los Encantados and the Spanish-Venezuelan tradition La Corte de las Brujas. The other magical version, which is included near the end of this chapter, was given to this book by the wonderful Lorraine Monteagut, PhD, and it is very practical too.

You can choose just one, or you can use both. You can also borrow elements from both altars and create your own.

Devoting Space

The first thing you will need is a small ritual space in your bedroom. Depending on the space of your bedroom, this can consist of a small table in the corner or in the center of a completely empty wall. It could also be the wide windowsill of a bedroom window, although that is not the best option for reasons of practicality and privacy.

A nightstand is the right size and height for this work since we normally work while sitting on the floor in front of the altar, but you are welcome to use a bigger or higher table if you find it more comfortable as a sorcerer. For example, due to my height and the fact that I prefer to remain standing, I like to keep high altars, especially so pets cannot reach them and make disasters.

Once you've selected your altar, use a dark-colored tablecloth to cover it entirely—to the floor. The recommended colors for this cloth are blue, indigo, purple, or black. These are colors associated with the night and the guardians of the world of dreams.

Add a resistant base next. I like this mainly for the visual aspect, but I also recommend it for practicality in order to not place all the elements of the altar directly on the tablecloth. It is better if you can get a metal tray with a round, wooden base. This is usually easy to get in arts and crafts stores. One idea given to me by a friend was to use a thin and long piece of agate in dark colors.

Gathering Altar Items

Now that you have the space for the altar and the altar itself, it is time to focus on the elements that will complement it and help you to carry out your magical work. Do not feel pressured to find all the elements in a single day. You can always start with the simplest and handiest elements, such as salt, a glass of water, and candles from the market, while you take the time to acquire all the other elements. The altar will be there; it's not a one-time thing.

Candleholder

Add a candleholder (preferably metal). On this altar, we will place just one candle each night, only adding another candle if a spell specifically requires it. Because we are working with the night, dreams, and shadows, the light of the candle will be one of our many anchors to the physical world. Often, we will use a single candle that will be continuously lit and extinguished for several consecutive nights.

Censer

Place a heat-resistant censer that's either metal or ceramic. This can also be a small cauldron, which is widely available in a variety of sizes at botanicas, or it can just be a heat-resistant plate. You will use this object to burn incense cones or herbal incense with the help of a piece of charcoal.

Crystal Ball

Another item for your dream altar is a crystal ball. There are some small ones on the market that fit perfectly in your hand, and these are just right for a small altar. These crystal spheres help you to receive omens and visions of the future, and they are especially suitable if you are trying to remember a dream. To do so, light a candle, take a deep breath, and carefully observe the candle's light in the ball and the visions that it shows you.

Dagger or Athame

You will also need a ritual knife, which can be a consecrated knife of your magical tradition, such as a small dagger or athame. These instruments are not accessible in all countries or in all cultures, even today with the accessibility of the internet. For this reason, these instruments are commonly replaced by a small blade or knife, which you can bless by anointing it with water from a nearby river and a few drops of rue and sandalwood oil or rose oil, or by leaving it in the window under the full moon night.

You will use this blade only to cut plants for your rituals, and you will keep it under or behind the altar as a protective amulet so the blade or knife never reaches you or touches you to hurt you.

Jar for Herbs

You will also need a small glass jar with a lid to store your sleeping herbs. (Make sure you don't add any toxic or poisonous herbs.) These are the herbs that you will use to prepare your infusions, burn as incense, or fill sachets and charm bags for dream magic. You can buy and have multiple jars in order to keep all your herbs separate and not mix them. Simply identify them with tags or stickers and keep them closed in a fresh place.

Mirror

Find a small mirror for your altar and anoint it on a new moon night with an infusion of mugwort and rosemary for clairvoyance and good fortune. According to Latin American folklore, a mirror washed with sagebrush water allows us to see spirits that approach with bad intentions.

Moon Image

To represent the night and the lunar cycles, I suggest you add a figure of the crescent moon or a drawing of a moon to your altar space. Sometimes I would replace my handmade drawing with a photograph of the moon printed on good quality, which I would write a little rhyme about the moon and dreams on the back of. You are welcome to take inspiration from this too. This representation can be also the Moon tarot card or a drawing of it.

Mugwort Plant, Small (Optional)

If you have enough space and natural light in your bedroom, a mugwort plant in a small pot on the altar will bring you clairvoyance, good omens, mental clarity, and good luck in all matters related to dreams, lucid dreaming, and astral projection.

Paper and Ink

Always keep ink or pens and loose sheets of paper on your altar to write recipes and infusions or to draw your dreams. It wouldn't be a surprise if you woke up one day to see that you managed to write something on the paper in your sleep.

Pentagram

The symbol of the pentagram (a five-pointed star within a circle) is not something typical of Latin American Indigenous cultures, but even so, the pentagram is a valuable emblem of power for witches. It not only represents the elements, but it is also the drawing and representation of a star, and that is the representation that we seek to bring to the altar—a star that illuminates the darkest nights, a flash of light that works as an anchor, manifesting itself in your nightmares (in case they happen) to bring you back to the light.

You will need either a wooden pentagram, which you can find in a store, or a provisional drawing of a pentagram that you can make yourself on paper and keep on the altar. The pentagram symbolizes the elements of creation, the conscious spirit gaining power over the elements that govern each plane of existence, the human form as an icon of power, and the power of the witches that are infinite and changeable.

The pentagram on the altar acts as a magnet that will keep you grounded during the meditation days, provides protection, and works as a small oracle that will alert you through different ways within your power if you are in a dangerous situation or if someone is intervening with your magical work.

Psychic-Protection Gems

All those gems, stones, and minerals that help strengthen the psyche and protect your mind and aura can be scattered about your altar or placed in a small saucer on it. You can include small figurines made of crystal quartz, black onyx, jet, and tiger's-eye if you wish.

Salt

Your altar will need a saucer or small pot full of salt. It can be kitchen salt, coarse salt, or even bath salt infused with aromatic oils. You will use the salt symbolically to channel the earth, but it will also independently absorb any negative vibrations that arrive in the space and surroundings of the altar. Remember to replace the salt every so often—either every two to three weeks or every night of the new moon.

Seashells

Seashells represent the sea, the waters of creation, the beginning of life, and from the Latin American Indigenous vision, the world of spirits. Seashells that you have collected on the beach or that someone has given you can be a beautiful and powerful complement to your altar. They channel the waters and connect us with the ocean from wherever we are; they provide a feeling of harmony and calm; and they are (as well as the shells of turtles) a powerful talisman of protection against psychic attacks and night visions.

Vase (Optional)

In your sacred space on the altar, you can keep a small vase or a tall glass of dried plants that help you to relax and sleep, such as lavender, eucalyptus, mint, and white chrysanthemum.

Glass of Water

You will need a glass of water for your altar. You can fill this glass with tap water from the kitchen, but if you are able to use water from a river, a lake, rainfall, or any other natural source, that would be helpful. If you use sea water (salt water), you can add seashells to better channel the strength and spiritual energy of this powerful element. If you use water from a river or a similar source, you can collect some small stones from the site and place them on the altar as a way to bring nature with you.

EXERCISE
Ritual to Activate the Altar

Once the altar is set up and ready and sacred space has been built, it's time to activate it and use it; this is a ritual you can do to make that happen. This work uses a rose. In Latin American spiritualism, roses represent the cycle between life and death. The spirits of roses are a form of psychopomp capable of moving between the world of the living and the world of the dead as the cut roses end up withering.

You will need:
- White rose in a glass of water or vase
- Stick of rose or vanilla incense
- Censer or heat-resistant plate
- Lighter or matches
- Fan
- Blue candle in candleholder
- Rose, gardenia, or eucalyptus essential oil
- White or light blue paper
- Pen with blue ink

Place the rose on the altar, put the incense in the censer, and light the incense stick. Using the fan, move the fragrant smoke from the incense in all possible directions and around your surroundings.

Anoint the candle with a few drops of one or more of the oils, place it on the center of the altar, and light it.

On paper and with the pen, write your name seven times and draw a picture. It can be any picture that comes to mind at the moment. Do it calmly and without distractions. After drawing, fold the paper and place it under the altar as a personal signature. Keep it there or save it later in your journal.

Three Altar Guardians

Your dream altar is a magical portal to your dreams. That's the reason you will have guardians to protect you and to guard your altar against any bad entities or spirits.

The three guardians or keyholders represent the three states of dreams: the conscious or guided dream, the common unconscious dream, and the lucid dream. The latter one is also what gives us access to different forms of projection.

These three guardians are always present under different forms in each dream we have. They respond to a common name once you find them, and they usually have the same appearance once you discover their names. They have different individual names for each dreamer, and discovering their individual names, although not a priority, will take you to one of the most complex levels of elevation and work. They are powerful spirits, and they will not reveal their names right away because they need to trust you first.

Once you discover the names, it is your duty to keep them secret if you want to advance on your path. However, it is important to write down these names, so I recommend you keep the written names completely secret and do not share them with anyone. Someone is your friend today, sure, but tomorrow who knows? They could make use of those sacred names to enter your dreams and cause all kinds of imbalances.

The figures of the three guardians must be made and interpreted by you. If you want external inspiration, I recommend looking for illustrations of the tarot card the Hermit, which looks exactly like these guardians. Their faces are kept in complete shadow under their cloaks, under which they keep all kinds of magical objects, enchanted scrolls, and relics of your past lives.

Dream Magic Insight
THE DREAM ALTAR
BY LORRAINE MONTEAGUT, PHD

Sleep is a ritual often overlooked in our magical preparations, but the sleep state offers us opportunities for transformation every single day. Why not treat it with the reverence we reserve for other rituals? I have found in my own practice that keeping a separate dream altar in my bedroom helps me build a healthy routine around sleep and inspires lucid dreaming. Here are a few tips for setting up a dream altar of your own and incorporating it into your daily rituals:

Create Your Space

Find a spot in your bedroom that you can peacefully visit every night before you go to bed. This doesn't have to take up too much space. I use a nice big window ledge by my bed. You might use the top of your dresser or your night table. You should be able to comfortably sit or stand in front of your altar.

Once you've found your spot, clear the space of all objects that don't belong on your dream altar. Clean all surfaces with a diluted solution, such as Florida water. You might clear the air around your altar with a sustainable smoke bundle.

Set Up the Altar

It's time to set up the altar of your dreams! This can be as simple or as elaborate as you'd like. I like to represent all the elements on my altar. Here are a few examples of element-related altar items you might pick and choose from:

- *Earth:* Flowers, herbs, gemstones
- *Water:* Chalice, photographs, heirlooms
- *Fire:* Candles, incense, smoke-clearing bundles
- *Air:* Journals, spell books, grimoires
- *Space:* Divination tools, such as pendulums, tarot decks, runes

Check the correspondences of the things you use. For example, the herb mugwort is especially potent for lucid dreaming, while lavender is soothing and supports rest. Quartz helps clear your mind, amethyst helps tap into intuition, and obsidian and tourmaline protect your energy while you're sleeping. Water charged under the light of the moon makes a nice offering.

Using the Altar

Visit your altar right before sleep. Make sure you've already done all your other get-ready-for-bed rituals and that you're comfortable. What are you wearing? What's the temperature like? Once at the altar, I like to interact with each item in a small way. I might add water to a cup, light some incense, open my spell book to a page and read aloud, or pull a tarot card. This is your practice. Follow your curiosity and intuition.

The most important part—the heart of the dream altar ritual—is your intention. For this, you'll want to put anything down that's been weighing heavy on you or that's been rattling around in your mind. You might say this to yourself silently, speak it aloud, or write it in a journal. Tell yourself that this will still be waiting for you when you're back from the dream world. Next, ask for the dream you'd like to have. Maybe you have a person you'd like to see or a place you'd like to visit. Try to detach from problem-solving and ask yourself what you really want. Again, you can do this any way you'd like, whether in thought, speech, or writing.

After you've set your intention, it's time to say goodnight. You might use a form of divination to receive a message before you tuck yourself away. Snuff out your candles. Say a prayer. Get yourself to bed. And hopefully you'll dream.

When I wake, I like to journal my dreams so I remember them. Use your altar water to water your plants. Do not drink it, and refresh it the next evening.

TRIBAL TALES
CHÁCOBO PEOPLE

The Chácobo are the Indigenous ethnic group that inhabits the northeast of Bolivia. The tribe is made up of less than two thousand people and has a well-structured hierarchical organization with a chief followed by several other minor chiefs. They are mostly nomadic people of hunters and fishers.

For the Chácobo, the main figure of their culture and religion is Káko, a mischievous hero whose story is similar to that of Prometheus, the Greek hero who stole fire from Olympus. Káko entered the world under the ground and was guided by the Yushini, the souls of the dead whose names have been forgotten and therefore do not remember who they were. Once there, Káko stole the fire of Asijka, or Ashija, the old witch who had appropriated fire and the art of growing plants.

Once he had the fire in his hands, Káko rose to the surface, finding his way through a dark cave. He used the fire to force the banshees to rest and descend to the world beneath the floors. He shaped the world to make it what it is today because the world had no form.

With the fire in the hands of the people, the Chácobo could cook their food, light the caves, and keep warm at night. They no longer had to beg the old witch for fruits and food. After that, the witch remained a prisoner in the dark world. She could only manifest through dreams and nightmares, in which she begs people to bring her fire to warm her old bones in exchange for the power to change shape at night.

The Yóbeka is the spiritual leader of the tribe, often considered in anthropological terms to be the shaman. This spiritual worker receives an initiation at a very old age while chewing tobacco in the surroundings of the Ivón River, a sacred place for them. It is considered the river that covers the cave through which Káko escaped. They also ingest *Banisteriopsis caapi* (the vine from which ayahuasca is cooked).

CHAPTER 11

MOON PHASES & DREAMING

Sorcery and magic have been strongly influenced by the lunar phases—not only from the Wiccan perspective but also in many esoteric paths in Latin America. The initiatory path of Los Encantados in Chile, Bolivia, El Salvador, and Guatemala; *La Tradición Espiritista Nativista* (Spiritist Tradition) in Venezuela; and the path of the *Dama de las Aguas* (the All-Waters Lady) in Brazil are all esoteric paths where the moon has a strong presence and influence that must be taken into account. This is not done in a compulsory way, and it is mostly a suggested practice to complement various ritual services with the lunar cycle.

According to a scientific study from the University of Washington, the lunar phases, in one way or another, do have a series of effects on our daily activities. The quality of the night's illumination by the moon and other factors have a tremendous influence on the stages of sleep and its quality too.[33]

Part of this study even shows that on days before the full moon, we sleep fewer hours and it is more difficult for us to fall asleep, while on nights with waning moons and before the new moon we sleep more hours and go to bed earlier.[34]

This study, although medically accurate because it has been tested by the scientific community on various population groups in various cities, does not add anything new or contradict anything that has not already been handled for years in the esoteric field. For example, the nights before the full moon, we feel more nourished by the lunar energy, and it is more difficult for us to

....

33. Casiraghi et al., "Moonstruck Sleep."
   Kronfeld-Schor et al., "Chronobiology by Moonlight."
34. Cajochen et al., "Evidence that the Lunar Cycle Influences Human Sleep."

fall asleep, and in folklore, it also has an enormous influence on the paranormal phenomenon of werewolves. The nights before the new moon, we sleep more because we are perceiving less moonlight every day in the atmosphere and our body feels more exhausted at night.[35]

Dream Witchery Timing

When it comes to magic and sorcery, the lunar phases are linked to the way in which our spells, rituals, and enchantments unfold.

In astrology, the sun represents the outer self, the way we present to others, and the way we are perceived when they look at us, while the moon represents our inner self, our subconscious self, and everything that dwells in our inner self. In short, the moon and its phases are associated with the inner world, the processes of inner transformation, and what activates them or keeps them in constant operation. It affects everything that drives you to act from within, whether for good or for evil.

In modern magic, we make use of the energy that the lunar phases manifest to reinforce our spells and various rituals or even to perform, manufacture, and consecrate our amulets. For example, the new moon represents beginnings and restarts, which is why it is a suitable time for the realization of spells and amulets focused on starting new processes and academic

....

35. Röösli, "Sleepless Night, the Moon Is Bright."

studies, studying new forms of magic, and performing rituals that attract something new (a new love, a new friendship, a new job). The full moon represents abundance, celebration, fullness, and light that reveals everything, and it is the perfect time to perform spells that thank, celebrate, and duplicate abundance, wealth, and progress. The waning moon, on the other hand, is the phase when the moon is losing light and plunging into shadow to renew itself. This stage of the cycle relates to magic meant to lower some form of energy, nullify spells and curses, or decrease the power that a witch has upon us.

If the moon is associated in the esoteric world with the manifestation and direction of our energy, and if it is associated with everything that inhabits us internally and transforms us in the astrological realm, it is important to consider how these lunar aspects also influence our sleep phases and the dreams we have. After all, dreams are part of our internal processes, and they are full of energy of manifestation and transformation.

EXERCISE
Dream Time Exercise

In witchcraft, we commonly talk about how the moon and its phases dominate certain forms of magic and sorcery, how the lunar phases affect the waves and the cycles of sleep, and which phases are the most effective for each spell we perform or talisman we craft. While all such discussions are good, it is important that we take the time to study how these phases affect us personally, which is why this exercise here is so crucial.

You will need:
- Calendar or digital app that shows the lunar phases
- Dream journal
- Pen or pencil
- Personal calendar

With the help of a calendar or a digital app that provides information about the lunar phases, locate and identify the next new moon and take note of this day in your dream journal. From there, draw or mark on your own calendar the next three phases. For example, if next Monday is the new moon, the Monday after that is the waxing moon, the following Monday or Tuesday is the full moon, and the following week opens with a waning moon.

This is a fairly simplified setup, but it is definitely one that is easy to follow for those who are not so familiar with the deeper aspects of astrology. In short, this method is simple but useful.

When the night of the new moon arrives, go to sleep and keep your journal close to you. When you wake up the next day, proceed to write about your night of rest. What kind of dreams did you perceive, assuming you had any? If there was a nightmare, or if you had any trouble sleeping, perhaps some anxiety or insomnia, write that down too.

From then on, on each of the following nights until the next new moon, keep these notes up to date. Although the stars affect us all in a general way, each individual has a unique energetic trace, which means each person reacts in a different way to certain aspects. This goes far beyond conventional basic astrology. Instead, it is an individual practice that invites you to work with your own energy field and understand how it reacts and manifests according to the moon.

After years of studying various astrology books and performing this exercise, I noticed that on new moon nights I fall asleep faster, while on full moon nights I tend to have more anxiety. On some nights before the full moon I can stay up until four in the morning without feeling sleepy, which leads me to spend hours awake in bed, rolling from side to side trying to sleep. The nights after the full moon, I begin to sleep more soundly and even for more hours.

I have suggested this exercise to others, and they usually have quite different results, often contrary to my own. Many sleep better with a full moon, and some of my colleagues tend to have greater nocturnal anxiety with the new moon. These nights of the new moon are also when nightmares are more common.

This personal information is of vital importance because it helps us, although not in great depth, to better understand how our psyche works and how it can connect to planetary movements and lunar cycles. This knowledge does not just help in the magical, astrological, and social aspects but in an entirely individual and more spiritual aspect too.

For example, if, after having been disciplined and performing this exercise for about three consecutive lunar cycles, I noticed that the waning moon causes me anxiety, perhaps I can use this information in my favor. Perhaps I could choose not to carry out the performance of certain spells and magical works during this phase because my emotional state could completely affect the work I am doing.

If, on the other hand, I discover that during the nights of the waxing moon I tend to sleep better and feel more rested in the mornings, perhaps I can think ahead and plan my more complicated rituals for those days or for the days before the full moon.

The Moon Phases and Dreams

The lunar phases have diverse effects on all individuals, plants, spirits, and animals, so it is not surprising that they can also affect our sleep states and night visions. In the following sections, we will study some of these effects in more detail and examine how the movements of this natural terrestrial satellite affect our dreams and the way we perceive them.

New Moon

The new moon is the moment during which we sow intentions of growth. Everything that is new or in a period of renewal is celebrated and empowered with this lunar phase. There is little light in the sky and dark nights motivate us to prolong our rest. However, it is common for us to wake up in the morning with a feeling of exhaustion, as if we had not rested enough.

During these nights, rituals and spells dedicated to exploring the individual shadow, the dark parts of our mind, our fears and nightmares, as well as analyzing in-depth past situations that have not allowed us to move forward, take on greater power.

The dreams during these nights are open to exploration, although they are often the darkest and most enigmatic dreams—perhaps even disturbing. They are also the ones that invite us to study our psyche and explore in detail the night visions that appear to us.

New moon nights invite us to take our first steps in the world of dreams, to prepare our dream pillow and our journal, as well as to burn incense outside the home to dissipate negative energies, ward off evil spirits, and invite fairies to assist us from their wonderful kingdom.

Waxing Moon (Increasing Light Phase)

The waxing moon is the lunar moment of growth and overcoming. It is when we witness the moon covering itself with more light each night as time progresses. Plants and animals begin to receive more light and energy from the moon; Earth and all its inhabitants are nourished night after night.

This phase is a good time to perform spells and rituals that seek to grow or increase a feeling, energetically charge a situation, or transmute or redirect energy in a different way. It is also a good time to enact spells and rituals dedicated to personal growth and individual evolution.

During these nights, dreams begin to manifest with little clarity, and we often only manage to perceive a few clues and traces of what is really there. Dreams are perceived as dark situations under a thick fog, and it is common for dreams to be seen as repetitive night after night.

Full Moon

The moon has covered her beautiful figure with a dress made of silks and silver light. The creatures of the night feel more powerful, stronger, and even more beautiful. There is a breath of invulnerability in the air, and witches feel it more deeply than anyone. Full moons are times of celebration, greatness, evolution, and wholeness.

Nights of the full moon are the most powerful for the realization of magical works and talismans that seek to liberate and empower a person, situation, or feeling. On these nights, we bless our outside rituals with the presence of the moon and bathe our talismans in moonlight.

Dreams are perceived with greater clarity, understanding, and eloquence during this phase. The deities of the world of dreams give us the keys to access profound wisdom and invite us to meditate to deepen our dreams and improve our intuition.

Whether you wish to have dreams that delve into the past or future, perform a ritual to make a dream repeat itself more clearly, or enter the dreams of another sorcerer, this is the time when our energy manifests most fluidly and invites us to try. It is the most suitable lunar moment to practice lucid dreaming, draw a dream map, or carry out those healing and protection rituals that we have not dared to put into practice in the past out of fear.

Waning Moon (Decreasing Light Phase)

During the waning phase, the moon is losing clarity every night and beginning to darken again. It is the lunar moment in which we should cast spells or make amulets that seek to weaken, divert, or completely annul an energy, situation, or emotion. This can include ending a vice, dispelling a negative entity from our lives, forcing out a feeling or a situation that does not make us feel comfortable, counteracting the effects of some spell or curse made against us, or completely voiding the powers of a sorcerer who cursed one of our loved ones.

This is the lunar phase when our dreams begin to lose clarity, and we again feel like sleeping for longer stretches of time. Our dreams begin to lead us to delve less into the day-to-day and more into our subconscious. We are coming again to the new moon.

EXERCISE
Tracking Your Sleep with the Moon Phases

The study mentioned at the beginning of this chapter was a fairly generalized study. It is much more interesting and impactful if you do an individual study, and you can do this in your dream planner. Draw a total of twenty-one lines or columns. Then, for twenty-one nights starting with a new moon, record your activity before and after sleeping. For example, write down:

Before going to sleep:
What time did I go to sleep?
What moon phase is it?

After waking up:
What time did I wake up?
How did I sleep?

Evaluate the quality of your sleep and value it on a scale from 0 to 10 with 0 being the best. Make a note of any dreams you had and any images, symbols, or communication clues. Also track how much energy you feel you have lost or recovered during your rest.

Evaluating your sleep in this way, day after day, will tell you how the lunar phases influence your sleep hours. This information will be useful in the future because you will know which nights and lunar phases you feel more recharged or tired during, and that will help you decide when to perform a spell or make an amulet.

EXERCISE
Moon Phase Rituals

In witchcraft, the lunar phases are studied and followed in detail to make the most of the available lunar energy. Being a Dream Witch makes you a night sorcerer, a messenger of the moon and the shadows. To put this concept into practice, I have created a series of short rituals to perform with the lunar phases to take advantage of the energy that surrounds us night after night.

New Moon

On the night of a new moon, light a white candle and a piece of charcoal on a heat-resistant surface or in a small censer, and sprinkle a tablespoon of dried rose, marigold, and Roman chamomile petals on the hot charcoal. Add another tablespoon of petals every five to six minutes to keep the aromatic smoke in the room.

Inhale this enchanted incense deeply from a safe distance and close your eyes for a moment to clear your mind. Allow the incense to nourish and cleanse your energy field before sleeping.

Waxing Moon

Three to five nights before the full moon, mix a few drops of frankincense or myrrh essential oil with a few drops of lavender essential oil. Moisten the surface of a blue, violet, or purple candle with this oil and light it.

Using the flame of the candle, light a piece of charcoal inside a censer or on a heat-resistant surface. Wait a few minutes until the charcoal is completely white or red hot, and burn equal parts marigold and cayenne flower petals on it.

With the help of a fan, move the smoke of the incense in different directions of the room while you breathe slowly and deeply. Add another bunch of dried flowers to the charcoal and visualize the smoke of the incense. Focus on perceiving the shapes, movement, and aromatic notes of the incense.

In your dream journal, write down any images or visions you gather from the incense and compare these notes with those from other sessions in the future.

Full Moon

Sometime after sunset and before midnight on a full moon, open your bedroom windows; light a white or silver candle on your altar; pour a cup of clean, cool water into a glass; light a myrrh or sage incense stick; and light an herbal stick of blue sage or palo santo.

Using a fan, move the incense around the room. Close your eyes for a moment to clear your mind and take three slow and deep breaths. Open your eyes slowly and visualize the smoke around you. Calmly look toward the crystal sphere on your altar and carefully visualize any form that manifests within it or on its surface.

Between every three and ten minutes close your eyes again. Take three deep breaths and open your eyes. Visualize the smoke and the crystal ball. Repeat this visualization process for a maximum of five times.

Take note of your visions in your journal. You can repeat this exercise on each full moon and compare your results.

Waning Moon

When waning, the moon is getting darker every night, so let's make use of this time to cut off old vices and thought patterns that are no longer useful to us.

If you simply wish to meditate, light a white candle. If you wish to break or nullify an energy or emotion, light a black or a dark blue candle. Once your chosen candle is burning, light an incense cone with a flower aroma, such as roses or peonies. On a sheet of paper, write in ink the vices or thoughts that you want to let go of.

Close your eyes for a moment and meditate on the list of things you want to eliminate. Prolong this moment for as long as you consider necessary. Once you feel ready, open your eyes and take a deep breath.

Pronounce the following incantation and burn the paper from its ends in the candle flame. Let it burn completely inside a small cauldron with earth and salt.

> As the light fades, I leave you in the shadows.
> As the night drags on, I let you go.
> Just as the moon loses light, you lose my interest.
> As the world darkens, I let you go.

EXERCISE
Dream Visions Moon Cycle Mojo (21-Day Spell)

This spell is made to broaden your vision and your perception of the dreams you have, and it gives you the perfect opportunity to put your dream diary to use. You can take notes in it during the twenty-one nights of the ritual.

Based on my experiences and those who have previously put this spell into practice, one of two possibilities will occur: either your dreams will become more frequent and feel shorter at the same time or you will spend several nights in a row without visualizing any dreams, probably during the last nights of the ritual.

By using this spell, you will put into practice something that is fundamental to dream witchery and magic as a whole: constant discipline. While there are surely many other similar spells out there for the same purpose that take only a few hours to perform, this particular spell leads you to work on this personal goal for a short period of time every day for better and more rewarding results.

You will need:
- White or purple candle for the first night
- Incense (cones or wands) of lavender, vanilla, or myrrh for twenty-one days
- Lighter or matches
- Piece of garnet (associated with dreams and good fortune)
- Piece of celestine or celestite (dream magic, healing)
- Piece of crystal quartz (purification, balance, energy)
- Lavender essential oil

- Purple, blue, or white drawstring bag
- 1 tablespoon dried rose petals
- 1 tablespoon dried eucalyptus leaves
- 1 tablespoon dried mint leaves
- Crystal glass, which you will drink water from every night

Before you begin, find a calendar with the moon phases. Check for the next new moon phase in an air sign (Gemini, Libra, Aquarius) or in a water sign (Cancer, Scorpio, Pisces). Mark this date on your calendar and gather all the necessary elements to start the spell.

After a shower with your favorite essential oils on the chosen new moon night, light the candle and an incense stick or cone on your personal altar. Anoint the three rocks with a few drops of lavender essential oil. Hold the anointed gems in your hands, and with your eyes closed, recite:

I see beyond what my eyes see,
and I feel beyond what touches my skin,
so I move beyond my feet.
In the dark night, I find light.
In the world of dreams, I find the path that others ignore.

Recite the incantation as many times as you consider necessary. It can be three times, it can be six times, or it can be twelve times—whatever number of times you consider correct. After that, place the gems inside the bag and add the herbs and a few drops of lavender essential oil. Close the enchanted bag and (very carefully) seal the edges with wax from the candle.

Now hold the bag between your hands and repeat the same incantation as before. This time you are going to say it three times. When you are done, the magical bag is ready.

Fill the crystal glass with water and place it beside your bed. Hold the bag in your hand (preferably the left hand), and recite the previous incantation. Take a sip of the water and place the bag under your pillow to sleep.

Each of the following twenty nights, light an incense stick or cone a few hours before going to sleep, preferably between six and nine at night, and then repeat the previous step of drinking water, reciting the incantation, and placing the bag beneath your pillow before going to sleep.

☾

Dream Magic Insight
LUNA LUNITA FOR GETTING MORE MONEY
BY HECTOR SALVA

Here, a money spell by our own Houngan, Hector Salva, who teaches us through this spell to manifest financial abundance by anchoring our financial projects to lunar energy in order to make them grow spontaneously and constantly.

This is a full moon working designed to fill your pockets. As the moon grows so will your wealth and abundance. In this particular recipe, you'll build a magnet for prosperity that grows in power as you use it.

You will need:
- Small hand mirror
- White cloth
- Dried thyme, basil, and parsley
- Seven-day white candle
- Pinch of cinnamon and sugar
- Dry uncooked rice
- Lighter or matches
- White ceramic bowl
- Magnet
- Magnet food (iron filings)
- White ceramic bowl

Recommended moon phase: Start this recipe on the first quarter moon (about seven days before the full moon).

Each night, take the mirror and reflect the moon in it. You will do this until the first night after the full moon. As you do so, repeat the following incantation for about ten minutes:

> **Luna Lunita maravillosa y Bendita, as you grow and I double your light, so does my money grow more and more.**

Wrap the mirror in the white cloth. The night after the full moon, place a pinch of the herbs in the white candle. Add the sugar and cinnamon as well. Light the candle and repeat the chant as you prepare the bowl.

In the bowl, unwrap the mirror and place it face up in the center. Cover it with rice and herbs. Add the magnet and feed it with its food. Cover the bowl with the white cloth. Place the candle nearby. Every day, while the candle burns, repeat the chant into the candle for ten minutes. When the candle goes out, place the covered bowl in a high place.

You can reuse this recipe by pulling out the mirror and repeating the spell. When done, put the mirror back in the bottom of the bowl and complete the white candle burning as before. Each time you reuse the spell bowl, it becomes more powerful. With time, you'll be able to simply start the working and begin to see quick results.

There's just one special note that's very important: The mirror must never see the light of day or the sun once you begin. If it does, the complete spell will be rendered useless. Everything will have to be thrown away, and the process must be repeated from scratch.

TRIBAL TALES
KALINAGO PEOPLE / ISLAND
CARIBS / *LOS INDIOS CARIBE*

The Caribs of the Lesser Antilles were one of the first
American peoples known to Europeans. Well-known throughout much of
the coasts of South America, the Kalinago people, now also known as Caribs,
Caríbals, and Karipona, were a group who, at the time of Columbian contact
in the fifteenth century, occupied northern Colombia, much of Venezuela,
and several Lesser Antilles.

On the islands of the Caribbean Sea, they disappeared as an independent
ethnic group as a result of European colonization, but in Venezuela, Brazil,
and the Guianas, they continued to give rise to the modern Galibis (*kari'ñas*)
and other peoples.

In the Spanish chronicles, they are usually opposed to the Tainos, who
were presented as a peaceful people with a high culture. The Caribs were
seen as a warlike and savage people who practiced cannibalism. In fact, their
name is the origin of the terms *cannibal* and *cannibalism*.

Although most of their descendants practice the Catholicism that was
forced on their ancestors, some of the families still preach a form of polythe-
ism and animism that consists of ancestor worship, family mystery rites, and
associated ceremonial magic related to lunar phases and eclipses. In these
polytheistic cults, the gods manifest themselves as wild animals or cosmic
events (eclipses, meteor showers, electrical storms).

Unlike other Indigenous tribes of South America, dreams do not form a
vital part of their traditions. However, dreams play an essential role in the life
of the ceremonial sorcerer and medicine man. The dreams are interpreted
directly by the town healer at a high price, either publicly or in private. These
are full of esoteric symbolism, which may be associated with the future or
the past lives of the consultant.

The symbols in these dreams can often be interpreted as esoteric rituals
of a ceremonial nature that seek to be recreated. For example, if an individual dreams that they are at home surrounded by people and a cat and there
is water in the dream or someone playing a musical instrument, the dream
is recreated in a ceremony with the individual standing in a nearby river,

animals brought to the ceremony to be fed in the place, and people dancing or playing musical instruments around the individual in question, seeking to give life to the dream and receive power or visions through it.

The Caribs were well-known historically for being cannibals. During ceremonial rituals, they devoured the victims of war or any individual from another tribe who had caused harm to one of the Caribs. The ingestion of human meat and other organs could cause all kinds of infections or diseases to the warriors, especially when mixing these foods with their fermented drinks based on vegetables and fruits. The combination could generate intoxication and near-death experiences. Visions and dreams from these experiences were reinterpreted by the priest of the tribe as visions of the gods and ancestors to celebrate the triumph of the warriors.

Among its many gods, whose names mostly do not prevail to this day, is the snake. The snake is revered as a guardian of the spiritual world, a mother goddess who feeds on other animals to bring balance to the jungle. A warrior or a priest who was bitten by a snake and somehow survived its venom would be seen as a tribal hero who was blessed with the mark of the highest deity. The mark of the bite would be covered with black, red, and green paints made from various minerals and herbs.

The visions and dreams present during the period of intoxication of the bite are interpreted as Yias (visions that the serpent goddess has transmitted through the poison). These visions represent the origin of the world and the creation of all things.

CHAPTER 12

DREAM PILLOW

A pillow is a container that is used to support the head at bedtime and provide the user with comfort. A dream pillow is a magical container of aromatic herbs, dried flowers, and other elements that is used to induce happy dreams or deep nightmares according to the intention of each sorcerer.

There are hundreds of recipes and spells that require placing an amulet or a bunch of herbs under the pillow or bed. This placement allows you to channel the energy of the spell's element while you sleep. If, for some magical-esoteric reason, you need to place two or more elements under the pillow or bed, as long as these elements seek the same purpose, you can combine them with natural cotton flowers and fill a small pillow to keep them all together. What at first glance appears to be a small pillow can actually be a powerful tool of sorcery.

Creating a Dream Pillow

Although you can easily purchase a dream pillow online, there are two other options: make one or buy one in person. I highly recommend option A. If you craft it yourself, the pillow will have your energy and your intentions. If you choose option B, make sure you can open the pillow or in some way see the interior content of it before you purchase it. The magic of the pillow is inside; it is more than its attractive exterior design.

There are many different recipes and ways to make a dream pillow; some are more elaborate than others. When crafting a dream pillow, be entirely sure that you are making one with the best you have, including the best ingredients, time, and dedication. Put all your energy and effort into it, and always keep in mind that if you make one yourself, even with the help of someone else's sewing skills, it is important to put in all your intentions. In short, why are you making one?

A dream pillow can be made for many different reasons, and you can find a variety of recipes for each purpose. When it comes to romance, for example, there are multiple common spells that suggest making one of these pillows to help you dream of a loved one. For good fortune, in Venezuela and Peru, small pillows filled with rosemary and leaves of the money plant, or Swedish ivy, are obtained. They are used to dream of lottery numbers. White pillows filled with feathers and white flowers collected during the Night of San Juan, or Saint John's eve, are made to gain protection against negative entities and evil spirits. For the health of someone who is in the hospital, a small pillow filled with fresh healing herbs and a silver coin is placed under the individual's head to help them recover faster. Pillows filled with lavender flowers and mint and eucalyptus leaves are used to fight insomnia and gain rest.

In many parts of Latin America, including Peru, Guatemala, El Salvador, Venezuela, Colombia, and Paraguay, just to mention a few, it is common to find dream pillows in markets and botanical stores, and they are commonly given as gifts to other people. On Valentine's Day, a lot of pink dream pillows filled with rose petals with a small pocket to add a photograph are sold and given to partners as gifts to dream of their love.

I like to make dream pillows for gifts because they remind me of the concept of a charm bag. A charm bag or mojo bag is like a little magical pillow. It is a handmade amulet with a specific magical purpose that connects with your intentions and your energy, beginning with the creation of it and the action necessary to activate its power.

Considerations

Surely you don't want a pillow with sharp ends that could cause any discomfort while trying to sleep, so make sure to choose a comfortable and thick fabric for your pillow. When using herbs and flowers, make sure to use the soft parts of the plants, such as the leaves, roots from garden herbs, and petals. These parts can also be pulverized in a mortar to make sure they do not have sharp ends. Remove all the twigs and spikes that could break the surface of the pillow. If you consider it necessary, you can add two parts cotton for each bunch (approximately 10 to 12 ounces) of herbs and flowers you use.

If you are going to use any complementary oil to perfume the pillows, such as rose or myrrh oil, just add a few drops inside the pillow or in the herbal blend you prepare for filling. Do not use it on the external parts of the pillow.

Pillow Fabric

I recommend that the pillow's fabric be cotton or silk. Remember that it is the pillow on which you are going to sleep, and certain types of fabrics and other materials do not react well to skin and sweat. They can be highly irritating or release chemicals during use.

I prefer using white fabric (to represent purity and tranquility) or dark blue or indigo fabric (to have deep and meaningful dreams), but those are not the only options. You can use a pale pink fabric if you want to have dreams focused on romance and love. A black fabric, like deep night, will help dispel nightmares, although this color can also produce a certain feeling of anxiety during the night depending on the individual's level of psychic sensitivity.

Pillow Filling

The filling of the dream pillow can certainly vary depending on the result you are looking to have. Later in the chapter, I list several herbs, flowers, and other elements that you can use, and I include some recommended mixtures that have worked quite well for me. An even longer list of plants and herbs awaits you in chapter 13.

At least half of the herbs and flowers used in magic and sorcery are associated in some way with psychic energy, dreams, and predictions of the future. Instead of focusing on a specific plant, which may or may not be available in your region, do a local search first. Make a list of the herbs and flowers found around you, and then compare which of these herbs are included in this book. This same tip will come in handy with any other magic book.

When filling your pillow, use equal parts of each herb. The total amount will vary depending on the size of the pillow; use between 10 to 12 ounces of herbs for a large pillow and 6 to 8 ounces for a very small one.

Essential Ingredients

There are two things that I recommend be in every dream pillow. The first is a piece of crystal quartz no bigger than a coin; this will stimulate your psychic energy and provide clarity during dreams. The second is mugwort or yarrow, as both plants have a positive reputation among psychics, diviners, and sorcerers and will be of great help to you. They are good not only for channeling and sharpening your natural psychic abilities but also for bringing clarity to your dreams and developing a more acute reasoning capacity for their interpretation.

Basic Dream Pillow Recipes

Here is a brief list of mixtures to create at home according to your pillow's purpose.

- *To stimulate your dreams:* Mugwort, lavender, roses, chamomile flowers
- *To bring prophetic dreams (version 1):* Mugwort, bergamot, heliotrope, jasmine, a piece of crystal quartz
- *To bring prophetic dreams (version 2):* Mugwort, roses petals, jasmine flowers
- *To prevent nightmares:* White roses, calendula, chamomile flowers
- *To fight insomnia:* Hops, catnip, mullein, a piece of onyx
- *To find your perfect lover:* Rose petals, jasmine and magnolia flowers, a small piece of rose quartz

- *To heal:* White roses, chrysanthemums, eucalyptus, mint, a piece of crystal quartz
- *To protect you against psychic attacks, curses, and the evil eye:* Rosemary, frankincense, and myrrh

EXERCISE
Creating a Dream Pillow

Making a dream pillow is not complicated at all. It only takes a couple of hours of your dedication; some inexpensive materials; several herbs, which are easily available in the nearest botanical garden; and no more than that.

You will need:
- Fabric of your choosing
- Scissors
- Thread (I recommend the use of golden thread, as it is linked to multiple uses in magic from the grimoires of San Cipriano to more modern esoteric books. It also helps differentiate magical outfits and artifacts from common ones.)
- Needle
- Fillings that correspond with your magical purpose
- Camphor or eucalyptus incense stick
- Incense holder
- Lighter or matches

From the fabric, you only need to cut two pieces of cloth about the size of your hand in a square or rectangular shape (you can even be a rebel like me and cut the pieces in a circle or star shape). Sew the two pieces together with the needle and thread, leaving only one part open. Place the fillings inside.

Once all the corresponding elements have been placed inside the pillow, sew the last side closed with a needle and thread. Then light a stick of camphor or eucalyptus incense and move the pillow around the incense smoke on all sides. This will fully activate its energetic and therapeutic properties. Place the pillow on the bed a few hours before going to sleep.

A Pillow for Another Person

If you read the disclaimer on ethics and morality at the beginning of the book, you will remember that in traditional Latin American witchcraft we do not consider doing good on someone's behalf without asking them to be unethical or immoral, as it happens to be in Wicca and modern Western witchcraft under the influence of traditional British witchcraft.

Making a dream pillow for another person—either at their request as a magical work or as a present that can be offered to them—is easy. If you want to give someone a unique gift, something truly special, a dream pillow is a practical choice, as it can be done according to the person's wishes and further personalized.

If, for example, your best friend has trouble sleeping, or you know that your neighbors are going through a difficult situation, you can offer a dream pillow as a small gift to help them. If an individual is experiencing difficulties conceiving, a dream pillow filled with assorted grains to represent abundance, red flowers to represent the movement of blood in the body, and tulip bulbs to symbolize spring may provide them with extra support to manifest the fertility they are looking for.

If you want to make use of any herbs, resins, or minerals to help someone during their rest but you want to do it with some discretion and not attract attention, you can simply take a bouquet of the plant in question or a tiny piece of the resin to their home. Once there, you can hide it inside their pillow or under the mattress.

For example, a bunch of rose petals under the mattress of someone who is sitting watch during the nights will bring that someone peace of mind. A handful of bay leaves inside the pillow of someone who is looking for a job and has not yet found it can make a difference.

EXERCISE
Prophetic Dream Pillow

Dreams have almost always been associated with visions of the future, omens, premonitions, and warnings of what is about to appear on our horizon, and there are multiple herbs and natural elements that can be added to a magical dream pillow to attract these visions of destiny. For this spell, I have combined many of those elements in a single mix to provoke that long-awaited vision.

You will need:
- Lighter or matches
- Three candles
- Camphor incense stick
- Incense holder
- Pillowcase
- Equal parts cotton balls and pillow stuffing
- 2 tablespoons mugwort
- 1 tablespoon storax resin
- 1 tablespoon lilac blossoms
- 1 tablespoon juniper root powder
- 1 tablespoon cedarwood powder
- 5 pieces of crystal quartz (optional)
- Gold, silver, or white thread
- Needle
- Scissors

Recommended moon phase: New or waxing moon

At night, place the candles and incense stick on your altar and light them. Fill your pillowcase with all the cotton and pillow stuffing, herbs, and crystals one by one. Thread the needle and start to sew the pillowcase shut calmly and serenely. Smell the incense and enjoy its fragrance while you carry out this little ritual. Sew the pillowcase from one side of the opening to the other and then back; take your time to do it.

Once you have finished sewing, cut the thread and leave the pillowcase on your altar. Let the incense run out and the candles burn down completely. Lightly shake your pillow before placing it on your bed and going to sleep.

For three more nights, light a stick of incense on your dream altar a couple of hours before bed to clear the energy and allow the night visions to reach you without much hindrance.

Variation

If you wish to know how your relationship with a specific person will be in the future, add the following items to the pillowcase before sewing it closed:

- Photograph of the person
- Piece of paper with the person's full name and zodiac sign
- 3 tablespoons of crushed and powdered rose petals
- Pinch of coarse salt

This variation will help you see if you and the individual will be lovers, friends, or enemies; if they will receive the promotion they are looking for; or if they are going to carry out some threat to you.

Consecrating Your Pillow

In sorcery, there is a difference between making an amulet and consecrating an amulet. Making an amulet (or dream pillow, charm bag, etc.) is the process that goes from choosing the lunar phases for the execution of the spell and selecting the colors and materials to being clear in our intentions. Consecrating is the process of activating the energy—of taking an object and turning it into something truly powerful. This is the step that can easily distinguish an inexpert novice who buys a premade talisman on the internet (always a valid option also) from a more experienced witch who acquires the implements separately and makes their own amulet with the confidence and experience that it will work for a specific purpose.

This is no different than cooking soup. Making the amulet is like choosing the right vegetables, meats, spices, and broth for the food. Consecrating the amulet is like finally turning on the burners and stirring the soup in the cauldron so the ingredients mix together.

A dream pillow made with your own hands for a specific purpose requires choosing and combining each herb, each fiber, and the colors of the threads. Your power of decision has been present, guiding each step of the process. The magic is there, existent and acting, but that moment when you consecrate your pillow, just like any other amulet, is when you activate its power and take it to another level, guiding the energy of your enchantment to manifest it in the right direction.

EXERCISE
Consecration Ritual

This spell can be performed at any time of the day, but it has a greater effect if it is performed on a new or crescent moon day in the morning.

You will need:
- Red candle (symbolizes action)
- Blue candle (symbolizes the mind and dreams)
- White candle (symbolizes purity and rest)
- Incense holder
- Myrrh or frankincense incense stick
- Lighter or matches
- Small saucer with a few drops of lavender and eucalyptus oil
- Small saucer of water
- Saucer of sea salt
- Some pine needles
- Dream pillow you have already made

On your altar or in your magical workspace, open up a large and orderly space to work. In front of you and in the chosen space, visualize the shape of a triangle. This triangle should be wide enough for you to place the pillow inside it comfortably. Place the candles in the corners of the triangle, and station the incense holder and all the other elements outside the triangle.

Place the incense in the holder and light it, then light the candles from left to right. Once the incense is burning and the candles are lit, moisten three fingers by dipping them in the oil and then the water. Flick your wet fingers to carefully splash your surroundings and the ritual space.

Take some salt and the pine needles in your hands and throw them gently in the center of your triangular space in order to definitively cleanse its energy. Now take the pillow with both hands and carefully place it in the center of the triangle. Take three deep, slow breaths, and recite this incantation:

> **I bless you, I activate you, and with my energy I consecrate you.**
> **With the four elements, I activate you.**
> **With fragrant smoke, I consecrate you.**
> **With fire and light, I protect you.**
> **With water and oil, I purify you.**
> **With salt and herbs from the sea and the land, I bless you.**
> **With my hands and mind, one more time I bless you.**

Once you have finished reciting the incantation, touch the oil and water again and sprinkle the liquids on the pillow. Take more salt and pine and sprinkle them on the pillow as well.

Close your eyes, take a deep breath, and with your eyes closed say:

> **You are blessed, activated, and consecrated with my power, and the elements have witnessed it.**

Open your eyes, remove the pillow from the ritual space, shake it in the air, and proceed to put it away until it is time to make use of it. Let the candles and incense burn until consumed, and discard their remains and everything else used for the spell in the trash.

A Different Sort of Dream Pillow

Lucumi funeral rites are full of symbolism, secret elements, chants, and religious rituals. Many of the elements in these funeral rites occur in public, in a cemetery or even in a market, but even so the symbolism, origin, and importance of these rites are never explained to those who have not received initiation.

When a family relative who belonged to the Lucumi tradition died, my mother went looking for all the religious garments this person owned in order to carry out the necessary rituals. It was my task to help Mom at every step—in the cemetery, in the river, in the church, in the market, and other places. Wherever she went, I followed along. The person in question, however, died at a very old age, and we had no idea where these specific garments were stored. We had nothing.

Then, one night, Mom wove two small square pillows and filled them with herbs, keeping one pillow with her and placing the other under the head of the deceased. While she wove the little pillows, she prayed without distraction:

> **To you who left us, to you who went ahead of us, although your consciousness is free from the body, let me see in my dreams the memories you left in your body.**

Her words were something entirely improvised and something that she had not written anywhere. The spell did not even rhyme, nor did she have any pretense of trying to. But it worked. About three or four days after the funeral, my mother arrived with all the individual's esoteric and initiation belongings—everything that we could not find earlier. She had learned their location in a dream. She never told me exactly what her dream was like, but I have kept this recipe ever since.

This was definitely not a ritual that I had witnessed before, read about before, or heard about before. It was not even a Lucumi ritual. My mother was a witch, a bruja, creatively crafting a practical and functional spell out of nothing, without resorting to books or more instruments and tools than those she had at hand. With her permission, I have shared the simple spell here just as I wrote it in my journal years ago:

> *The two tiny pillows had small five-pointed stars embroidered on them in gold thread, and at the tip of each star a small crescent moon. The pillows were filled with sage, apazote (Dysphania ambrosioides), francipan flowers (Plumeria rubra), and flores de maravilla (Tithonia diversifolia). Place one under your pillow and another under the deceased to learn their memories.*

Dream Magic Insight
DREAM PILLOW TO TRAVEL THE ASTRAL WORLD
BY PHOENIX COFFIN WILLIAMS

I created this spell several years ago because I wanted to hang out with friends that I had met on the internet in the dream world. In this spell, I guide you to create a small pillow about the size of your palm. Later, if you want, you can make a bigger one.

You will need:

- Two pieces of indigo or purple fabric in a rectangular shape
- Indigo or purple thread
- Needle
- Indigo, purple, or blue candle
- Lavender and rose essential oils
- Pinch of ground cinnamon
- Pinch of ground nutmeg
- Lighter or matches
- Rose, lavender, or mint incense stick
- Incense holder
- Holy water (optional)
- Small bowl
- 2 tablespoons rose petals
- Handful of dried lavender
- 1 tablespoon ground orange peel
- Bag of small cotton balls and (optional) pillow stuffing
- Piece of paper
- Pen or a black sharpie

On your altar or in your magical workspace, realize the prayers and invocations to the gods, deities, or spirits of your pantheon as you normally would do for ritual. If you do not have a specific pantheon ritual to follow, I invite you to pray the following incantation:

To the divinity above me and around me,
to the divine energy that surrounds me at all times,
to the divine presence that cares for me everywhere,
to the force manifesting itself in all acts of kindness and love,
here and now I request your guidance.
I request your strength; I request your assistance.
Guide me in my purpose and magical work of this day.
Thank you.

Breathe deep, close your eyes, and talk with the spirits present. Let them know of your intention to enhance your ability to dream and move between physical barriers.

Now, with the fabric pattern sides facing each other, start sewing three sides of your pillow with calm and patience. While you do so, imagine the spirits and their divine energy are present in the room. Talk to the energy and your spirits, affirming your intention for this work by saying things related to this magical work, such as "I can dream of my boo, and we will have a sweet time together, although we are so far apart right now" or "I walk freely in the world of dreams."

If you are creating the pillow for other purposes, you could say, "I'm dreaming so true that my dreams of prophecy will help me know what's coming my way for sure," "My dreams are so on point I will get those lottery numbers if I wanted," or "My dreams warn me of danger and bad conditions."

Once you have sewn three sides of your pillow, flip it inside out so the raw seams you have just sewn are now on the inside. At this time, you should anoint your candle with two drops of lavender oil and two drops of rose oil. Drop a few sprinkles of cinnamon and nutmeg onto the candle and light it. Light your incense stick as well, and pass your pillow around the candle and through the smoke of the incense.

If you are using holy water, sprinkle a bit of this on both sides of your pillow right now.

In the bowl, combine all the herbs for this spell: the roses, the lavender, and the orange peel.

Continue talking with your spirit guides about all of the things you wish to manifest with the pillow, and start adding the cotton or stuffing to the pillow. Sprinkle a bit of lavender oil over the herbs, and add some of them to the pillow, praying for your wish over them as you do so. Add some more cotton or pillow stuffing, put a few drops of the rose oil in it, and add a sprinkle of the herbs, making sure you continue your prayers. Continue this pattern until your pillow is as full as you would like.

When you feel your pillow is filled, take up your pen and draw your dream symbols on the paper. You can draw an astral doorway, eyes, stars, moons, or symbols that you personally find appealing to psychic work and dreams. Anoint the paper with the lavender and rose oils and place it inside the pillow. With your needle, sew up the last edge, finishing up your prayers. Leave the pillow by your altar until the candle goes out.

To use this pillow, take it to your sleeping area. If your dream pillow is small enough, place it inside your pillowcase with your everyday pillow. If you chose to make a large one, put a pillowcase over it and place it on your bed.

On the nights you wish to use this pillow, as you lay in bed in darkness or dim light, state your dream intentions three times. This could be "Tonight I dream true" or "Tonight my lover and I reunite in our beautiful and joyful dreams"—whatever your intention is. Allow yourself to drift asleep while being relaxed and soothed by the light smells of lavender and rose.

Dream Magic Insight
LAVENDER DREAM PILLOW SPELL
BY JENNIFER SACASA-WRIGHT

Whenever I have trouble sleeping, am having bad dreams, or need to dream of something in particular, I turn to dream pillows. Making them can be an easy spell that mostly uses things on hand.

There are a number of herbs you can add to a dream pillow for varying results. A few are:

- *Lavender:* Brings peace, comfort, and calm; it aids in calming stress and depression. It eases headaches and helps relax you to sleep. It is a protector.
- *Mugwort:* Helps the dreamer remember their dreams; it increases clarity while encouraging relaxation.
- *Rosemary:* Ensures sleep and keeps away bad dreams
- *Marjoram:* Eases nervousness and restlessness during sleep; it adds warmth, safety, and comfort to dreams.
- *Mint:* Adds clarity, vividness, and color to dreams

You will need:
- Material to make the pillow from (you can use an old T-shirt or pillowcase)
- Scissors
- Muslin to make a small pillow from or a small sachet bag to fit inside your pillow
- Thread (the color of your choice)
- Sewing needle or machine
- Lavender (enough to fill the muslin/sachet bag)
- Herbs of your choice
- Fluff (can be new or from an old pillow)

To make a square pillow 5 x 5 inches large, cut two pieces, each 6 x 6 inches in size, from the material you have chosen. This will give you an inch of sewing room.

If using muslin instead of a sachet bag, you need to sew a pillow 3 x 3 inches large. Cut two pieces of muslin, 4 x 4 inches in size, to give you the inch of sewing room you will need.

Starting with the muslin, sew three sides and half of the fourth side together with a half-inch seam. Whether sewing by hand, my preferred method, or with a machine, envision sleeping with your pillow while you sew. See yourself holding it or having it under your pillow. See yourself getting restful sleep, sleeping through the night, smiling, having great dreams, and waking up rested. Hold these visions in your head while you sew, imbuing your pillow with your magic of manifestation. While doing this, chant the following out loud, under your breath, or in your head:

> **With stitch one,**
> **I have begun.**
> **With stitch two,**
> **my goal is true.**
> **With stitch three,**
> **It shall be.**

Turn the pillow right-side out by pulling it through the unsewn portion of the final side. Fill it with lavender and your herbs of choice and sew the hole shut. If using a sachet bag, fill it with all the herbs and sew the top shut so the bag is sealed.

With the material you have chosen for the larger pillow, put the wrong sides facing out and sew three sides and half of the fourth side together with a half-inch seam. Do this while chanting and holding your visions of manifestation.

Turn this larger pillow right-side out by pulling it through the unsewn hole. Put the muslin pillow or sachet bag inside the larger pillow and fill around it with fluff. You do not have to use too much fluff—just as much as you like. Sew the opening shut.

Your dream pillow is complete. Sweet dreams!

TRIBAL TALES
THE INITIATION CIRCLE
OF PAORIMA

Paorima's initiatic circle happens twice a year and everyone is welcome. The very few descendants of the Paurima, one of those small forgotten tribes that today has moved to live in the big cities, meet on the Sorte Mountain, a famous set of mountains in Venezuela dedicated to the Aboriginal queen goddess Maria Lionza.

Once in the mountains, they wait until sunset. Then they begin a long pilgrimage that must last until dawn. This walk around the river is accompanied by the sounds of drums made from skin and maracas made from coconut shells, small stones from the river, and many seeds. Everyone walks together during the night, their path illuminated by flashlights and lit candles inside plastic cups and large empty paint cans.

At this point, the place of the initiation is not chosen yet. It is where they see the first light of dawn arrive at the edge of the river that is considered the site designated by the spiritual guides to carry out the initiation.

During the following days, which can number between four and eight, tents, tables, and wood stoves supported by cement bricks are set up. This area will be the sacred precinct for the following days and nights. All those who have been invited to the celebration, to this sacred rite of passage, are invited to live here, to take notes, and to learn about the ritual, either to keep the tradition alive (which each year fewer individuals attend) or to document it.

The participants must wait until they have slept for at least three nights in the same place. Then, on the dawn after the third night of prayers, feasts, divinations, and chants, comes a whole day of initiation work.

For those previous three days, the elders and the women have woven a long rope with flowers and dry herbs mixed between the threads. This great rope, which has been made collectively, is used to mark a huge circle on the ground that is as big as a small house. In the center of the circle, a deep hole is dug to feed the earth. Within this circle, fruits, flowers, and vegetables are deposited; the ground is watered with a whole cup of broth; and a couple of animal sacrifices are performed. The young people (two or more—never just one) receiving the initiation dance around this circle with only their shoulders covered with

237

a piece of leather in the form of a shoulder pad decorated with feathers and bones of various animals.

The young people dance and dance until exhaustion, not drinking any more liquid. They must dance until they are dehydrated because they are performing the Sabiuco, a sacred and pre-colonial rite that symbolizes the waters of a human (body sweat) feeding and nourishing the earth or returning to it. The less water found in the hungry, thirsty, and exhausted bodies of the young, the more space there will be for the spirits to inhabit them.

From there, a large tent is erected around the place and only the priests and initiates can enter. They must remain inside for the following days, the number of days varying from group to group. For some, it may be two, and for others, it may be five or six days. Only those who are in the tent know what happens there.

CHAPTER 13

DREAM HERBS & PLANTS

In this chapter, you will find a summary of the diverse plants, flowers, and herbs commonly associated with dreams. But before we begin, please note that some of these plants can be moderately toxic, and it is strongly advised that you study them before using them for various purposes.

There are two types of plants mentioned in this chapter. The first kind are calming or relaxing (chamomile, for example). These plants are recognized for their sedative effect and are commonly ingested as a tea or infusion for it. The second type is made up of the plants that have an esoteric purpose linked to the realm of dreams, lucid dreaming, and astral travel.

Among the plants listed, you will see some that are quite common and some others that may not be the most common. No, you do not need to have them all, but if you do get any of these, purchase them in the market or in a botanica. If you come across any of these during some trip, it will be good that you know their energetic relationship and use in relation to the magic of dreams.

Mugwort

Mugwort (*Artemisia vulgaris*) is commonly associated with clairvoyance, psychic energy, prophetic dreams, and psychic and mental protection in general. It is an essential herb for every Dream Witch and spellcaster.

Mugwort comes from the *Artemisia* genus, a large and diverse grouping of plants and herbs named after Artemis, patron goddess of women, priestesses, and virgin maidens.

Mugwort is associated with brujas and sorceresses in the folklore of many Latin American countries, and it is considered the ally of witches. In Colombia, it is common to hear of mugwort as "the herb of witches," while in Venezuela it is "the grass that grows where women meet at night to agree with those who are not alive."

It is perhaps the most common ingredient to find in dream pillows. My first contact with this herb was at home when Mom made dream pillows for my sisters. Their pillows were made of white fabric and filled with mugwort and red rose petals, both elements entirely dry. Mother said, "The mugwort is to give clarity and psychic protection during dreams, and the roses provide spiritual strength." My pillow was stuffed with mugwort and dried white chrysanthemum flowers for mental clarity and spiritual strength.

Mugwort and Psychic Powers

Mugwort, like many other herbs and flowers that we use in magic and sorcery, does not bring or create something new. It does not make you psychic or create feelings of love and security out of thin air. What this herb does is find these energies and feelings and help express them, externalize them, and encourage them to grow favorably for us.

Mugwort is your ally to externalize, control, and manifest your psychic power. A bouquet of mugwort dried in the sun and tied with red thread around the neck is a perfect amulet to increase your clairvoyance with the passing of days and strengthen your mind against external psychic attacks. A pot of mugwort by the window will protect you from psychic attacks during the day, while a sprig of mugwort under your pillow will keep you safe from psychic invasions and influences while you sleep. Sprinkling powdered mugwort around and in the corners of a room prevents mediums and psychics from invading your mind, while burning dry mugwort on hot charcoal as incense is one of the most effective ways to strengthen your clairvoyance and psychic clarity before conducting a divination session.

One of the traditional rites in Venezuelan spiritualism consists of mixing mugwort powder with dried chamomile flowers in a bottle of white wine and drinking it for seven days in a row. This helps to develop clairvoyance and awaken all our psychic senses.

When you are having difficulty understanding certain information during a tarot card reading, or any other oracle reading, you can burn some mugwort as incense and move the cards around the incense smoke to bring clarity and dispel any doubts that get in the way of your reading.

Mugwort and Dreams

If you have the time to do a quick search on the internet or explore your local pharmacy, you will notice that most herbal teas and sleep aids include mugwort among their ingredients. This is not because mugwort will create dreams out of nowhere but because it is such a good ally of your psychic side that it will help you remember your dreams more clearly. It will also guide you in the process of understanding and deciphering your dreams, helping to dispel any confusion about them.

For example, holding a bouquet of mugwort in your hands and doing a short meditation before going to sleep will lead you to have longer, clearer, and much more vivid and concrete dreams. This powerful plant enhances your psychic powers, allowing you to differentiate dream processes and even have lucid dreams.

To gain protection while you practice some kind of exercise for astral projection or unfolding, or if you have been recently having nightmares, light a charcoal stick on a heat-resistant plate. On the charcoal, burn three parts dried and powdered mugwort with one part of dried garlic in a corner of your bedroom. It is not the most exquisite fragrance in the world, but it will scare away everything from astral larvae, which interrupt your dreams, to witches trying to enter them.

RECIPE
Mugwort Infusion for Sleeping and Dreaming

To make this mugwort infusion, simply begin by boiling water. Once the water is hot, add a bunch of dried mugwort and let it rest for about ten minutes, mixing occasionally.

This mugwort infusion can be made for three magical purposes:

1. To drink as tea (without honey or sweeteners) before meditating or going to sleep
2. To be added to your bathwater for a restful bath before going to sleep or taking a nap
3. To wash your mirrors and crystal balls, which creates an extra layer of clairvoyance that allows you to see the presence of spiritual entities in the surroundings

Mugwart Clay Doll

Attending to one of their many clients, my mother and my closest aunt created this human-shaped clay doll at home. They did it following the instructions of a spirit of an Indigenous witch, who had been channeled through a medium.

My mom, always looking to be practical, added about six drops of homemade mugwort essential oil to the clay. But that wasn't all; she also added rosemary, lemon, and ylang ylang, making a truly mesmerizing combination of aromas. After the figure was ready and out of the oven, they covered it with yellow paint, which they also added a few drops of mugwort essential oil to.

Once the doll was ready, they placed it inside a small cauldron with dried herbs and flowers. They then lit five yellow candles and sprinkled a few drops of wax from each candle on the figure.

My aunt wrote an impromptu rhyme on paper to reflect the wishes of her spell (to convince the client's boyfriend to commit to her through dreams). They recited the incantation so many times that they may have lost count; they must have recited it forty or fifty times.

When the last of the candles burned out, they took the clay figure and placed it inside a cloth bag with the herbs from the cauldron, sealed the bag completely, and took it to the car. They then went to bury the figure in a nearby park near sunset to be sure that the ritual would be ready before the enchanted one went to sleep.

Within about six or seven weeks, the charmed man in question made a marriage proposal to the client. This would be the first of her three husbands.

EXERCISE
Mugwort Clay Doll Spell

The following is the spell that my mother and aunt used. I recommend you make the figure at home on a Tuesday before noon.

You will need:

- Rose incense
- Censer or heat-resistant plate
- Lighter or matches
- Water
- Clay
- Needle (or any other engraving tool)
- Rosemary, lemon, and ylang ylang essential oils
- 1 cup mugwort oil
- Yellow and green paint
- Cauldron
- Assorted dried flowers (enough to fill the cauldron halfway)
- 3 tablespoons dried mugwort powder
- 5 yellow candles
- A thin stick

Light your incense and wet your hands with water. With the clay, create a human figure. You can represent the sex of the person or not. If they have any distinctive physical traits, such as a large nose, long hair, a very pronounced jaw, or big hands, you can also represent them in the figure. Once the figure is finished, engrave the name of the person in the chest or trunk of the figure from top to bottom using the needle or any appropriate tool available to you.

Anoint the figure completely with three drops of each essential oil, then allow it to dry for about sixty minutes (or go by the amount of time the bag of clay is likely to say in the instructions).

Once the time has passed and the figure has dried properly, add a few drops of mugwort oil to the paint. Using your fingers, paint the figure completely green on the left side and yellow on the right. As you do so, visualize the person in your mind, moistening your fingers occasionally with the mugwort oil as you continue to perform this operation.

Once the figure is complete, place it in the cauldron. Add the flowers and mugwort, light the candles around it, and sprinkle a few drops of the hot candle wax onto the figure.

Rub a little more of the mugwort oil on the figure, and keep quiet for a time of thirty minutes without pronouncing any words. Let the magic act in complete silence. After this time, recite a few words to enchant the figure, such as "May your dreams be filled with my image and my presence every night" or "In your dreams and visions I immerse myself; in my charms I wrap you."

Once the candles are completely consumed, collect the figure with the flowers and herbs, and bury it altogether in a nearby park or in a pot with soil.

Mugwort Flower Essences

Flower essences work with different concentrations and solutions of each plant. They also use water memory, or water's ability to retain information (according to science) or spirit (according to brujeria) from any element dissolved in it. In that way, for example, flower essences channel the frequency of certain plants and maintain it in the long term. Flower essences are easy to get online, but I like to suggest that they be purchased directly from a homeopathic pharmacy specializing in Bach flower remedies and flower essences.

To channel deep and peaceful dreams, add essence of mugwort to your bathwater with the essence of apple, using about ten or twelve drops of each. Meditate in the bathtub for about fifteen to twenty minutes before going to sleep. This exercise will also help you attract mental clarity and clairvoyance when sleeping.

If you are looking to produce more dreams, are having difficulty sleeping, or are having dreams that are not very clear, you can prepare a hot bath as directed, adding ten to twelve drops of mugwort and apple flower essences plus one to two dozen white rose petals. Light a white candle, and immerse yourself in the bath. You will sleep better and have clearer dreams.

African Dream Herb

This is an interesting plant. It is a liana, or a sturdy vine that grows from the ground, with the appearance of a large woody snake that is well-known as the African dream herb (*Entada rheedii*) and the cocoon vine in Jamaica. The big seeds of this plant are found near rivers and swamps of Africa and tropical areas of Africa, South America, and Asia.

This plant is used in African traditional medicine to induce lucid dreams and facilitate communication with the spirit plane and otherworlds. The seeds of this plant are used to craft jewelry for protection and good luck. The priests and priestesses of the tribe or town prepare the dried seeds with a mix of different local herbs. Once ready, it is consumed or smoked as tobacco before sleep to induce a vivid, longer dream.

Ashwagandha

Ashwagandha (*Withania somnifera*) is known commonly as Indian ginseng, poison gooseberry, or *hierba mora mayor* (in Latin America). The specific epithet "somnifera" refers to the sedative properties of the root of the plant. However, its traditional use in Ayurveda is similar to that of ginseng in traditional Chinese medicine.

Its name in Sanskrit was translated as "horse aroma" because of the particular aroma it gives off. Even with that strike against it, its dried leaves can be burned in small quantities in the bedroom several hours before sleeping to cause a sedative atmosphere.

Although it is not a typical plant of the Caribbean, it can be obtained in the esoteric markets or botanicas for very high prices. It is commonly burned in very specific rituals as votive incense to induce a feeling of relaxation and sleep in the place.

A dry twig of this plant with a blue cord tied around it can be kept near the bed to induce lucidity and clarity in the dreams of the witches.

Bálsamo del Perú (Peru Balsam)

Peru balsam is a balm extracted from the plant *Myroxylon balsamum*, known as *chicarra* or *sandalo Hispano* (Hispanic sandalwood), which can be found in different regions of Mexico, Peru, Brazil, and El Salvador. Although it is widely used in the cosmetics industry, it is one of the products that causes the greatest allergies in the skin, so its use is not recommended without professional supervision.

The black balsam is popularly associated with witchcraft in several countries. On the borders of Brazil and Venezuela, it can be found at a good price per bottle, and the written name of a person can be added to the bottle before it is thrown into a river to promise that the target will not be able to rest in peace for a long time. Anointing the name of a person that was written on a wooden log at midnight with the balm is a curse that will keep the individual from sleeping peacefully for nine nights. The only way to nullify this curse is to throw a bunch of coarse salt into the river and later take a bath in it at midnight.

Blue Skullcap

Known commonly as blue skullcap (*Scutellaria lateriflora*), this plant grows in the humid forests of North America. It belongs (as well as all *Scutellaria*) to the family of mint plants, the same ones commonly used to create certain types of menthol and essential oils, varieties of mint tea, and some alcoholic beverages, such as the mojito.

The fresh flowers of this plant are placed under the pillow to induce long and deep dreams, especially in combination with rose petals. Sun-dried skullcap flowers can be combined with eucalyptus and ground into a powder to burn on pieces of hot charcoal as incense. This is done to honor local spirits and provide calm to the souls of the recently deceased. A fresh branch of this plant can be planted near the bedroom window as a perfect natural charm to prevent other witches from entering your dreams at night. If a child is suffering from nightmares and it is believed that there is some sorcery involved in the matter, tying a bouquet of dried skullcap around the legs of the child's bed will help them to find confidence and personal strength during sleep. It will also dispel any bilocation effect that a witch may be using.

Calea

Calea (*Calea ternifolia* or *Calea zacatechichi*) is a flowering plant native to Mexico and Central America (mostly Costa Rica). It is known in English as bitter grass.

This plant enjoys a very good reputation in Mexico, where it is used as a common remedy to reduce fever despite its bitter taste. For various populations of Mexico, this medicinal plant goes by different names, which all allude to its bitter taste. For example, the Zoque Popoluca people call it *tam huñi* (bitter gum), and for the Mixe people, it is known as *poop taam ujts* (white bitter herb).

The Indigenous Chontal people of Oaxaca make use of various parts of this plant (mostly the roots and its large leaves) in their divination rituals and magic related to the world of dreams. According to their folklore and tradition, this plant, drunk as a tea with a very bitter taste, can induce prophetic dreams, clarify the signs that are sought in dreams, and help one to remember dreams.

For the followers of the magical-religious tradition of the Nahuatl, this plant is chewed or drunk in tea to help remember dreams clearly. In the botanics of Central America, it is common to find people who recommend keeping a few dry twigs of this plant next to the bed to have happy dreams and remember them clearly the following day.

Burned as incense, calea is used to induce sleep therapy in people who may suffer from various symptoms related to a spiritual illness or a psychic attack that causes insomnia. Pillows filled with sun-dried parts of this plant can bring a deep sleep full of signs related to the fate of the person who uses it. It can be mixed with tobacco leaves for the realization of magical cigars, and its smoke helps to dispel evil spirits that adhere to people from the world of dreams. Burned alone, its smoke can help the sorcerer enter the dream world. Its leaves can be burned during divination processes to support clairvoyance, and its roots can be mixed with blue sage and chamomile in a charm bag to be kept under the pillow to induce sleep and prevent psychic attacks.

This plant is difficult to germinate, but according to the magical tradition that surrounds it, it grows quite fast when it is sown on a new moon. It tends to dry out and die quite quickly when it is planted by a witch who has bad intentions regarding the use of this plant.

Even though this plant can produce a strong allergic reaction and cause vomiting and stomach upset, its popularity in dream-related rites does not diminish. It is popular to even being used as tobacco in religious rituals to induce deep dreams that lead us to remember the past.

Cañaduz or Caña de Azúcar (Sugarcane)

Sugarcane (*Saccharum officinarum*) was introduced to the Americas during the second voyage of Columbus. Due to the climate conditions and the work of enslaved people, this plant proliferated in the following countries, many of which ended up becoming the largest sugar producers in the world: Panama, El Salvador, Cuba, Guatemala, Honduras, Brazil, Nicaragua, Mexico, Argentina, Bolivia, Paraguay, Peru, Ecuador, Uruguay, Dominican Republic, Puerto Rico, Colombia, and Venezuela.

In Latin America, sugarcane is washed with water from a river and is given to children to chew to combat the evil eye, and sticks of sugarcane are placed in the corners of rooms to attract fertility and to have visions related to unborn children and familiar spirits. When a sugarcane stick well positioned on the wall suddenly falls to the ground, it is believed to herald pregnancy or death. In the traditional oral folklore of Indigenous populations, the trunks of this plant grow taller and thicker where enslaved individuals died.

EXERCISE
Spell to Appear in the Dreams of a Beloved One

This is a traditional folk ritual that is performed the same way in several countries. It requires a long sugarcane stick, which has to been given to you by someone else.

You will need:
- Thick toothpick or nail
- Long sugarcane stick
- Piece of thick white cloth

Use the toothpick or nail to etch the name of your loved one three times into the surface of the sugarcane, and tie the cloth around the name several times. Hide the sugarcane under the individual's bed, between two mattresses, or on top of the bed as a companion, and they will begin to dream of you. Within the next three nights, the dreams will become longer, clearer, and more frequent, and they will not stop occurring until the person has a conversation with you.

It is said that if the sugarcane breaks under the bed, it is because the person carries a powerful protection amulet or is guarded by a witch or spirit.

Chrysanthemums

Chrysanthemums, which belong to the genus of the same name, represent strength, vigor, unity, and skill. They channel wisdom, divine connection, protection, and strength of spirit.

Red chrysanthemums are kept at home to make love always find its way back. Placing red chrysanthemums next to the lovers' shared bed augurs deep dreams and full of romance between them, while tying three red chrysanthemums with black string and throwing them at someone's door is a way of cursing them with dreams of disappointment and breakup.

Yellow chrysanthemums attract financial abundance and good relationships and are widely used in spells for money and wealth.

White chrysanthemums represent purity and attract healing, and they are widely used in rituals of cleansing, elevation, and spiritual initiation. Keeping white chrysanthemums in the bedroom will attract clear dreams with concrete messages for your interpretation. They also give you mental strength.

Cornflowers

In Latin America, cornflower (*Centaurea cyanus*) is known as *azulejo*, and the plant's blue flowers are used in magic for all purposes related to dreams, daydreaming, clairvoyance, and psychic protection. Its intense blue gives you a suitable focus for meditation sessions. The fresh flower is burned in a flame or bonfire to keep you from repeating your most recent dreams.

Cotton Flower

Cotton flowers grow in Venezuela in practically all places, and I remember a huge tree of these flowers growing next to a parking lot in the city of Caracas, where my parents have lived for the last few years.

These flowers symbolize pure love, clarity, purity, and spirituality. They are burned in a small saucer near a door to let the spirits of relatives and ancestors leave, and they are anointed with magical oils and thrown in front of houses to bless or curse inhabitants.

A handful of these flowers in the bedroom absorbs unwanted visions and dreams. It will also attract sweet dreams and divine protection. A cluster of these flowers on your dream altar portends good omens and brings clarity and peace of mind during your magical work.

Kava Kava

Kava kava (*Piper methysticum*) is a shrub that is cultivated for its calming effects, being able to produce muscle relaxation and drowsiness, and the roots of the plant are used to produce a drink with sedative, anesthetic, euphoric, and entheogenic properties. Kava kava is consumed throughout the Pacific Ocean cultures of Polynesia, including Hawaii, Vanuatu, Melanesia, and parts of Micronesia for those attributes.

To have deep and extensive dreams, simply hang the sun-dried root of this plant in your window.

Purple Passionflower

Commonly known as maypop, wild apricot, and wild passion vine, purple passionflower (*Passiflora incarnata*) is a climbing liana that reaches 29.5 feet (9 meters) in length with large, aromatic flowers of attractive color. Although historically the plant has been used as an herbal medicine to cure sleep problems, its intake without supervision or medical guidance is not recommended. Purple passionflower essential oil is a sedative, which is why it is often used in cases of insomnia and anxiety attacks/crises.

The yellow plant substance that surrounds the flower seeds accumulates in small saucers and is surrounded by white candles and offered to the souls of the deceased at midnight. It is believed that its exotic aroma, sweet taste, and sedative effect will influence those who have passed away and have not yet found eternal rest.

Its flowers can be grown to attract happy dreams and long nights of rest. If the plant turns dark and odorless in the place where it was planted, it indicates that a body was buried in the surroundings, and the soul of that body has not yet found rest. If, on the other hand, the plant begins to grow unexpectedly near the house, it is an indication that a walker between dreams is living nearby.

You can mix the dried and powdered flowers of this plant with chamomile flowers and eucalyptus leaves. Keep this magic blend sealed in a glass bottle, and use a teaspoon of it in the shower water before sleeping to provide relaxation and calm.

As a personal note, my mother usually carries (among her countless belongings in her huge purse that seems bottomless) a sachet with this mixture of powders. She always mentions that it is to blow on the graves of the deceased when they are being "used" by some palero,[36] or death-worker, a drainer, or some witch on the way to cause harm to others. It would cause a calming effect on the soul of the deceased and, at the same time, a spiritual sensation similar to physical fatigue.

EXERCISE
Magic Dream of Walpurgis Ritual

In North America, orchids and cayenas (*Hibiscus rosa-sinensis*) enjoy enormous popularity—probably because their level of care is quite complicated, making them unusual flowers. The passionflower enjoys similar popularity in South America, as it is mostly imported from other areas (Central America), and the high temperatures in Brazil, Colombia, and Venezuela affect its beauty and durability.

....

36. A palero is a practitioner initiated into *Palo Monte* or *Las Reglas del Congo*, a magical-religious Afro-Caribbean tradition that also separates itself into several other paths. It's originally from Cuba and very common in South America.

This spell uses purple passionflower, which you can buy online today in all its forms (fresh, dried, pulverized, etc.), and you should realize it a week before Walpurgis Night.[37]

In Spain and South America, the night of Walpurgisnacht entertains a certain popularity. It is named "the night of all the witches." This festivity has gained enormous notoriety through popular songs, children's stories, and the odd movie.

You will need:

- 1 cup dry purple passionflower
- 1 tablespoon ground cinnamon
- 1 teaspoon star anise
- 1 teaspoon almonds
- 1 teaspoon sweet cloves
- 1 teaspoon verbena leaves
- Mortar and pestle
- Dark cloth bag or a crystal jar
- Lighter or matches
- 2 white candles
- Charcoal
- Censer or heat-resistant cauldron

Place the passionflower and the other herbs in the mortar and grind everything together calmly for about ten minutes, or until it's reduced to a uniform mixture. Store this mixture in a cloth bag or glass jar near the window to keep it dry.

On Walpurgis Night, light the two white candles and a piece of charcoal in the censer or cauldron in the evening hours. Proceed to throw small amounts of the mixture on the charcoal as incense. As the smoke rises, recite twice:

> O witches who dwell and listen from beyond,
> answer my honest call to create a bond.
> Come here to embrace those who respect you.
> On this night, our kingdom bless you,

---

37. Saint Walpurgis Night, or *Vappu*, is an annual celebration that occurs between April 30 and May 1 to honor Saint Walpurga.

here where I call you and invite you to enter.
Come here with all your talents and all your blessings.
Bring your power and your secrets through dreams.
Reveal for seven nights your deepest secrets, no fear.

Proceed to meditate, visualizing the figures that the smoke forms until it ends. Take note of the figures that are present, as well as the dreams that you receive during the following nights.

Quimbombó (Okra)

Okra (*Abelmoschus esculentus*) is also known as *gombo, bamia,* and *candia* in Cuba, Venezuela, Colombia, and Peru. This plant arrived in the Americas from Africa during the transatlantic slave trade, which is why it is widely linked to African and Afro-Caribbean cults.

Okra flowers are dried in the sun, crushed, and added to baths to allow people to heal the emotional wounds of their ancestors through a ritual by the river. Okra fruit is traditionally used to curse or heal by writing people's names on its surface before or after sunset respectively. If you have nightmares, place five pieces of fresh okra under the bed in a bowl with water and a pinch of salt, let it rest for five nights, and then throw it in the trash to get rid of any bad energy.

Rose

Roses (*Rosa*) provide magical and energetic protection, spiritual guidance, and emotional stability, and they also give extra power to dreams focused on seeking a loved one.

One of the most common and well-known plants in the world, the rose is also among the most used in the esoteric market and is often featured in various books for spells of protection, love, and good fortune. The uses of roses in magic and sorcery are as varied as the uses of quartz. Essentially, roses (as well as quartz) can increase the frequency and energetic power of other plants and minerals when combined in the same spell.

You can burn roses to curse the person who gave them to you, or you can leave dead roses at the entrance of someone's house to sponsor the death of a loved one. You can give a yellow rose to someone and make sure they keep it close to their bed so you can appear in their dreams. Smear honey on the stem of a white rose before gifting it to someone to ensure they will have a long and prosperous relationship with you. You can even plant white roses around your front door to indicate to the guardian spirits, "Here you are welcome to protect and manifest." You can also create a bouquet with dried roses and hang it over the kitchen to bring protection, guidance, and good fortune. To have new dreams, placing a bouquet of white roses by the bed is the right thing to do. Wearing a wreath of white roses from dusk to dusk effectively connects you with the spirit world and thus contacts guardian spirits. If a witch has cursed you, and you know who exactly it is, you can diplomatically give a bouquet of white or yellow roses to them. If they accept the flowers (even without knowing the reason), it immediately cancels the curse thrown on you.

A common spell in the spiritism of the Caribbean is to partially cover the bed with rose petals to dream with a loved one. If you do it on a new moon and place a photograph of your loved one under the pillow, they will be the one who will dream with you.

Tulsi

Tulsi (*Ocimum tenuiflorum*) is popularly known as holy basil around the world, *albahaca morada* in Latin America, and *balanoi* in the Philippines. It is a native plant to the Indian subcontinent. Tulsi is cultivated and used as an essential oil for traditional medicine purposes. It is also sold to be used as an herbal tea.

This plant is commonly used in Ayurveda, and it has a place within the Vaishnava tradition of Hinduism. Its leaves are worshipped as the avatar of Lakshmi, and it can be found planted in courtyards of Hindu houses or Hanuman temples. The offering of its leaves is recommended in ritualistic worship of Vishnu and his avatars like Krishna and Vithoba.

Tulsi wood can be used to make prayer beads for rosaries and amulets, either to venerate the custodial deities of the home or to pray for protection. Its flowers manifest the power of mediumship in people who have constant contact with them. When dried, the flowers can be burned in a censer or on a plate over the altar space to help you meditate before sleeping, thus elevating the senses to other planes.

Valerian

Valerian (*Valeriana officinalis*), our smelly garden friend, is commonly associated with rest and sleep. Yet, when you've been into practicing magic and brujeria for more than two decades, you simply remember it as one of the worst-smelling plants in your apothecary.

Valerian is mentioned in multiple spells for love, sleep, and fame and recognition. It is highly effective in love spells, including those made to project yourself into the dreams of your loved one, as well as in some curses in Venezuela and Colombia to make the man fall asleep every time he has an unfaithful encounter with his lover.

When dried, this herb has an aroma similar to old, wet clothes. If used in spells, it is important to accompany it with other plants that help cover its fragrance. For example, a charm bag for love made with this plant can also contain dried roses and lavender or roses and gardenias.

When burned as incense on a piece of hot coal, the fragrance is not better, but burning it at home is highly effective as a small ritual to nullify those spells that cause sleeplessness and ruin your rest.

EXERCISE
Coven Clairvoyance Ritual Invocation

This ritual is to be performed between two or more people (not individually) on Saint John's eve, which is one of the most magical nights of the year in Venezuelan folklore. It is when we have big events, dancing in crowds around the fire and burning paper dolls with our wishes written on their heads. This spell helps create a powerful link between the sorcerers who carry it out, generating group energy focused on a single goal and helping to unlock the sorcerers' natural psychic and intuitive abilities.

You will need:
- 1 teaspoon dried and pulverized mugwort root
- 3 sweet cloves
- 3 red rose petals
- Pinch of powdered valerian
- Small mortar and pestle

- Bottle of red wine and glasses for each person in the ritual
- Lighter or matches
- Black candle
- White candle
- Charcoal
- Censer or heat-resistant plate
- 1 tablespoon dried parsley

In the mortar, grind and mix the mugwort, cloves, rose petals, and valerian. Add a pinch of the blend to each glass.

Light the candles and the charcoal, placing it in the censer or on the heat-resistant plate. Add a pinch of parsley to the hot charcoal. Serve the wine in equal amounts in the glasses with the herbs.

Sit with the other participants in front of or around your altar and talk openly about the visions you wish to have and the dreams you wish to generate while sipping slowly from the cups before midnight, occasionally adding another pinch of parsley to the censer.

Once you have finished the wine, extinguish the candles. Each participant then goes to their bed to sleep and receive visions.

Yerba de la Pastora

Also known as sage of the diviners, yerba de la pastora (*Salvia divinorum*) is commonly imported from Mexico to the rest of the world for its psychotropic qualities. The Mazatec shamans, who became very popular thanks to María Sabina, the most famous Mazatec *curandera*, make use of this, among many other native plants, to induce various trance states during their rituals.

The leaves of this plant are chewed to bring about deep states of sleep. When burned as incense, it invites communion with the spirits, opening the pathways between the worlds. As a divination method, dry leaves are used to predict the future by observing the positions and movements they take on the water's surface.

Complementary Plants and Herbs

Here you will find a list of complementary plants for spells and rituals related to dreams. The following plants have briefer explanations than the previous ones, which is because they are used in dream spells as complements and not as the main herbs. They are also imported from other countries and, therefore, given a minor use in our esoteric cults.

Almonds

Eat almonds (*Prunus dulcis*) before bed to have happy dreams full of joy and abundance and to help manifest those dreams in reality. Place a little blue bag filled with nine almonds and the name of a loved one written on paper under the pillow or on your dream altar to give them visions of yourself in their dreams.

Angelica

If you usually have prophetic dreams, putting angelica (*Angelica archangelica*) inside your pillow will give you greater clarity, understanding, and vision of them. Place a bowl of dried angelica root under a sick person's bed to help them heal and throw it away the next day before dawn.

Anise

Anise (*Pimpinella anisum*) prevents nightmares, increases psychic power, and is related to stimulating the senses. When prepared as a tea with chamomile flowers and a pinch of powdered valerian root, it helps achieve deep sleep and rest to enhance your night visions.

Ash

Ash (*Fraxinus ornus*) is highly recommended to prevent nightmares, psychic attacks, evil eyes, and curses related to canceling people's sleep and rest. It also helps to see the enemy's face in dreams. A small mojo bag with anise and rosemary seeds grants powerful protection against spells and curses made to invade our dreams.

In Venezuela, this plant, which is imported from the United States, is sold in botanicas for quite high prices as an herbal amulet of protection. To protect yourself against negative entities and spirits, dry and pulverize any part of this plant and mix it with the water you shower with for three consecutive mornings.

Basil

Basil (*Ocimum basilicum*) is the perfect plant when it comes to divinatory arts and omens. Add it to pillows (preferably with mugwort) to attract premonitory dreams or to decipher the omens that you have been receiving in recent dreams. Burn nine dried basil leaves by the entrance of any building to dispel misfortune enchantments. A jug of fresh water with basil leaves can be sprinkled at the same entrance to keep away people with bad intentions.

Bay Laurel

The leaves of bay laurel (*Laurus nobilis*) can be crushed and burned to activate and elevate our psychic and extrasensory abilities. They are also recommended for burning before divination sessions or the performance of a spell or ritual for prophetic dreams. Chewing bay leaves before a divination session is a common practice in several South American spiritualist traditions, as bay leaves are believed to stimulate clairvoyance and premonitory abilities.

Bay laurel also helps with prophetic dreams, good omens, money, and protection of your financial abundance. The leaves can be burned in the morning to bring inspiration and clarity of mind.

Bergamot

Bergamot (*Citrus bergamia*) is mostly related to money and prosperity, but it has such a delicious fragrance that you can add it to your pillow and it will make you very happy. You're welcome. Bergamot focuses on the mind and energy, protecting against astral larvae.

Bible Leaf

Bible leaf (*Tanacetum balsamita*), also called costmary, produces flowers that can be dried and kept close to deepen your wisdom and broaden your intuition while you sleep.

Box Elder

Box elder (*Acer negundo*), also called ash-leaved maple, is used to create spells and herb amulets for prophetic dreams, clairvoyance, and building or strengthening your psychic shield while you sleep.

Calendula

Calendula (*Calendula officinalis*) is used for mental and emotional healing, as well as psychic protection. The Cuban immigrant population in Venezuela introduced the belief of bringing bunches of these flowers to the *Virgen de la Caridad del Cobre* (Our Lady of Charity) at the beginning of each month. It is said that these flowers grow where the virgin walks and blesses her followers with love and good fortune.

Chamomile

Chamomile (*Matricaria chamomilla*) is used for health and healing, sweet dreams, well-being, prosperity, relaxation, and protection. It is an excellent addition to all sleep-related teas and infusions due to its relaxing effect. A yellow bag filled with chamomile flowers and a photograph of a person will make the individual feel sleepy much of the time.

Eucalyptus and Mint

Eucalyptus (*Eucalyptus globulus*) and mint (*Mentha spicata*) work perfectly together to provide peace of mind and tranquil sleep. You can combine these with bay leaf and basil to make the perfect pillow of prosperity and abundance. The dry leaves of both plants can be burned as incense in a baby's room so the infant has peaceful rest.

Jasmine

Jasmine (*Jasminum officinale*) is perfect to ward off nightmares and all kinds of dreams that cause you anxiety or emotional discomfort. It can be drunk as tea after a divinatory session to help you reflect calmly on the things learned and the visions obtained.

Lavender

Lavender (*Lavandula angustifolia*) is used for relaxation, calm, and protection, providing an elegant and fresh aroma to your hours of rest. You can combine it with lilac flowers to create a therapeutic healing dream. Burn its flowers to support rituals related with astral projection and all kinds of meditation.

Magnolia

In addition to having one of the sweetest fragrances you can find, magnolia (*Magnolia virginiana*) provides calm and tranquility when trying to sleep and meditate. You can fill a pillow with dried magnolia parts and lotus flowers to sleep on after a long day of meditation.

Mimosa

Mimosa (*Mimosa pudica*) flowers and oils are used to promote meditation and healing. It brings calm, relaxation, and prophetic dreams.

Mullein

Mullein (*Verbascum thapsus*) has yellow flowers that provide protection against nightmares and foster a sense of security and comfort.

Rosemary

Rosemary (*Rosmarinus officinalis*) is associated with the magic of protection and money. It is very good for helping to focus the mind during magical workings. A small bunch of rosemary hung with red thread from the doorframe prevents the evil eye from entering the home.

St. John's Wort

Healing, divine protection, blessing, and consecration are all benefited by St. John's wort (*Hypericum perforatum*). In Latin America, it is commonly known as *corazoncillo* or *corazon de San Juan* (San Juan's heart), and it is used to exorcise evil spirits, either by burning it as incense with other plants or by hanging a bunch of the fresh flowers from the frames of the windows and doors so evil spirits leave.

Vervain

Vervain (*Verbena officinalis*) is a protective plant that is excellent against spiritual and astral entities that attempt any damage, and it is especially powerful for nocturnal rites of protection. In Venezuela and Colombia, where this is a rather expensive imported plant, its flowers are offered exclusively to *San Benito, el Moro* (Benedict the Moor), who helps the homeless and marginalized people.

Dream Magic Insight
A SLEEPING SPELL TO AID IN PLANT COMMUNICATION
BY EMMA KATHRYN

Working with plants spans the divide between the many beautifully varied magical and spiritual practices that abound throughout the world.

Plant work within traditions such as obeah combines spirit work with the more mundane aspects of plant work. This means that the spirit of the plant is also worked with in a way that enhances the magical and medicinal properties of the plant, which can add real depth to your spellwork. Using plants in this way for spells and magic involving sleep and dreams mirrors the crossing and blurring of realms found within plant work, thus making it potent magic indeed.

This spell focuses on plant communication and the wisdom plants can offer us as witches. Such knowledge can help build our crafts and strengthen the bonds between us and the other beings we share this world with across the different realms.

You will need to set aside some time before bed for this spell. I always think it's worth setting aside a whole evening so you can fully relax. Setting time aside for yourself is essential for self-care and well-being, so do not feel guilty for taking this time for yourself! It will be worth it, you'll see!

You will need:
- 2 tablespoons valerian root, dried and ground or chopped
- 2 tablespoons dried lavender
- 2 tablespoons dried mugwort
- 2 tablespoons dried lemon balm
- 2 tablespoons passionflower
- Several tealight candles
- Lighter or matches
- Charcoal disk
- Fireproof dish or cauldron

- Teapot and mug (a pan will also do)
- Pen and journal or paper

Begin by having a ritual bath. Run a bath and add a teaspoon of each herb, light one of the candles, and chant:

> **Plants of sleep, prophecy, and dream,**
> **let what is hidden now be seen.**
> **Speak to me in the depths of night**
> **while my soul does take flight.**
> **Show me what I need to know.**
> **As I will, it makes it so!**

If it's not possible to have a bath, steep the herbs in warm water and wash your hands and face. Dress in whatever you are comfortable with.

Next, light the charcoal disk and place it in your fireproof dish. Light the candles and spread them around your working space to create a gentle light. Take a teaspoon of each herb and mix them together. Sprinkle the mix over the charcoal. Make a brew of the herbs, using one part of each, or mixing to suit your tastes.

While the tea brews (or mashes, as we say in my small part of the world), chant over it again. As you do so, enter a meditative state. As the steam rises from the tea, breathe in the aromas and visualize the essence of each herb, plant, and spice. Try to pick out each delicate scent. Notice how each contributes to the overall effect.

When you are ready, pour a cup of tea and enjoy it by candlelight. Really immerse yourself in the act of drinking. Breathe in the scent as you bring the cup to your lips. Taste each individual ingredient within the mix. Notice what comes through first—what lingers. As you drink, visualize yourself taking in the potent energy of each ingredient used.

After the final sip, repeat the chant. Extinguish the candles and go to bed, following your normal nightly routines.

When you wake in the morning, make notes in your journal. It's a good idea to do this straight away so you can recall any important information from your dreams. If you cannot recall your dreams, don't worry. It's still important to make notes about how you feel. Really pay attention to your body and your thoughts, not only upon waking but throughout the day too.

You can repeat this exercise as often as you need to. It's a good idea to do it weekly, as sometimes it might take a while for any understanding gleaned from your dreams and from the plants to be understood. This is where keeping a journal comes in handy, allowing you to go back through your notes. It's amazing how hindsight and experience can shed light on things we might not have understood at the time.

You'll also notice, over time, that this exercise also increases and strengthens your relationship with the plants, either when growing them or working with them in other contexts and situations. The more you work with these plants, the clearer their communications will become and the more you will learn about yourself, the plants, and your craft.

TRIBAL TALES
THE MATACO OR WICHÍ

The Wichí are a well-known Indigenous group in
South America. Its tribes extend along the headwaters
of the Bermejo River and the Pilcomayo River in Argentina (where they
are known as *matacos*) and Bolivia (in this country, they are called *ween-
hayey*). They are also found inhabiting different parts of Paraguay and Peru.

The belief system of the Wichí peoples has been defined as an ethnic and
native fusion of animism and Indigenous shamanism.

Historically, the Wichís have shared their tribe and travels with the
Chorotes and Chulupies (other Indigenous groups) with whom they share
certain beliefs in animism, as well as in the use of cebil seeds and tobacco.
They all use these plants to cure diseases, illnesses, and physical ailments,
as well as to predict the future in the visions of smoke and the forms that
tobacco leaves take when burned.

The Yopo and the Cebil

The healers and sorcerers of the Wichí tribe are the authentic masters in the
use of certain herbs to heal, although their use can cause stomach upset and
spasms in those who ingest them. These herbs are part of their traditional
medicine, which was not slow to spread (although losing its enormous cultural and metaphysical value) to other parts of Latin America. In certain esoteric and botanical stores, they can be obtained, albeit illegally, for a fairly
affordable price.

Among their healing plants, the most popular is the Anadenanthera,
a tree that can reach 66 feet (20 meters) in length that is native to Argentina, Brazil, Bolivia, Peru, and Paraguay. Two specific varieties derived from
this species enjoy enormous magical and cultural value. First is the yopo,
cohobo, or parica (*Anadenanthera peregrina*), which has a highly resistant
wood, which is used to create furniture, and beans that are highly toxic and
hallucinogenic. The second is the cebil, curupay, or huilco (*Anadenanthera
colubrina*), which grows in Ecuador and Cuba and from which a fermented
sweet drink is produced.

The use of these herbs goes hand in hand with the idea that by entering a deep state of sleep, or induced trance, the sorcerer or healer can move between worlds and find in them the ability to heal themselves and others by treating the diseases from the root of its origin.

They may use a fine powdered herbal mixture to lull the patient to sleep or many other methods of inducing a trance. If the Wichí goes into a trance with the patient, he can heal him from the spirit world, where both act as forms of energy.

The Wichís collect the seeds of these trees during the first months of the year through a ceremonial rite. The seeds are traditionally dried in the sun for several days inside large woven baskets, while some more modern groups of the tribe prefer to roast them over a slow fire. In any case, the seeds are later stored until the moment of being used. When the day arrives, the seeds are pulverized between songs and prayers, and their powders are mixed with the tobacco leaves to be smoked by the priest while patients and those attending the ceremonies inhale the smoke.

Another method, perhaps even more elaborate, consists of mixing these powdered seeds with powdered tobacco leaves and powdered snail shells. This mixture is inhaled through an instrument similar to a small flute with two holes on one side, which is made of carob wood or bird bones.

Among the many effects of cebil, it is said that it leads patients to visit the world under the ground, which is where they can find the origin of their discomfort and combat it. It can also help the individual to free themselves from any harmful spirits attached to them. Those blessed with the gift of vision can awaken their instincts and visions through this tribal ceremony.

According to Julio Cezaro, one of the traditional Wichí sorcerers, the smoke of the cebil that has been inhaled blocks the senses of the physical body, allowing the soul to work without anguish or distractions from a higher plane in the ailments of the body. On this plane, made entirely of air and spirit, the soul is capable of moving between worlds, entering the dreams of others, or manifesting itself in the physical world in the form of birds and other animals.

CHAPTER 14
DREAM INCENSE, RESINS & OILS

Incense, resins, and oils are used in sorcery in two main ways. First, they can be used as the primary tool of a spell or spiritual offering. Second, they can be used as a ritual complement to create and channel the specific type of energy we seek to manifest in a spell.

Resins, like incense, are commonly burned over hot coals to create a fragrant smoke that raises our spiritual frequency and removes distractions during the performance of a spell.

Oils and perfumes are used in witchcraft to bless or curse places, objects, and people. They are also used to anoint dolls, talismans, jewelry, and candles for mystical and ritualistic purposes.

Incense Basics

Incense is one of the most common tools in witchcraft—and also one of the most popular forms. Incense is manufactured through many different ways, and it has countless uses. Beyond aromatizing environments, certain types of incense are used to eliminate bacteria from the air; to change the aeonic frequency of a place; to dissipate negative energies; to stimulate healing processes; to keep evil spirits away; to attract and influence various emotions, such as love, courage, detachment, and self-esteem; or even to generate psychic visions and empower transmutation rituals.

In multiple books and teachings related to magic and sorcery, you will find long lists about the types of incense that you can make use of to attract, influence, or disperse each type of energy (healing, protection, abundance, etc.) or emotion (love, joy, sadness, etc.). I will focus on the use of incense in relation to dream magic, dream walking, and astral travel.

There are many types of incense. The most common is probably loose incense (my personal favorite) because the pure elements—herbs, soil, resins—burn without needing other oils blended in the mix. Cones are perhaps the cleanest and easiest to clean at the end, and wands are the most common of all and available in a wide variety of fragrances.

When I light the incense in the morning, I always like to recite:

May my abundance and my energy flow upward, just as the incense flows in the morning. May my prosperity go higher, just as the smoke of my incense.

Over the years, this phrase has taken many forms, and each one has become my personal mantra.

A Note about Incense Safety

During meditations it is important not to have distractions or fire risks, so make sure you have a suitable censer, small cauldron, or heat-resistant plate to use for the incense. Keep any cloth, paper, or flammable material away from it. Also try to light the incense away from fire alarms to avoid any nuisance.

EXERCISE
Method for Burning Homemade Herbal Incense

Burning homemade incense is one of the most powerful ritual practices in my opinion. It is fine to light a stick or cone of incense from the market; it is quite practical. However, when you do light a piece of charcoal, wait until the piece changes color, apply the incense in small doses with an incense spoon, move the smoke in different directions with your fan, and apply more incense occasionally while the charcoal is still burning, the entire practice is pure ritual ceremony, allowing no distractions of any kind or comforts. Here, I show you how to do it correctly.

You will need:
- Charcoal
- Lighter
- Small cauldron, censer, or heat-resistant plate
- Teaspoon
- The combination of dried herbs and/or loose incense to be burned
- Hand fan

Although today there are a dozen tools that can be used to carefully light a piece of charcoal, they take a little away from the whole magical experience for the less experienced, and that is why I am going to teach you how to do it exactly as my multiple teachers taught me.

Very carefully hold the piece of charcoal with one hand (you can use good tweezers if you prefer). With the lighter, light one end of charcoal. Hold it for just a few seconds—until you notice that it has some minimal sparks. Once the charcoal has sparks it means that it is lit and will start to burn in a few seconds, so quickly place it in the cauldron, on the plate, or in the censer and keep it there for a minute. You will notice the charcoal begin to burn bright red and slowly turn white. This means that it is lit and ready to use.

Using the teaspoon, collect the dry herbs to burn. Deposit these on the burning charcoal. You will immediately see how it burns and releases the aromatic smoke.

Wait five to ten minutes before placing more incense on the charcoal in the same way. If you notice that it has stopped producing smoke, you can use the fan to subtly vent some air toward the charcoal to produce more smoke.

Variation

Many rituals require you to move incense through various places, rooms, and spaces. But due to inexperience, many novices make the mistake of holding the censer or cauldron with their own hands. In many cases, these tools are made of metal or ceramic, which will burn their hands when heated. Or, worse, the inexperienced individual may throw the incense carelessly, failing to realize that hot incense may fall onto a bed, curtain, tablecloth, or table and cause a fire. For rituals with movement, always place the censer or cauldron on a heat-resistant plate so you can move the incense around without burning yourself.

To begin, place the censer or cauldron on the plate. Use a mortar to mix all the herbal elements and crush them. Place half of the mixture in the censer. Light the piece of charcoal and place it on the mixture in the censer. Once the charcoal starts to burn and look an intense red around the edges, slowly add the rest of the mixture, completely covering the charcoal.

Carrying the plate, proceed to move the incense smoke to the corners of the room where you will perform the spell or ritual. Between small periods of time (about three to five minutes) move the charcoal and mixture with a stick or wand to prevent it from going out.

Incense Recipes

Choosing the right combinations and portions of different elements to create your own incense is not easy. It takes some time and experience to learn which combinations are the best. For example, if an incense formula only specifically requires valerian but does not specify which part to use, a novice might not know that the best thing to do is use the powdered roots of the plant and not the leaves or flowers, which would completely eclipse any other herb used in the combination. (It's for this reason that the plant is also used in very small doses.)

The most common fragrances we are going to use to complement our rituals for dreams and psychic magic include:

- *Myrrh:* Blessings, sacred protection, high ritual magic
- *Frankincense:* Protection against the evil eye and psychic attacks, consecration
- *Dragon's blood:* Protection against all kinds of curses and transformation
- *Rose:* Love, unity, emotional protection, connection with ancestors
- *Camphor:* Cleansing, spiritual work, removing obstacles
- *Mugwort:* Divination, psychic empowerment, dream magic
- *Palo santo:* Divination, cleansing, protection
- *Sandalwood:* Love, financial abundance, prosperity, attracting money

The following is an assortment of incense combinations for different purposes. The directions are written based on how I prepare them to my own liking and functionality. According to your tastes and preferences, you can always slightly alter the quantities of my recipes and others. Also note that all recipe lists only include the herbs and other such ingredients. You should always have a mortar and pestle (or something similar) in your workspace to mix ingredients in—plus a way to burn the mix when the time comes. It goes along with the assumption that you should have and use a lighter and censer when appropriate, not because an author told you to do it; it is simply something important and basic to have in your space.

RECIPE
Incense of Dreams

This recipe results in a practical and easy-to-use incense that disperses astral larvae (minor negative entities that cling to the surroundings) and psychic disturbances. It also helps to focus the psychic energy of the magician who is about to cast the spell. Among the elements used here, mugwort is the most important, as it is a plant par excellence burned by psychics, seers, mediums, and cartomancers before making a reading or holding a divinatory session.

Sea salt is included in this recipe, and it is burned to disperse anxiety, which can quickly turn into all manner of distractions. The brown sugar is burned to attract and reinforce positive thoughts, which will help keep your mind focused on the ritual, replacing the anxious thoughts that obstruct the process.

You will need:

- 3 tablespoons mugwort
- 1 tablespoon frankincense
- 1 tablespoon jasmine flowers
- 1 tablespoon star anise
- ½ tablespoon myrrh or copal
- Pinch of brown sugar
- Pinch of sea salt

You can double or triple the listed amounts to make more incense and store it in a glass jar, cloth bag, or wooden box to preserve it until you need it.

RECIPES
Incense to Manifest Prophetic Dreams

Normally, sleep incenses are a combination of aromas and essences that help bring about deep rest, such as chamomile flowers, white sage, camphor, mint, spearmint, and eucalyptus.

If creating a homemade incense that allows us to slightly stimulate our psyche in order to produce visions of events in the future, the past, or even current events occurring somewhere, it is important to accompany these calming scents with elements that increase or stimulate our clairvoyance, such as mugwort, myrrh, copal, or camphor.

Another important step when making incense to induce prophetic dreams is to focus our mind on what we want to see, either by using a brief and silent meditation to visualize what we are looking for or by writing down the situation or event that we wish to see.

These mixes should be burned in the room or space where we expect to receive the visions, either in the bedroom a few hours before sleeping or on our altar before a divination session. The following is a short list of recipes that have been quite effective for me and are easy to use and implement in your individual practice.

For the first recipe, you will need:

- 1 teaspoon dried mugwort
- 1 teaspoon powdered rose petals
- 1 teaspoon acacia leaves

For the second recipe, you will need:

- 1 teaspoon dried mugwort
- 1 square camphor
- 1 handful of rosemary (for psychic protection)

For the third recipe, you will need:

- 2 teaspoons dried mugwort
- 1 teaspoon dried lilac blossoms
- 1 teaspoon cinnamon powder

For the fourth recipe, you will need:

- 1 teaspoon dried mugwort
- 1 teaspoon cardamom powder
- 1 teaspoon coriander powder
- 1 teaspoon dried wormwood

RECIPE
Incense to Drive Away Nightmares

To use this incense to chase away nightmares, blend equal parts of the ingredients. Then, light a candle and burn the blend of herbs in the flame as you move around the bedroom, focusing on not avoiding or forgetting any corners or the doorway. Let the incense burn, then walk very carefully over the smoke three times.

You will need:

- Dried juniper berries
- Copal
- Dried chamomile
- *Cyclamen* or lavender flowers

RECIPES
Incense to Sleep

Insomnia is one of the most common issues that practitioners of sorcery face day after day. It is so common that we mention it in most of our books. When you work so often with energy (your own and that of others), you manage to gain a certain sensitivity to the most subtle energy changes in your environment. These can be reflected by generating certain forms of anxiety, physical discomfort, and insomnia—practically the most basic symptoms of a cursed person. Your energetic body is perceiving changes that your physical body is not yet able to notice, and because of this, you feel that you are in a constant state of alert.

Smoking incense in your bedroom a few hours before sleeping not only helps decontaminate the air against various bacteria and germs in the atmosphere, but it is also an effective and simple method to clean and balance the energy of the place, allowing you to achieve a greater state of rest at the time of sleep.

Due to all of the reasons I just mentioned, I will share with you a variety of effective recipes to burn in the bedroom about twice a week. You will need equal parts of each ingredient in all the following recipes.

For the first recipe, you will need:
- Dried acacia
- Sandalwood
- Cypress

Burn this blend to enhance and raise your psychic abilities. Acacia is related to the myths of Osiris and the power of clairvoyance.

For the second recipe, you will need:
- Mugwort
- Frankincense
- Acacia

Burn this recipe as votive incense to let the ghosts and spirits manifest around you. Mugwort (the mother herb) is related to most of the spells for clairvoyance and mediumship, but it should be used in moderation, as it is toxic in high amounts, especially for pregnant women.

For the third recipe, you will need:

- Mugwort
- Blue sage
- Acacia

Blend these herbs together, burn them on a piece of charcoal, and meditate for twenty-five minutes, watching the smoke around you to open your spiritual vision to the otherworld. You can add to this same incense a pinch of dragon's bloodroot and rosemary to see and detect bad ghosts and omens around you.

RECIPE
Incense to Dream Five Nights

Prepare a good quantity of this incense to burn for five nights in a row. It is perfect for freeing your mind before going to sleep and allows you to more easily capture the night visions you are looking for. Between the second and the fourth night it will probably keep you from falling asleep, but after the fifth night, you will resume your normal hours of sleep.

You will need:

- 1 part storax balsam (resin)
- 1 part copal
- 1 part mugwort
- 1 part peppermint

Crush the ingredients in a mortar and then place some of the mixture in a censer. Store any extra incense in a mason jar. Light a piece of charcoal in a heat-resistant container, and place the incense mixture around the charcoal, adding more mixture every two to five minutes. Move the incense around the room and bed. Repeat for the next four nights using the mixture from the jar.

RECIPE
Incense of Dreams Gift

If someone who is not familiar with sorcery and spells wants to relive a recurring dream or understand it better, you can give them a handful of this homemade incense. It is easy to make and gives a light enough result, meaning it will not overwhelm the person.

You will need:
- 1 teaspoon honeysuckle blossoms
- 1 teaspoon cedarwood chips
- 1 teaspoon myrrh
- 1 teaspoon mugwort leaves

Mix all the ingredients together, and store the mixture in a box, cloth bag, open amulet, or small bottle. Give it as a gift along with one or two pieces of charcoal so the recipient can burn it at home. Maybe even add a little fan to the gift so they can move the smoke around the bedroom an hour before sleeping.

Incense Spells and Rituals

Since you have duly advanced in working with incense, it is time to take our craft to the next level and make use of them. We will not use them to attract, move, enhance, or dissipate a form of energy but to complement and accompany more powerful spells and rituals that require your experience, dedication, and concentration.

I invite you to design your own formulas and create your own rituals with what you have learned. In addition to the spells you craft, here are some powerful rituals. One will increase your clairvoyance, and the other two can be done to bless and protect your bedroom.

EXERCISE
Jar of Dream Incense Spell

With this spell you are going to create a blend of dream magic, which you can occasionally burn as incense to elevate your subconscious mind during dreams (lucid dreaming), to gain greater clarity during your dreams (clairvoyance), or to catch a glimpse of the future in your dreams (oneiromancy).

You will need:

- Clean glass jar with a lid
- Equal parts anise, eucalyptus, mint, marjoram, jasmine, hibiscus, rosemary, and yarrow
- Piece of crystal quartz
- Piece of labradorite or celestite
- Rose or lavender incense stick
- Incense holder
- Lighter or matches

Time: Between sunset and midnight on a Wednesday

In the clean jar, mix the herbs together, then add the crystal quartz and labradorite or celestite. Seal the jar completely, safely position the incense stick in the holder, and light it. Wave the sealed jar several times in the smoke, drawing circles in the air. Store the jar in a dry, cool, dark place, such as a cabinet outside the kitchen or a large closet.

On nights that you wish to practice a spell or meditation related to your dreams, light a piece of charcoal in a small cauldron and burn one to two tablespoons of this incense over the charcoal.

As a Charm Bag

On a night of a crescent or full moon, use three tablespoons of this herbal mixture to fill a blue or purple felt bag. Add a few drops of lavender or rose oil, close and seal the bag completely, and light a blue candle. Keep this charm bag in the bedroom to enhance your clairvoyance while you sleep or rest.

EXERCISE
Ritual to Enchant and Protect the Witch's Room, Version I

When it comes to dream magic, the practitioner's room is an extension of sorcery itself. This is not so different from other paths. For example, witches who specialize in working with nature might like to have plants in their bedroom to clear the oxygen, or they might add flowers to their bedroom décor to bring more color into the room. Witches and brujas in Latin America, although this sounds like a stereotype, usually have three magical workspaces. These spots are so important that they seem to be the three altars of the witch:

- *Kitchen:* This is where bottles of spices and flavors are used for all kinds of spells. In Venezuela, Cuba, and Colombia, it is the kitchen where the most important altars in the house (the spiritual vault, the altar dedicated to the deceased) are kept, so your spirit can perceive the delicious aroma of the food and be kept where wine and other drinks are served.
- *Patio or garden:* This spot usually contains all kinds of aromatic plants, poison ivy, and spices. It is the place where we plant our seasonal flowers and poison ivy, where we bury amulets (among other things), and where we put our bowl to rest at night to prepare moon water.
- *Bedroom:* This is where the grandmothers hang photos from mirror frames, embroider the names of their enemies on curtains, and usually have a small altar with images and figures of saints to pray to before going to sleep. This is a clear remnant of the influence of the Spanish and Portuguese peoples among our modern Indigenous families.

For dream magic, the bedroom is most important, and its purpose goes beyond being a simple sleeping area. Witches have all kinds of amulets under the bed; mojo and charm bags under the pillow; multiple pillows of different colors and sizes, which do not match each other, that are always full of herbs and dried flowers on the bed; amulets and dolls hanging from the windows to attract the favor of some spirits and to keep others away;

and countless rosaries, oracles, talismans, and necklaces hanging from door handles.

If the body is a temple for our spirit, the bedroom is clearly the temple for the witch's body. It is where we sleep while the spirits assist us at night and take care of our valuable sleep and astral travel.

This ritual is carried out to bless the bedroom and manifest good energy and spiritual protection. It can be carried out on any day as long as you have the complete freedom and privacy to carry it out.

You will need:

- 5 sheets of paper
- Black ink
- Tape
- 5 pieces of crystal quartz
- Cone of vanilla or myrrh incense
- Censer, small cauldron, or heat-resistant plate
- Lighter or matches
- Tall white or blue candle in candleholder

On each sheet of paper, use the ink to draw a pentagram (five-pointed star inside a circle). Stick a pentagram on each of your bedroom walls at the height of your head using the tape. Set one more under the bed and place a piece of crystal quartz at each of the pentagram's points.

Place the incense in the censer, on the plate, or in the cauldron and light it and the candle. With the censer in one hand and the candle in the other, move around the room, illuminating the pentagrams on the walls one by one.

After casting light on the four pentagrams, place the candle and the censer in a safe place near the bed. Sit in the lotus position on the bed and take a deep breath. Visualize the pentagrams on the walls and picture light coming from these drawings. Watch as the dense golden light that comes from these tiny portals spreads from the walls to all over your environment, moving around the room and entirely protecting the place.

Next, close your eyes and continue with the visualization exercise. Continue to visualize the light moving around the room, showering the space with safety.

EXERCISE
Ritual to Enchant and Protect the Witch's Room, Version II

This is a short spell that shares a purpose with the previous ritual. Using good energies, it works to bless and exalt the spaces used for rest and magical work, such as your altar and your bedroom, and all other spaces that require channeling calm and removing all kinds of distractions.

You will need:
- Brown candle
- White candle
- Sandalwood or myrrh incense (in any form you prefer)
- Incense holder or censer, small cauldron, or heat-resistant plate
- Lighter or matches
- Wooden bowl half full of water
- 1 cup Saint John's wort
- 1 cup rose petals
- 1 cup ground verbena
- 6 drops poppy essential oil
- Rubber gloves (optional)

Light both candles and your incense (in an appropriate vessel for the type of incense) in a corner of the chosen space to consecrate it. In the bowl, mix the herbs and the oil together with your hands (preferably with your bare hands, but if you feel you need gloves, use them). Blend the ingredients for five to ten minutes with your closed eyes, breathing deep and visualizing all kinds of beautiful images that bring you a feeling of joy, kindness, safety, protection, healing, beauty, and love.

Once all the ingredients are combined, start dotting the corners of the room with the mixture calmly and with a sense of safety. You can do this in silence or with background music. You can do it naked or with your ritual clothing—however you feel most comfortable. Through this ritual, you are claiming this space as your own and commanding the energy of the site. Continue with this process, marking all corners of the room, plus around the door and window frames, several more times.

Once you have finished with the ritual, let the candles and incense burn to the end. Throw the rest of the water and herbs out of your home or around it; you can even water the door with this mixture.

Resins to Blend in Your Dream Spells, Charm Bags, and Incense

Resins can be burned as incense using a piece of charcoal. They have a higher chemical/elemental concentration, which is why the smoke seems to be thicker and more charged with aroma. Like incense, the aromatic smoke from the resins alters the energy of the site and allows us to better focus our energy before and during magical work.

When using resin, it is smart to get multiple small pieces, not large pieces. For example, if you place a large piece of frankincense or myrrh on a hot coal, it can end up melting, covering the coal and making it cool and useless. With that in mind, make sure you have enough resin in small pieces and a good mortar to grind them in before using.

Here are some common resins to consider:

Amber

Amber is related to clairvoyance, psychic vision, and all forms of mediumship and precognition. In short, amber is the mugwort of resins. One or two pieces of amber inside a pillow helps balance mediumship within dreams.

Copaiba

Copaiba is a highly oily resin that is extracted from Copaifera trees, which are native to Brazil and have begun to grow in other parts of South America. The bitter aroma of this resin is linked to the traditional folk medicine of Brazil, where it is used as a common medicine for multiple diseases. The oil is used by the Indigenous peoples of Panama and Brazil to ward off nightmares, malevolent spirits, and ill-intentioned witches. The resin is allowed to dry for several days to remove all traces of oil, and it is burned to venerate and awaken the spirits of the trees.

Copal

This resin has a calming effect on moods. For this reason, I once filled an entire pillow with copal and chrysanthemums as a gift for my older sister, who suffers from depression. According to her own words, it helped her sleep better each evening.[38]

Damla Sakızı (Mastic)

Originally from Greece and enormously popular in Turkey, from where it is shipped to different parts of the world, this yellow-golden resin is used in combination with frankincense for the divinatory game *üç göz, bakmak, üç kehanet* (three eyes for three omens or three eyes watching three omens). In this secret, juvenile game, three people are seated in a circle around a censer. Mastic is then burned with frankincense as incense while each person covers their right eye. Using only the left eye, they all try to see a figure in the smoke. If two or three of the people see the same figure at the same time, it is an omen of fate.

Frankincense

Frankincense, also called olibanum, is associated with the high states of consciousness that we consider sacred and the support of a cosmic force or entity superior to ourselves. A small bunch of frankincense placed near your bed can help you feel more comfortable and more secure while you sleep.

Myrrh

Myrrh provides divine and spiritual protection during sleep. Whether you are engaging in night meditation, lucid dreaming, astral projection, or any other form of out of body experience (OBE), a small bunch of myrrh and frankincense will give you the protection you need while your body remains on the physical plane and your consciousness travels outside of it.

Sandarac

This resin is mostly imported from Morocco and different parts of Africa. In Latin America, it is linked to the practice of folk magic of the Spanish. It is not highly fragrant; however, when it is mixed with copal and frankincense or with copal and myrrh and burned, it can clear the energy of a

....
38. Copal comes from the Nahuatl word *copalli*, which means "incense."

home before receiving visitors. It can also be burned to honor the spirits of the night during magic and spiritualism sessions.

Essential Oils

Just as plants extract all the energetic benefits of the earth, so do the essential oils that come from the plants. The aromas of essential oils contain those plant microparticles that relax us and induce certain states of calm. Essential oils have been widely studied by botanists and herbalists around the globe. In fact, they are still being studied in order to further learn how they treat all kinds of problems related to anxiety, stress, and depression.

Essential oils are a great ally to have when combating insomnia. Insomnia itself has a large number of allies that we find in our daily routine, including a poor diet, caffeinated drinks, alcohol, muscle pain caused by overwork (or lack of daily movement), general malaise, and daily irritability that ends up causing emotional wear and tear. These things alone—or combined—leave us unable to take advantage of the hours of sleep.

While there are many scientific studies that support the use of these oils as treatments for ailments, in this chapter we are going to focus on their esoteric uses. In addition to helping us sleep and relax, they also help us induce episodes of deep sleep and raise our state of consciousness during them.

There is no single method to use when it comes to essential oils. In fact, there is a great variety of methods that can be used based on budget and individual taste. For example, before arriving in the United States, my method of using essential oils was to put them in a glass bottle near a window and then place some long wooden sticks inside the bottle. This acted as an air freshener so the aroma was diffused about the room throughout the day; I chose this method because bathtubs are not all that common in my home country. Now, living in the United States, I use essential oils in the bathtub two to three times a week, either by adding a few drops directly to the water or by making homemade salt bombs loaded with an infusion of these oils.

In places where people commonly gather at the edge of rivers to wash clothes, as we used to do in different parts of my country, a bar of unscented soap is used to clean the clothing. Those washing the clothes then apply homemade perfumes crafted from herbal and floral oils, which they brought with them, to the fresh water for the last rinse. This way, the clothes have a nice scent at the end.

In the United States, you can buy a plastic spray bottle for only one dollar and fill it with your favorite combination of oils. If you do this, misting spaces, sheets, and nightwear with your relaxing oils will be a simple task. And let's not forget air fresheners and oil diffusers, which come in all sizes, colors, shapes, and forms; these are often suitable for moving the vapors of essential oils around a large room for extended periods of time.

Most Common Oils for Sleep

The following is a short list with the most recommended oils in relation to sleeping and combating insomnia. Keep in mind that essential oils can sometimes cause allergic reactions when applied to the skin. This can be due to multiple different factors, and it is important to remember to never apply pure oils directly to the skin. Dilute them in water under the instructions of a chemist or expert specialist since all oils can have different concentrations. Always do an oil test on your skin half an hour before use.

Bergamot Essential Oil

One of the most popular citrus oils, bergamot fragrance is heavily marketed in the perfume industry, which is why it will certainly smell familiar to you when you first work with it. Bergamot oil is widely used to calm anxiety. If combined with a few drops of orange or lemon oil, it is perfect for recharging energy in the morning after a sleepless or difficult night.

If you have a night job, you can create homemade glycerin-based soap with bergamot and orange oils to use in the mornings. This will give you an extra feeling of energy.

Chamomile Essential Oil

The essential oil of Roman chamomile is one of the best-known natural relaxants. It helps fight nervousness, irritability, restlessness, and common insomnia. Because of its fragrant and light aroma, it is one of the few oils that a qualified pharmacist would recommend you use on young children to help them fall asleep. You can apply a few drops of this essential oil directly to your pillows before going to sleep to provide an extra feeling of calm and serenity.

Clary Sage Essential Oil

Clary sage is one of the most valued oils on the market. It has a fresh, sweet, and woody fragrance. It is commonly used in sorcery to consecrate, reactivate, and charge spells and amulets related to financial abundance, prosperity, and family or marital love.

Although not directly related to the field of dreams, a few drops of this essential oil can be combined with the essential oils of lavender and sweet orange in an air humidifier in the morning to energize the environment after a tiring night.

Lavender Essential Oil

Lavender essential oil is one of the first oils people choose for sleeping due to its floral and herbaceous aroma. It is relaxing and almost hypnotizing, making it an ideal oil to fall asleep with, even in chronic cases. You can mix a few drops of this essential oil with a tablespoon of olive oil and use it to massage the neck muscles, letting it function as a relaxing and antispasmodic oil.

Lemon Essential Oil

Lemon oil is one of the most beneficial essential oils that exists. A few drops of this oil with a tablespoon of pure honey is the immediate solution to multiple physical discomforts. It is also a great natural solution for cleansing the throat before and after each ritual or to slightly relieve flu symptoms.

Sprinkle a few drops of lemon oil on each corner of the bed before going to sleep to lighten the atmosphere and provide a feeling of comfort and relaxation. A glass of water with five drops of lemon oil in it can be drunk in the morning by those who talk in their sleep to soothe the throat and clear the respiratory tract.

Lemongrass Essential Oil (Hierba luisa, Caña Santa, or te de limon)

Lemongrass oil is mostly recommended to combat feelings of anxiety, depression, and anguish, especially in Venezuela, where it is a common oil to use against anxiety specifically. A mixture is made with four parts of olive oil and one part of lemongrass oil, and a few drops of this formula are added to water and drunk in cases of anxiety attacks and emotional discomfort.

To carry out magical work, it is important to be rested, as well as physically and mentally present at all times, so if it is difficult for you to fall asleep and achieve rest, a few drops of this oil in a diffuser in the bedroom will do wonders.

Marjoram Essential Oil

Marjoram has one of the most soothing and relaxing fragrances in the world of essential oils. It is a facilitator of sleep and rest par excellence. Used in an oil diffuser, it helps you to have cleaner and healthier air. Combined with a few drops of valerian or chamomile essential oil, it is a fairly strong sedative that you can aromatize the bedroom with if you wish to have a long session of restful sleep.

You can create a pale pink or light blue dream pillow filled with dried chamomile and lavender flowers, two or three small pieces of polished crystal quartz, and a few drops of marjoram and orange essential oils to create the perfect resting pillow.

Mugwort Essential Oil

The essential oil of mugwort, also called Artemisia, is of high value to practitioners of witchcraft and magic, but it is commonly confused in the botanical market with wormwood oil. Both have a similar taste and bitter aroma. Therefore, it is important to check the source of the oil and its quality. Artemisia oil is tagged and sold as armoise, while armoise oil is commonly made with plants from the genus Artemisia, which also includes tarragon and sagebrush.

Please note that mugwort oil can be highly toxic, especially for pregnant women. Due to its high concentration of camphor, it is considered a neurotoxin, so it should not be ingested or applied directly to the eyes, mucous membranes, or skin. While many traditional witchcraft books and recipes suggest using mugwort in baths for sleep, vivid dreams, or insomnia, as I have also done throughout this book, most of these recipes call for dried and pulverized mugwort in small amounts, not the oil. Again, the oil is highly concentrated and can be dangerous.

One last important note: Do not also confuse the flower essence of mugwort with the essential oil. Flower essences are often applied to bathwater without causing much inconvenience. These are distilled from the flowers and are not the same as the concentrated essential oils.

To safely use the oil in magic, try a dropper. The oil can be added to a floral potpourri in the bedroom, for example, to conjure happy and peaceful dreams. It can be rubbed with a cloth into candles for the performance of dream spells, such as those used to enter the dreams of others, project messages in the dreams, interpret dreams, or conjure vivid dreams.

Orange Essential Oil

There are two different varieties of orange oil: oil extracted from sweet orange and oil extracted from bitter orange. Both are highly recommended, not only for their fruity-floral fragrance but also for their benefits to the nervous system. The scents can provide a feeling of joy, deep calm, and well-being. Mix either variety with chamomile oil in a diffuser and turn it on a few hours before bed to prepare the room for resting.

The calming and sedative properties of orange oil quickly and effectively counteract insomnia and anxiety, as well as the sensations of nocturnal depression, accumulated stress during the day, and nervousness. If you want a deep sleep but at the same time are looking to find something within your dreams (a prediction of the future, an answer, a signal), orange oil is more suitable than others because its energetic quality allows us a feeling of alertness, even while we are sleeping.

Rose Essential Oil

Although rose essential oil is often used in the beauty industry, combining it with orange or chamomile oil makes it an incredible ally at bedtime. When either used in a diffuser for the room or added to a bathtub, rose essential oil is one of the most suitable if you want to have a restful night's sleep after a very busy day.

Tangerine Essential Oil

Citric oils, such as orange and tangerine, are extremely popular for their peculiar fragrance. They have a relaxing, calming, and sedative effect. Tangerine essential oil has a fruitier note and is suitable for the room of young people who are suffering from insomnia or stress. We could even dare to recommend its use in the room of someone who suffers from anxiety because its fragrance is a natural calming agent that revives the spirit.

Valerian Essential Oil

Known for its relaxing and calming qualities, valerian provides a sedative sensation and restful, healing sleep. It is commonly used in an oil diffuser or air humidifier a few hours before bed. Six to twelve drops of this essential oil can also be added to a massage lotion or cream for a relaxing massage session before bed.

The seeds of the valerian plant, as well as its flowers, are also used to formulate all kinds of spells and talismans related to rest, sleep, and relaxation.

RECIPE
Essential Oil Mixture to Protect Your Dreams

You can use this mixture in a diffuser, to bless altar candles, or to lightly spray on pillows.

You will need:
- 3 drops carnation oil
- 3 drops sandalwood oil
- 3 drops vanilla oil

Dream Baths

In Latin America, baths charged with oils, herbs, and flowers have an enormous and growing popularity. These magical baths combine the naturally purifying and transforming power of water with a variety of floral oils and herbal essences to achieve a specific purpose. In this book, we will make use of baths related to the world of dreams and lunar phases.

These baths should be preferably prepared at home. They can be prepared in two ways: either in a bucket to be applied in the shower or directly in a bathtub, which is where they will probably offer greater relaxation to the sorcerer or the patient in question.

The following four baths combine the energy of the lunar phases, which strongly influence the hours of sleep, with different essences that will lead you to delve more easily into the world of dreams.

Basic Instructions

Make a schedule with the lunar cycles and have everything prepared for each bath at least two days in advance.

For each recipe, boil all the ingredients in a cauldron or large pot. Let the mixture boil for about five minutes, then let the mixture rest for about thirty minutes. You can store the completed mixture in a jar until it is bath or shower time. To use the mixture, combine it with some warm water before you bathe.

When it is time for your bath, I recommend that you light a couple of blue candles on a saucer in the bathroom. Afterward, you can take the candles to your altar and leave them there for the rest of the day. This will make you feel calmer. Remember to extinguish them if you are going out. Relight when you return. Never leave a candle unattended. If they are still burning when you are ready to go to bed, extinguish them before sleeping and light them again in the morning.

RECIPE
New Moon Dream Bath

Once this bath is applied to your body, close your eyes for five minutes and visualize a dark moon in the night sky. Watch it darken, disappear, and blend with the dark night before your eyes; visualize the starry sky that forms in the space around you. Slowly open your eyes and proceed to dry yourself.

You will need:
- 1 liter water
- 2 tablespoons almond oil
- 1 tablespoon coconut oil
- 12 drops mugwort floral essence
- A bunch of chamomile flowers

RECIPE
Crescent Moon Dream Bath

Once you have applied this bath to your body, close your eyes, take a deep breath, and visualize a dark, starry sky around you. Then, picture a crescent moon in front of you that is slightly eclipsing the sky with its pale white light. Visualize the perfect shape and color of this bright and soft light. Feel it reflect on you and illuminate a part of your body. Take the time you need to carry out this meditation. At the end, open your eyes slowly and proceed to dry yourself.

You will need:

- 1 liter water
- 3 tablespoons olive essential oil
- 12 to 20 drops mugwort flower essence
- 12 to 20 drops apple flower essence
- 12 petals of white flowers (preferably roses)

RECIPE
Full Moon Dream Bath

This bath can be done in the middle of the full moon night, the night before, or during the next day before dark. Once you have applied this bath over your entire body, close your eyes, breathe deeply, and visualize a dark space abundant in tiny stars. Picture the bright crescent in front of you and watch the moon cover itself in light in totality. Visualize this splendid full moon forming in front of you and perceive this ostentatious silver light covering every inch of your body. Let yourself be bathed in this light, and do not stop the visualization of the full moon until you personally feel that it is time to end. After this, proceed to open your eyes and dry yourself.

You will need:

- 1 liter of the most natural water you can find
- 2 tablespoons almond oil

- 21 white flower petals (preferably from chrysanthemums or roses)
- 2 tablespoons pure honey
- 1 teaspoon ground star anise
- 12 drops neroli essential oil

RECIPE
Waning Moon Dream Bath

Once you have applied this ritual bath to your entire body (which you can complete with a bar of natural soap of myrrh or sandalwood), close your eyes and proceed to breathe slowly and deeply. Visualize an illuminated starry sky with an ostentatious full moon in its center. Watch how the moonlight slowly disappears from one side until there is only an illuminated half moon in front of you. Picture every detail of this crescent moon—its colors, its surface, its vibrant light—and take a deep breath before opening your eyes, accepting that another lunar cycle is ending. Once your eyes are open, proceed to dry yourself.

If you have been dreaming about an ending to a cycle, or if you have visualized in your dreams any situation in which you are letting go of something, repeat this bath to allow your dreams to give you a better, in-depth interpretation of what is about to happen.

You will need:

- ½ liter of water
- 2 tablespoons olive oil
- 12 to 20 drops mugwort flower essence
- 12 dehydrated and sun-dried roses
- 1 tablespoon sugar
- 1 tablespoon coarse salt

EXERCISE
Relaxing Mind Bath to Dream Deep

To keep your mind properly focused during a ritual, I suggest you carry out this bath one to two hours before you perform it. Take all the time you need in this bath, and repeat it before a ritual whenever you feel it necessary. Memorize the feeling of relaxation and calm—that feeling of "I'm ready." Memorize it as if it were a tarot card as to bring it back as a whole mindset every time you go to perform a ritual.

You will need:
- 1 to 2 liters of water
- Handful of dried mugwort
- Handful of dried chamomile flowers
- 2 tablespoons honey
- Myrrh incense stick
- Incense holder
- Lighter or matches

Boil the water and add the herbs and honey. Let the infusion stand and cool until it reaches a temperature you feel is comfortable for bathing.

If you have a bathtub, add the mixture to it. If you use a shower, use a small bowl to help you apply the water. Place the incense stick in the holder and light it before entering the bath or shower.

If you wish, you can add a few drops of bergamot oil to the mix to provide a sensation of awakening and protection.

Dream Magic Insight
HERBAL SMOKE MEDITATION TO INCREASE DREAMS AND VISIONS

BY ALY KRAVETZ a.k.a. THE BRONXWITCH

In my personal experience, dreams have often been elusive. For much of my adult life, my sleep had been dreamless, and I struggled with sinking deeply into the stages of REM sleep needed for visible dream experiences. As a witch, I know that herbal medicine is available to all of us, and I felt that a solution might exist among the plants and flowers that I call my friends. But one thing that I have also learned about working with herbs is that, just like working with people, each one is different and affects the user in a different way.

After years of experimenting with each of the herbs that I am going to share with you, I found a combination that, without fail, helps me to sink into deep states of sleep with active and clear dreams. I found that while you can use this combination of herbs as an incense or a tea (if you don't mind bitter things), it performs best when smoked and inhaled.

You will need:
- 1 to 2 pinches of dried blue lotus flower (*Nymphaea caerulea*)
- 1 to 2 pinches of dried Mexican dream herb (*Calea zacatechichi*)
- 1 to 2 pinches of dried mugwort (*Artemisia vulgaris*)
- 1 to 2 pinches of dried mullein (*Verbascum thapsus*)
- Smoking bowl, pipe, or natural paper of choice
- Lighter

Gather your ingredients, and be sure to use dried, not fresh, herbs only. A small amount, roughly a pinch or two each, is all that you need. Grind your herbs together until they reach a fine consistency and add them to a smoking bowl, pipe, or natural paper of choice. Make a ritual of preparing for bed, making sure you won't be disturbed. When ready, take a seat in a meditative and comfortable position.

Begin deepening your breaths, inhaling and exhaling through your nose. Hold your smoking herbs in your hands and say a prayer of thanks to each of them. State your intention and let them know that they are being called on to be with you as you sleep and to guide your spirit self into the dream world. Light your herbs and take three to four slow inhalations, giving yourself a minute or two in between each. No rush here. Take your time and imagine the smoke filling your body from head to toe with each inhalation.

When done, carefully put out your herbs. Extinguish any candles or incense you may have lit (remember safety first!) and go to bed. Keep a journal by the bed to easily record any middle-of-the-night or early-morning memories. Repeat this ritual every night or any time that you need to receive messages in your dreams.

TRIBAL TALES
INGA PEOPLE / THE AYAHUASQUEROS

The Inga or Ingano Indigenous people are the Quechua group whose territories are found in Bolivia, Ecuador, and Peru. They are also in the extreme southwest of Colombia, especially in the current department of Putumayo, and to a lesser extent in the north of Nariño and in Piedmont and Santa Rosa.

Ingan migrations are closely related to the practice of traditional itinerant medicine. The group's eclectic and polytheistic spirituality not only involves the practice of healing activities and the cultivation of magical and medicinal plants but also the exchange, delivery, and sale of the plants themselves. The Inga's study and exchange of knowledge with other nearby communities and Indigenous peoples also enriches them.

Among the Inga, the wise elders and priests are called *sinch* (which translates as "old" or "wise"), and they receive various functions as mediums and healers, which are called *taitas* and *curacas* respectively. The sinch carry out the practice of administering *Banisteriopsis caapi* (also known as yagé) or ayahuasca with psychotropic effects. The importance of this plant in Ingan medicine implies a strong relationship with the cultures of the jungle, especially Andaquí, Cofán, Siona, and Witoto.

The preparation of the sinch begins from childhood. They are chosen by the taitas and educated in the knowledge of nature, spirituality, life, society, and medicine. They cultivate medicinal and magical plants in *chagras* with spiritual guardians, which is organized as a microcosm that represents natural forces, men and women, and interethnic and social relations.[39]

....

39. There is no correct translation for *chagras*; these are places of worship where traditional plants and vegetables are planted and harvested for the consumption of the Ingas using traditional methods. These sites are also used as schools for traditional herbology and as sacred sites for prayer and spiritual connection, and they are of vital importance to the Inga people. Although men are welcome to be part of the chagra and share some responsibilities, it is the women who lead and make the decisions in these sacred places where multiple foods are harvested for the tribe and their offerings, such as cassava, yage, potatoes, bananas, papaya, tangerine, lulo, and beans.

CHAPTER 15

DREAM GEMS & CRYSTALS

Although crystals and minerals are not part of traditional Latin American witchcraft (their use is rather an influence of the modern era of witchcraft), they are the tool of many sorcerers and psychics. They carry an enormous power that comes from the root of the earth. Every time you hold a small mineral or crystal in your hands—as well as any other rock—you are often unknowingly holding a piece of human history, which may have been there for several hundred years, perhaps thousands of years, marinating in the powers of time and carrying enormous potential with it.

When we add crystals and rocks to any spells related to dreams, it is important to take some aspects into account. For example, some crystals and rocks have active colors, such as red, orange, or vibrant yellow, and they omit a busy energy. We must opt for gems with colors that invite mental calm and rest, such as shades of white, gray, or blue. These may be pieces of quartz, blue agate, lapis lazuli, or light-toned amethyst.

Another important factor to take into account is that some gems have energetic properties that invite rest, calm, inner peace, and relaxation, such as rainbow moonstone and blue calcite. Although they are a bright color that activates energy, some red gems, such as jasper and garnet, are recommended to keep the mind awake during a prolonged meditation session or to complement spells and rituals focused on lucid dreaming and strengthening the memory.

Moonstone (A Favorite for Dream Witches)

Do not confuse moonstone with white labradorite or opaline, which are often mistakenly marketed as moonstone due to their similar colors.[40]

Moonstone has been a favorite stone of jewelers since ancient civilizations thanks to its lunar appearance.

For modern witches, this gem has not lost that spirit and fame. Moonstone is still associated with lunar deities, especially the Roman goddess Luna (the divine embodiment of the moon), and it is found in dozens of modern witchcraft books for all kinds of altars and spells associated with said deities, either to venerate them or request prosperity, protection, health, and healing from them.

The correct, simple way to activate moonstone is to put it in a clean bowl and place that bowl where it will receive direct rays of light from the full moon, either on a window or on a patio.

....

40. Moonstone has something called adularescence; it is a unique optical illusion that shows a milky-bluish glow on the surface of the gem. Most times, if your moonstone is hit by light and shows a blue-pale glow, it is real. Labradorite is a dark gray, black, or sometimes bluish crystal sold as moonstone. Opalite (not to be confused with opal) is a human-made variety of glass that can also be sold as moonstone as a mistake.

Once the gem is activated, it provides protection, healing, and mental clarity to its wearer, which is why it also makes a good gift from a witch to someone they want to protect.

Keeping a bowl with pieces of moonstone and crystal quartz on your altar grants you power over the world of dreams and the spirits that come from it, encouraging them to serve your magical workings.

A sorcerer who has entered the world of dreams more than once understands the secret that this gem hides and its connection with lunar deities and spirits of the night.

Moonstone against Psychic Attacks

To protect yourself against nightmares and unwanted dreams, keep a piece of moonstone inside your pillowcase. If you feel any kind of energetic disturbance coming from the gem during the night, which can manifest as a strange sound inside your pillow or the sensation of someone putting their hands on your head, this indicates that some witch is trying to launch a psychic attack against you or invade your dreams. Remove the gem immediately from the pillow, wash it with clean water, and rub it with oil of lavender, rose, geranium, sandalwood, or bergamot. Then light an incense stick to cleanse the energy and a white candle to give clarity to your guardian spirits. Once this is done, return the gem, now cleansed and recharged, to the pillow.

RECIPE
Moonstone-Charged Oil

If you have been practicing magic related to dreams for some time and have experienced the difficulties that it can bring, I invite you to prepare this oil and use it to anoint yourself.

You will need:
- One or more pieces of moonstone
- Equal parts rose, jasmine, and geranium essential oils
- 2 tablespoons dried rose petals
- Glass bottle large enough to fit all the other ingredients

Recommended moon phase: Performing this spell on a full moon night is preferred, as it will provide clarity and understanding during the spell.

Mix all of the ingredients in the glass bottle. Once the ingredients are combined, anoint your hands, elbows, knees, and the point of your head between your temples and ears (watch out for your eyes) with the oil.

After having prepared this oil several times, I have started mixing it with 2 tablespoons of base cream, which is easy to find in homeopathic pharmacies, for practicality. I use this cream as a body lotion before going to sleep.

Other Gems and Crystals

While moonstone is often favored among witches, practically all minerals have a certain level of influence on our emotions and mood, and for the most part, they help balance our emotional state and our mindset. In short, they all have properties that can be employed during spellwork. The following is a list of the gems and crystals that have proven to be most effective concerning the magic of dreams and night visions during my practice.

Amethyst

Amethyst is the stone of transmutation par excellence, and it has a high-energy value in the metaphysical field. Place a piece of amethyst on your pillow if you are experiencing a day-to-day situation that needs to be completely altered. Amethyst is kept in offices and rooms to change negative energy and thoughts into positive ones. It is placed on altars to complement rituals that seek to turn a negative situation into a positive one, transform nightmares into good dreams, and help you recover from a night of anxiety.

Blue Agate

Imagine you have just experienced a day that you would consider to be one of the worst days of your life! Your stress is through the skies, and because of it, you have the feeling of never-ending anxiety. A piece of blue agate will bring you the sense of healing calm that you need at this time.

Blue agate is the perfect stone to use for sleep/rest spells and jewelry related to dream walking and dream vision. A blue agate crystal ball can be placed on your dream altar to avoid those anxious nights, giving you a good break.

Celestite

Celestite, which is also referred to as celestine, has a pale bluish hue and attracts serenity, inner calm, and inspiration. It is perfect to wear as jewelry if you wish to meditate deeply or develop a clearer vision of the spiritual world during your astral and spiritual journeys.

Chrysanthemum Stone

Chrysanthemum stone is often confused with the peony stone, one of the rarest gems and perhaps difficult to find outside of Asia. It has the especially powerful ability to bring inner calm and emotional balance. The gem also helps to understand the secrets hidden in nightmares. To meditate with the rock and use it to delve into your inner dreams and fears, the stone must be placed on a wooden, glass, or ceramic plate apart from everything else on your altar or in your ritual space. Incense with a floral aroma must then be burned around it.

Crystal Quartz

Crystal quartz acts as an energy filter that allows you to distinguish what is real from what is not. It also magnifies the power of all other gems. For that reason, it is commonly placed in charm bags and amulets with a variety of uses. It is an excellent gem to accompany you during meditation sessions if you consider yourself a novice, and it helps to magnify clarity and understanding in dreams.

Fluorite

Fluorite is used to complement spells that stimulate memory, as well as to attract balance, love, friendship, enthusiasm, and good humor, and it is a good addition to any amulets used to balance the mind and protect your mental well-being. It is also an excellent talisman of protection that you can have in the bedroom to keep yourself safe while you rest.

Gold

The Inca and Andean civilizations—in the days prior to the colonization of America—used gold to make all kinds of ornaments, including rattles, earrings, masks, necklaces, bells, and flutes. Gold was not seen simply as a precious metal but as a symbol of the power of the tribe or family that owned it. It was a divine gift that was believed to grant its bearer direct contact with divinity or a higher power. Gold, although not highly represented in the field of sorcery, has been used to build and decorate altars to creator deities and spirits from the world of water and the world of dreams.

The symbols seen in dreams and omens were engraved in gold on masks and other objects, and these items were then considered sacred emblems among the Mochicas.[41]

Gold was associated with the sun, the day, and awakenings, and silver, which there was also large deposits of, was associated with the moon and night among these Indigenous peoples of America. Therefore, funerary masks were decorated with gold and not with silver; the gold masks gave the deceased the opportunity to wake up once their soul reached the afterlife.

Lapis Lazuli

Lapis lazuli is a magical stone used in multiple traditions of witchcraft. If you look for it in books, you will find that there is much folklore and magical uses associated with this gem.

Give someone a small blue pillow filled with flower petals and a piece of lapis lazuli to grant them sweet dreams, good luck, and psychic protection.

Onyx

Perhaps the most misunderstood gem of all, onyx causes depression, nostalgia, and sadness for many. It is the gem that corresponds to Capricorn (the astrological sign of excessive rigidity and order) and Saturn (the planet of karma and constant revision), and most other things associated with this dark gem seem to scream "caution" too. Onyx acts like a black hole in space, devouring light and everything in its path, and it can be used to absorb bad vibes and negativity. Inside a pillow of dreams, it will absorb feelings of sadness and melancholy, but it should be avoided for everyday use. Although it is a great ally for witches, onyx can lead people to deep depression and inner sadness.

....

41. The Moche or Mochica culture, also known as Proto-Chimú, is an archaeological culture
   of ancient Peru that developed between the second and seventh centuries AD.

Rose Quartz

Rose quartz is not only well-known for its ability to attract love but for its power to strengthen ties of friendship and trust and establish understanding among family members.

A white or pink candle and an incense stick scented with rose or peony should be lit next to a piece of rose quartz before sleeping. The charged crystal should then be placed next to your bed to attract happy, positive dreams. It will also help you to wake up in a better mood.

A pale blue or pale pink dream pillow filled with three pieces of polished rose quartz in the shape of a heart and equal parts cotton, feathers, and dried rose and lavender petals will allow you to dream with a loved one.

Selenite

Selenite has a highly powerful energetic vibration, and a small piece of selenite on the pillow leads you to connect with your emotional and spiritual body in perfect sync. If you feel as if you are not acting like yourself lately or feel disconnected, a couple of pieces of selenite inside or under your pillow provides the emotional calm needed to perform an accurate inner review.

Smoky Quartz

Smoky quartz is associated with clairvoyance and secrets (two topics entirely contrary to each other). The darkened surface of this quartz symbolizes something covered by fog or clouds (secrets), while the clear areas represent and encourage our ability to see beyond these impediments (clairvoyance).

If you are trying to decipher a recurring dream that seems difficult (or even impossible) to interpret, do not hesitate to place a saucer with three pieces of smoky quartz (to represent the three primordial gods of sleep that tend to stay hidden within them) on the bedside table. With a dropper, apply three drops of mugwort essential oil to each crystal. This little ritual will lead you to have more clarity while you sleep and as you focus your vision on the elements that you need to interpret or decipher. As we mentioned in chapter 13, mugwort clarifies our vision and understanding of the spiritual world.

✦ ✳ ✦

EXERCISE
A Crystal Mojo Bag

Crystal quartz, jasper, and garnet are all allied minerals of dream magic. Separately they work very well in a subtle way, and together they are a powerful ally for your connection to the dream world. I invite you to use the following exercise to create a mojo bag, as it will be a good accompaniment to your magical rituals.

You will need:
- Blue cloth bag (a mojo bag)
- Piece of crystal quartz
- Piece of jasper or garnet
- 1 teaspoon rosemary powder
- Blue or white cloth ribbon (between 6 and 18 inches [15 and 45 centimeters] long)
- Lavender essential oil
- Lighter or matches
- White candle in candleholder
- Cone of myrrh or palo santo incense
- Censer, small cauldron, or heat-resistant plate

If you wish to perform a long meditation session on your bed or a comfortable sofa and do not want to fall asleep but keep your mind focused on a specific purpose, fill the blue cloth bag with the crystal quartz (clarity, intuition, healing), the jasper or garnet (focus, energy, psychic protection), and the rosemary powder (protection).

Make seven knots in the blue or white cloth ribbon. Use the ribbon to tie the cloth bag shut and sprinkle a few drops of lavender essential oil on it.

Light the candle and incense and place this mojo bag near them while you do your meditation session.

Dream Magic Insight
QUARTZ AMULET TO PROTECT YOUR MIND
BY MIRA A. GADE

As witches, we work with our hands, cultivating, grinding, and mixing plants and incense; shuffling our tarot cards; and turning the pages of our spell books. We are always aware of our actions and how each spell we perform will manifest its results in the near future. Protecting our exhausted mind at night is of the utmost importance.

This ritual is simple and easy, and you can perform it at night before sleeping to protect your energy against psychic attacks, disturbing spirits, and any residual psychic energy in your environment.

You will need:
- Lighter or matches
- White candle
- Heat-resistant saucer of some kind
- Essential oil mixture of lavender and bergamot
- Piece of crystal quartz no smaller than a small coin
- Square piece of blue or indigo fabric

After taking a cold shower and getting ready for bed, light the white candle on a heat-resistant saucer; it can be a small cauldron or a metal tray. Rub no more than two drops of the essential oil in your hands. If you do not like to work with oils directly on the skin for any of the various reasons, you can dilute the oil with water. Proceed to rub the crystal between your hands for about thirty seconds with your eyes closed with slow and deep breaths.

Open your eyes, bring the crystal close to your face, and whisper the following incantation into it:

With my hands, with my mind, and with my words I enchant you.
Protect me while I sleep and take care of me while I rest.
Take care of my space and take care of my sleep.

Nothing interrupts my rest without first passing through you and your power guard.

Extinguish the candle and place the crystal on the blue cloth. Be sure it is on a surface near the bed before going to sleep. Every morning, cover the piece of quartz with the cloth and keep it completely wrapped.

On any occasion you feel some type of energetic or psychic disturbance, repeat the incantation with the same crystal.

TRIBAL TALES
THE INITIATORY RITES OF CAMORA

Camora is the name given to a group of individuals of Brazilian descent who live in the Amazon regions, mixing with the natives and locals but without losing or mixing their beliefs. The Camora families are a very recent and slowly expanding group that is made up mostly of families hoping to flee from the cities and modernity. They move to the mountains and attempt a temporary period of nomadic life, touring various places before settling in one spot for a long period of time.

The Camora, although they identify themselves mostly as Catholic, practice their own form of folk magic. For this magic, devotees venerate the spirits of the deceased, practice spells at the edge of rivers (these must be whispered in the ear of the water to be fulfilled), and perform all kinds of ritual baths and irrigations. They also look to *A Virgem das águas* (the Holy Virgin of the Waters), a powerful female deity who embodies motherhood and fertility, life and death, the oceans and rivers, and all forms of water.

The Camora families prepare all kinds of fruit-based dishes and salads that are thrown into the river for ritual purposes. They light colored candles on the rocks at the edge of the river during their ritual baths and carry out a beautiful and simple but symbolically powerful traditional initiation at the edge of the waters.

Everyone is welcome to take part in these rites. Huge buckets filled with fresh water from four local rivers are gathered, and silver coins and precious stones are added to the bottoms of these buckets. All kinds and colors of flowers are thrown into them. They are mostly roses, sunflowers, and chrysanthemums from the nearby markets, as well as wildflowers that grow alongside the rivers. The flowers and other plants are stripped one by one and with great care to keep just the petals in the water. A huge amount of honey and molasses that was prepared at home is added.

Initiates then bathe naked using bars of coconut soap, and a woman dressed in white sitting by the river performs chants and prayers in a dialect that only they seem to know. It is a form of what they call "Portuguese de the coast." It is a term I personally have never heard anywhere else, although it sounds similar to French.

Priestesses dressed in white enter the river with empty coconut shells and use them to add to the river water inside the large buckets full of flowers, coins and crystals, and honey and molasses. These sweet mixtures are then poured over the naked bodies of the individuals participating in the initiation, and they stand with their palms open toward the sky, ready to receive all the gifts and blessings of God in their hands.

Those who have silver coins fall into their hands during the bath are particularly blessed. They keep the coins in a small clay cauldron of water that is replaced every night of the dark moon (new moon), as this little talisman will grant long life and health to them and their loved ones.

These initiation rites, although as fast as they are simple, represent what they call O Primeiro (the first of all dreams). In their mystical tradition, although mostly Catholic, the world was incomplete until the goddess from the waters emerged from the sea and saw a lifeless world. She then took a sharp stone from the ground and cut her belly. Blood and water flowed from her belly for many days and many nights. Because of the pain, the virgin goddess fell asleep. During the days, all the first creatures emerged from the puddles of blood. During the long nights, the waters cleansed the blood of the world, allowing the plants to grow and the rivers and seas to flow.

After many moons, the virgin goddess remained asleep, and her body was sunk at the bottom of the waters. Coral reefs grew around her. The sirens made her a crown of mother-of-pearl and coral, and the seas and rivers continued to grow from her womb.

Trying to wake up the virgin goddess, the sirens brought honey from the coasts. This honey was made by animals and wild creatures. The sirens wanted to give her the sweet honey to drink and thus wake her up, but the honey dissolved in the waters before reaching the goddess. Over the years, as they came and went from the coasts to the bottom of the sea, the sirens got smaller and lost their memory. They became fish, and they now swim from one side to the other looking for food and are always agitated because they know that their mission is not complete.

The large buckets used in the rite are prepared with flowers, honey, and molasses to represent this first dream of the virgin of the waters. The priestesses, who help bathe the initiates, are dressed in white to symbolize the mermaids in pearl dresses who took care of the goddess.

CHAPTER 16

DREAM SPELLS

Since ancient times, people have created all kinds of different spells related to the dream world. In Hispanic culture, we identify four types of dream spells: healing spells, spells for the incubation of dreams, psychic communication spells, and dream walking spells.

Healing spells are well-known in modern sleep therapy, as well as in the traditional magic of the South American healers. Often these healing spells are induced dreams that lead us to repair our body and mind while we rest. These spells also let the body find other alternative ways of healing and strengthening to improve our health.

The second variety of dream spell focuses on incubating a specific type of dream. This includes dreaming of a lover, dreaming of a better future, and dreaming with signs or good omens.

There are also spells that focus on psychic communication. It is with these spells that we allow ourselves to receive and send messages while we sleep. Those dreams include long-distance psychic communication, such as communication with spiritual entities and ancestors, master guides from the other realm, and others.

Finally, there are the spells that focus on developing the psychic and mystical abilities of the sorcerer and taking them to the next level. Those spells allow us to lighten our energy even more while we sleep. With practice and constant work, these spells let us to explore the confines of our mind and raise our state of consciousness, leading to lucid dreaming, astral projection, etc.

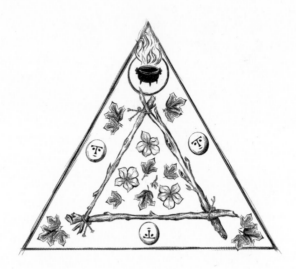

Dreamy Charm Bags

A charm, gris-gris, or mojo bag is a handmade amulet prepared to help you reach a specific goal or to stimulate a process. There are many types of charm bags in different cultures and magical traditions.

To create a simple charm bag, you first need a cloth bag in a color corresponding to your goal. Fill the bag with two or more elements that channel the type of energy you are looking for. To activate this amulet's power, it is advised that you make a circle with coarse salt (and perhaps a little rosemary), light a candle the same color as the charm bag and an incense stick, and hold the bag with you inside the circle. Perform a prayer or an incantation of your own to activate its power.

Charm bags are commonly kept close to the user (often tied with string around the neck or stored in a purse). In some situations, they are kept on the altar or in a specific place in the house. Charm bags associated with dream magic should be kept under a pillow, under the bed (on a saucer), next to the bed, or on a nightstand. And they should *not* be opened under any circumstances. If you must get rid of one, the most appropriate method is to burn it inside a circle of salt. You can also bury it at the foot of a tree or burn it at a crossroads and then bury the ashes.

EXERCISE
Charm Bag to Inspire Romantic Dreams

If you want to inspire romantic dreams in your lover, prepare this recipe.

You will need:
- Lighter or matches
- Red candle in candleholder
- Strawberry or rose incense stick or cone
- Incense holder or censer, small cauldron, or heat-resistant plate
- Pink cloth bag
- 2 or 3 pieces of rose quartz
- 1 tablespoon dried mugwort
- 1 tablespoon dried hibiscus flowers
- 1 tablespoon dried red or pink rose petals
- Recent photograph of you and your lover
- Lock of your hair
- Needle and thread or cloth tape (optional)

Recommended moon phase: New moon or moonless night

Light the candle and the incense, and place all your ingredients on your altar or workspace. Put soft and inspiring music on in the background. It can be a playlist of romantic songs that inspire the emotions you wish to convey during sleep: love, candor, seduction, lust, passion, romance, trust, etc.

With the background music playing, begin to calmly place all the ingredients inside the bag one by one (except the needle and thread), the last items being the photograph and lock of hair. Close the bag with a needle and thread, with candle wax, or by simply tying a knot with cloth tape.

Once the bag is sealed, hold it in your hands and recite this old incantation, duly translated, which comes from a Venezuelan lullaby:

Incantation (in English):

Into your dreams I step.
In them I anchor myself.
In them I find you.
In them I love you.

Original lullaby (in Spanish):

En tus suenos entro.
En tus suenos me anclo.
En tus suenos te encuentro.
En tus suenos te amo.

Once you have recited the incantation, blow out the candle and let the incense continue to burn. Place the enchanted sachet inside or under your pillow, and each night thereafter, light the same candle, recite the incantation in front of the candle, let it burn for twenty to thirty minutes, and blow it out again. Repeat this every night until the candle is completely consumed.

EXERCISE
Charm Bag to Focus Better in Your Dreams

Seeking clarity and understanding in our dreams is a never-ending task, which is why the more tools we can put into practice, the better results we can conjure up. Here is a practical and easy recipe to carry out.

You will need:

- Lighter or matches
- White candle in candleholder
- Any floral incense you have
- Incense holder or censer, small cauldron, or heat-resistant plate
- Blue, indigo, lilac, or pink cloth bag
- Piece of crystalline glass or a magnifying lens
- 1 tablespoon dried jasmine
- 1 tablespoon dried hop blossoms or tulips
- 1 tablespoon dried poppies

- Dried white rose bulb
- Pinch of dried lavender blossoms
- 1 piece of smoky quartz and 1 piece of crystal quartz (optional)
- Needle
- Blue or gold thread

Light the candle and incense, then fill your bag with all the elements (except the needle and thread) one by one while you chant the following incantation:

> **Crystal and glass, flower and grass,**
> **I enchant you in advance.**
> **Let me see the obvious, conscious, obnoxious;**
> **Show me what is hidden in front of me,**
> **opening my mind, clearing my dreams.**
> **Take me to see beyond the fog**
> **in any time beyond the clock.**

Close the bag, sew it shut with the needle and thread, then blow out the candle. Each night you wish to perform a dream ritual, hold the amulet and chant the incantation before going to sleep. Place the bag next to or under the pillow.

EXERCISE
Charm Bag for Prophetic Dreams

Craft this bag for divination, meditation, visualization, mediumship, and deep dream sessions.

You will need:
- Lighter or matches
- Blue or dark-colored candle
- Lavender incense (in any form you prefer)
- Incense holder or censer, small cauldron, or heat-resistant plate
- Blue or indigo cloth bag
- 1 tablespoon dried calendula flowers
- 1 teaspoon dried mugwort
- Frankincense essential oil

Recommended moon phase: This recipe is best prepared the night of a full moon.

Light the candle and incense, and fill the bag with the herbs, adding them one after another. Add two drops of the oil to the bag and close it.

Each time you are preparing to perform a spiritual session or mediumship experiment, light a candle and a stick of incense, then rub a bit of frankincense oil over the bag. Keep it close to you the entire session.

EXERCISE
Charm Bag for Sweet Dreams

This exercise shows you how to make a bag for sweet dreams that's not only perfect for you but perfect for gifting to someone you know is going through a difficult time or experiencing sleepless nights.

You will need:
- Blue, white, or rose-colored candle in candleholder
- Honeysuckle oil
- Sweet almond oil
- Lighter or matches
- Pink or rose-colored mojo bag
- 1 cotton flower
- 1 teaspoon dried bay or juniper leaves
- 1 teaspoon cane sugar

In the evening hours, anoint the candle with a few drops of both oils, then light the candle. Anoint the bag with a few drops of both oils inside and out.

Anoint your cotton flower lightly with the oils and place it, the dried leaves, and the sugarcane inside the bag. Close the bag and keep it near your bed or on your dream altar. Occasionally anoint it with a few more drops of sweet almond oil to keep it effective.

Magic Mirror of Dreams

Mirrors are energetic items that allow us to look at and monitor otherworlds. They are also portals to these otherworlds, so it is important to keep them clean and properly positioned where they reflect all possible light in a room. Due to the traditional belief that mirrors can duplicate everything they reflect, it is important to keep them away from the stove and prevent them from reflecting any garbage.

In magic related to dreams, mirrors are considered direct doors to our dreams. If a person is gazing into a mirror, an experienced seer can look at the mirror and see that individual's dreams projected in the reflection.

Any mirror placed in the bedroom must be purified beforehand. Mirrors, in their role as portals, can manifest dreams as well as nightmares, or they can be used by a more experienced magician to summon all kinds of nightmares, visions, and omens.

Mirrors have enormous and varied uses in magic. They can be a talisman for protection and communication with the world of dreams, the world of spirits, and the astral plane. Mirrors are also commonly used by magicians in magical wars to search for the hidden fears and nightmares of their enemies or to launch all kinds of psychic attacks against them.

EXERCISE
Easy Enchantments

Mirrors reflect good and evil back to their origin. With this enchantment and its variations, you can bless a mirror to act as an energy reflection in your favor. You can also seal it, preventing your nightmares or worst fears from projecting themselves into your reality while you sleep.

You will need:
- Dried mugwort
- Dried jasmine flowers
- Dried bay leaves
- Myrrh essential oil
- Piece of quartz crystal
- Bowl of water

- Hand mirror
- Dry cotton cloth
- Crystal glass
- Water
- Coarse salt
- Camphor oil

Recommended moon phase: New moon

On the night of a new moon, prepare an infusion with equal parts of the mugwort, jasmine flowers, bay leaves, and two drops of myrrh essential oil. Let the infusion cool and place the quartz in the infusion. Keep the infusion at rest for a few hours.

Use this infusion to wash the hand mirror completely, then use the dry cotton cloth to completely clean the mirror. Save the piece of quartz for when you will do this spellwork in the future. Place mirror in the bedroom.

Fill the crystal glass with clean water, coarse salt, and camphor. Place the glass under the bed, changing the water every three days.

Variation I

On a new moon night, fill a crystal glass with clear water and submerge a piece of crystal quartz in it. Replace the water every morning to have clarity in dreams and deep rest.

Variation II

To take care of someone's dreams, perfume a piece of blue or violet ribbon with lavender and mint essential oil. Tie a strand of the person's hair with a piece of this consecrated ribbon.

More Magical Baths

If you have enjoyed the bath exercises and recipes in this book so far, here are some more to incorporate into your practice.

EXERCISE
Bath Ritual for Dream Lovers

This ritual bath is to be performed between lovers to give them a quiet night of rest together loaded with confidence and protection. It will also allow them to feel more connected, even while they sleep, auguring a positive awakening.

You will need:
- Lighter or matches
- Red candle
- Light blue candle
- White candle
- Large bowl
- Boiling water
- 2 tablespoons fresh orange blossoms
- 2 tablespoons fresh red rose petals
- 2 tablespoons fresh white rose petals
- 2 tablespoons fresh hibiscus flowers
- 1 tablespoon star anise
- 1 tablespoon brown sugar
- Gardenia essential oil
- Lavender essential oil

Fill the bathtub with warm water and light all three of the candles. Prepare an infusion by filling the bowl with boiling water and adding all the elements (flowers, anise, sugar) except the oils. Let the mixture rest for about thirty minutes before adding it to the bathwater. Then, add six drops of gardenia essential oil and six drops of lavender essential oil.

At this point, the lovers can enter the tub and rest in it with their eyes closed for about ten minutes. They should use a timer so as not to exceed this time. After the ten minutes are up, the lovers can open their eyes and meditate or talk in the tub between fifteen to twenty-five minutes before going to sleep together.

You can complement this bath with rose soap or soap with lavender oils.

RECIPE
Bath to Unlock Your Mind

Prepare this bath to unlock your mind, relax your thoughts, and thus be able to achieve greater depth and clarity in your dreams. Simply mix all the ingredients in a glass jar, then add it to your bathwater and let it sit for fifteen to twenty minutes before using.

You will need:

- Bunch of dried hibiscus flowers or rose bulbs
- 6 drops of jasmine essential oil
- 6 drops of lavender essential oil
- 3 drops of neroli essential oil
- 3 drops of hibiscus essential oil

RECIPE
Bath for Dream Visions

Blend these ingredients and use them to take a magical shower before sleep. It will clear your mind and dreams so you see more than the simple evident facts.

You will need:

- Dried basil leaves
- Dried rosemary
- Dried hibiscus flowers
- Dried mugwort
- Dried rose water

EXERCISE
Soap to Have Beautiful and Happy Dreams

This exercise is not necessarily for a bath, but it is related. It creates a washing soap, not only putting what we know about oils and gems into practice but putting us to work with our hands.

You will need:
- White candle in candleholder
- Lighter or matches
- Glycerin soap base
- Large heat-resistant bowl and mixing spoon
- Lavender, roses, geranium, and bergamot essential oils
- Honey
- Heat-resistant silicone mold(s)
- Piece of oval or circular labradorite (optional)
- Piece of oval or circular crystal quartz

Recommended time/moon phase: A new moon or Wednesday night (Wednesday is ruled by Mercury, patron of communications.)

Light the candle and recite:

This mystical moment of crafting is blessed for all the spirits present.

Then, using a bain-marie or double boiler, melt the glycerin. Pour the liquid glycerin into the heat-resistant bowl, and add two to three drops of each of the essential oils. Mix well, adding the honey (2 tablespoons for each piece of soap).

Pour the mix into the mold(s) and add the gems to the soap. Let the soap dry in the open air for two hours. Then, proceed to unmold.

Make use of this soap exclusively at night, either a few hours before bed to keep your intuition and your energy field sharp or before performing any magical ritual.

Bonus Spells for Calm Nights and Good Dreams

I once created a spell to help my nephews sleep at night. They both have autism, and their medications would cause them severe anxiety and insomnia. Seeing as I am not a doctor or a professional therapist, there was not much I could do about that. But I could make this little spell, which was very helpful for me too; I was doing something useful.

Nightmares, sleep terrors, and insomnia are some of the biggest problems that many people face. Here are some bonus spells to make your dreaming time safe, calm, and even pleasant.

EXERCISE
Sleep Spell for a Child

This is the spell that I created for my nephews. If you have ever been to the Amazon, which is a great place to be and see, perhaps you will easily recognize the following exercise. This short and simple spell is similar to a ritual that we performed while exploring the Orinoco in Amazonas. At that time, we used snake oil and some dried herbs to stimulate rest.

Snake oil is a traditional liquor-oil highly popular in the towns of Venezuela, especially the version of the oil imported from Amazonas. It is used to soothe ailments and help with parasites in the body. Unlike the American snake oil of Chinese origin, which is often made with mineral oils, herbs, and sometimes animal fat, containing no true derivatives of snakes, this oil from Venezuela and Colombia is made with a mixture of pure vegetable oil, flowers of ajo sacha (*Mansoa alliacea*), piri piri (*Justicia pectoralis*) leaves, and leaves of wais (*Ilex guayusa*), as well as skin cuts and teeth from the snake known as *pucarara* or *surucucú* (*Lachesis muta*). This oil sometimes contains cane sugar as well.

For this spell, I changed ingredients to make a modern version of the recipe that is also more effective and less expensive.

You will need:
- Odorless cream base (find it on homeopathic pharmacies)
- Patchouli and gardenia essential oils

Begin with the odorless cream base and add six drops of patchouli essential oil and six drops of gardenia essential oil. Combine the cream and oils with both hands, spreading the mixture on them. Put your hands together in prayer, take a deep breath, and take a moment to visualize a circle of healing light forming between your hands. Feel this circle rotate, then sense the warm, healing light generate a tickle when rubbing against your skin. Continue visualizing for a few seconds.

Now open your eyes and visualize this halo of light separating into two as you open your hands. Place your hands around the head of the child (the patient), touching their temples with your fingertips.

Visualize both circles of energy and light spinning around your hands while you and the other person are in this brief trance where the energies are shared between one another.

Maintain this visualization for about two to five minutes. At the end, you simply have to "release" the light to the other person through your hands. Finally, physically release the other person, taking your hands off them.

EXERCISE
Consecrated Rope for Sleeping

Prepare this ritual to protect yourself during sleeping hours.

You will need:
- White or blue rope (at least 49 feet [15 meters] long)
- Cauldron
- Handful of dried rose petals
- Handful of dried jasmine flowers
- Handful of dried eucalyptus leaves
- Glass of brandy or orange liqueur
- Pinch of dried and ground ginger root
- Lighter or matches
- Purple or blue candle in candleholder

Recommended moon phase: Night of a new moon or a dark night

During a dark or new moon night, place the entire length of rope inside your magic cauldron. Add the next five ingredients one by one.

Light the candle and recite the following incantation five times with both hands holding the cauldron.

> **In this dark night, I summon the light to protect myself.**
> **This dark night, I call upon the dark to protect myself.**
> **This magical night, I recite this spell to claim long nights of rest.**
> **May my dreams and night be blessed,**
> **and may my dreams feel served.**

Pick up the rope and shake it. Tie the first end of the rope to the leg of the bed closest to the door, making a knot there. Move to the next leg of the bed, tying another knot there. Proceed the same way with each leg of the bed frame until you have managed to tie completely all sides. Once this magic operation is finished, you simply recite:

> **My spell is done; my bed and my dreams are protected.**
> **My spell is finished; this space is sealed.**

The remaining herbs and flowers in the cauldron can be used to create incense or to fill small protective magic sachets that can be given as gifts of protection to others. You can also bury them in the surroundings of your property.

EXERCISE
Pyramid Candle Spell

I performed this spell on an occasion when my nightmares, which were for some reason related to the moon phases, were becoming progressive. After performing this spell several different times, I found one of those pyramid candles, which were available in the market, to be pretty effective. If one is not available, you can use a large candle instead.

You will need:
- Purple or pink pyramid-shaped candle
- Orange and lilac essential oils
- Lighter or matches
- Small sprig of dried eucalyptus

Anoint the candle with the essential oils, light the candle, and burn the sprig of dried eucalyptus in the flame, then recite the incantation and let the candle burn out:

> My dreams are transformed; my dreams are manifested in signs
>   and guides that I can understand.
> Nightmares and visions that cause fear, in this home they have no
>   place.
> I keep them out of my mind.

EXERCISE
A Spell to Send Sweet Dreams to Someone

This spell is especially useful if someone close to you is going through a bad time. It will offer them nights of rest and moments of peace.

You will need:
- Photograph of the person (preferably a cheerful one)
- Pencil
- Wooden picture frame
- Scissors
- Yellow or white paper
- Three yellow candles in candleholders
- Eucalyptus, peppermint, and rose essential oils
- Lighter or matches
- Yellow or blue rope

Time: This spell can be performed any day you wish; just make sure you perform it before sunset.

On the back of the photograph, write the full name of the person and your good wishes under it. This sentiment can be something like "May you have sweet and beautiful dreams," "May your dreams always inspire you to pursue your goals and be better," or "May your dreams be full of joy and good omens." Place the photo in the frame.

Cut the yellow or white paper in the shape of a five-pointed star. Inside, write the messages and good wishes that you want this person to manifest in their dreams, such as "May your dreams help you through these moments, guide you, inspire you, empower you, and lead you to sound sleep, more and more. So be it."

Rub one of the candles with the oils and proceed to light it. With the rope, tie the framed photograph and the star together (preferably so the star remains covering the person's face).

Let the candle burn safely overnight, and light the second candle the next day and the third candle the day after that. On the third and final day, untie the paper star from the photograph. With the flame of the third candle, proceed to burn the star, consecrating the spell permanently. Place the photograph in a visible spot to keep this spell active for a long period of time.

EXERCISE
To Manifest Erotic Dreams

To have dreams full of romance and eroticism, brujas and sorcerers have several methods, and many of them, such as burning rose petals in the corners of the bedroom, opening a hole in the mattress to hide a bunch of lavender flowers and sewing it with red thread, or perfuming the rooms with floral incense before going to sleep, are very simple. Based on these easy but effective methods, I created this ritual, which uses simple and, at the same time, functional ingredients, that can be put into practice at home. Although the results take a few nights to manifest, I am sure you will be able to enjoy it too.

You will need:
- Charcoal
- Lighter or matches
- Censer, small cauldron, or heat-resistant plate
- Cup filled with equal parts of myrrh, dried jasmine, and dried roses
- Red cloth bag
- Red thread

To create and stimulate erotic dreams, light your charcoal; place it on the censer, in the cauldron, or on the heat-resistant plate; and add twelve pinches of the herb mix one by one. Let the smoke fill the room. Carefully, move the censer, cauldron, or plate to one corner of the room and add another pinch of herbs. Repeat that process in each corner, making your way back to the first one. When you have finished adding smoke to the room, wait a couple of hours to be sure the charcoal has been reduced to cold ashes and can't burn anything. Carry all the ashes in the red bag with what is left of the ingredients in the cup. Using the red thread, tie the bag like a necklace and wear it around your neck from dusk to dawn for several days, or if you prefer, you can hang it on the side of the bed.

Dream Magic Insight
NIGHT PLEASURE BATH AND EXPLORATION
BY MAWIYAH KAI EL-JAMAH BOMANI

The following is a sensual spell to transform sexual energy into dream abundance. The work aims to connect our physical desires to the astral plane via orgasms. It is a delicious snippet of sex magic that has the potential to challenge how we invoke magic outside of ceremonial venues. This exercise can be performed as often as you like; your orgasms are your business. After just one session, you will witness a deeper connection to your personal story of success. You will see what is achievable in your life and create a definitive road map to see your way through the rough patches. Your sexual energy and astral energy will produce an abundance within your life that makes traveling this path manageable and joyous. I hope you enjoy it.

You will need:
- Your favorite waterproof sex toy
- 9 drops of rose oil
- 9 drops of jasmine oil
- 9 drops of ylang ylang oil
- 2 cups dried hibiscus flowers
- 1 tablespoon cinnamon
- 1 tablespoon nutmeg
- Bar of lavender soap

Run your bath as you usually would. Place your toy within arm's reach. Then begin adding the oils, hibiscus flowers, cinnamon, and nutmeg. Stir the water and its contents with your dominant hand. As you stir, recite the following:

> **May my night pleasures bring me abundance in health, wealth, and financial stability.**

May the universe open my arms as I explore and align myself with
my greatest truth, my highest purpose.
As I sleep when all is done, may my dreams foretell the blessings of
sweet satisfactions to come.
I welcome the delicious emergence of multiple orgasms. Ase.

Quietly, enter the bath and begin washing with the lavender soap. Allow
the water to run over your body as you suds up and rinse. Repeat the chant
as you continue to wash. After the third wash, pick up your toy. Touch the toy
to your heart space and recite the mantra again. Now it's time to use your toy.
Go for what you know. As you enjoy your exploration, think about the goals
you have set for yourself. Envision yourself reaching every goal and experiencing the happiness that comes with feeling seen and blessed by the Spirit
of accomplishment. After reaching your orgasm, thank your Spirit, your Soul,
for partaking in this most sacred event. Wash your body once more. Repeat
the mantra one last time and then exit the tub.

Once you are dried and ready for bed, settle into the goals you visualized fulfilling during your orgasm. Focus on those experiences until you fall
fast asleep. By morning you will be well on your way to stardom.

TRIBAL TALES
A VENEZUELAN FOLK HISTORY
ABOUT MIRRORS AND MAGIC

In the Montaña de Sorte Natural Monument (Cerro María Lionza) in Yaracuy, Venezuela, you can find the Rio Vivo (River Alive). It is not really a river but a kind of tiny valley hidden between the mountains. In it, there is a common open grave full of broken mirrors of all sizes. Mirrors are thrown there once they have fulfilled their function.

Witches gather in the evenings for a great celebration. They drink aguardiente and smoke tobacco all night, sharing the light of bonfires, lanterns, and cell phones, providing a sense of familiarity and security in the middle of the night.

Those witches travel to the celebration from the cities with their mirrors, large and small, and they celebrate all kinds of curses and spells in front of these mirrors. The most curious thing here, however, is their masks.

When witches visit the mountain of Sorte on the day of the goddess Maria Lionza, tradition dictates that they must wear masks—obviously because you cannot let your enemies see you through the mirrors, for then they will know who you are.

Because of Maria Lionza and her *faeries court de ella*, the visions of the witches are just a pale reflection of what the water and the mirrors can see.

Once the long night of curses and spells is over, the witches head to Rio Vivo in a rowboat. There, they throw their mirrors into the grave until they break, ensuring their enemies and any spirits they send cannot see who cast the painful curse on them.

CHAPTER 17

DREAM HEALERS (CURANDEROS & YERBATEROS)

One of the main reasons why so many people travel to the Amazon, as well as parts of the Caribbean, for healing is because the Indigenous magic practiced by native witches, beyond being amazing folklore, is quite real and effective. The local herbal remedies and cures, which are prepared with native Amazonian flowers and pure water from waterfalls and streams, are potent and fast.

One of the most common symptoms of being under a spell or curse is constant insomnia—a sometimes contagious insomnia that ends up affecting everyone in the house. Many people dealing with this issue travel to Amazon and different parts of the Caribbean to cure their insomnia.

Insomnia, when caused by hexes or spells, can present as a feeling of anxiety mixed with physical exhaustion, a feeling of constant worry that keeps the affected person awake for long nights.

The affected person often begins to take all kinds of medicines. These medical syrups, pills, and treatments can easily work, but sometimes, these kinds of modern medicines can just alter the individual's metabolism and lead them to try stronger and stronger drugs and medications.

I am not claiming to be a doctor, and I am not against modern medicine, but watching members of my family constantly struggle with the effects of these very expensive treatments just made me consider my own approach and examine how important it is for many people to try alternative methods and cures. That's why it was so crucial for me to start learning with more dedication from the Indigenous practitioners and curanderos in the villages and towns. These individuals are not claiming to be "the only cure," but what they are claiming to be is a "medicinal, herbal alternative" to support your process while the first solutions and medicines do the work.

In a large number of cases, the same doctors who prescribe or suggest the medicine end up directing their patients to a healer. It is pretty normal to find a person coming to you who was referred by a medical specialist. If it is within their financial means, the person can travel to other corners of the world to have their conditions and ailments treated. However, insomnia in these regions has always been cured by healers and curanderos with the waters of the river.

Traditional curanderos learn to heal by studying and channeling the healing spirits of herbs and various plants. The curandero ends up being a physical healer, an herbal therapist, and a *brujo-hechicero* (an herbal witch and sorcerer). They are what we in South America commonly call a *yerbatero* or, in the more urban and modern vocabulary, what we call a *yerbero*.

These yerbateros and healers cure patients with local herbs. They do not go looking for the most expensive herbs brought from other parts of the world in the market just because a book tells them to. Instead, they learn which herbs grow in their environment. These herbs are literally close at hand, nourishing themselves day after day and night after night with the sorcerer's own energy. They sometimes grow by the side of the road, and they are often the plants that great books of herbal magic tend to underestimate.

Naturally these traditional herbalists—to use one name for them—learn to harvest the same local plants found in pots and small home gardens. Common herbs such as:

- *Rosemary:* For all kinds of respiratory conditions
- *Mint and spearmint:* To calm nervousness and help sleep
- *Eucalyptus:* To relieve coughs and clean the lungs
- *Ginseng:* To treat exhaustion and fatigue
- *Aloe vera:* To consume with water to cleanse the system; it works wonders on the skin.
- *Chamomile:* To help sleep and to treat digestive disorders
- *Dandelion:* For cholesterol
- *Parsley:* For kidney health
- *Echinacea:* For the immune system

- *Coriander:* For fatigue, insomnia, and stomach problems
- *Basil:* For the immune system; it is incredible when mixed in tea with coriander and chamomile to help sleep.

Although insomnia is not the only thing that these healers cure, it is one of the main reasons why people go to them. This is different than going to someone to buy a remedy. Patients go to be cured and learn to heal themselves. You don't go to a healer for them to heal you; you go to a healer so they can help your body remember how to heal itself, finding support for it in local herbs and flowers.

Suffering from insomnia can easily ruin a person's daily routine, and then the consequences of not having slept well arrive: headaches, bad moods, neck pain, fatigue, and feeling tired and negativity throughout the day. A person with insomnia can end up drinking more coffee than they need, which can cause stomach and kidney problems in the long run. The caffeine in the blood ends up causing more insomnia, and they get into a vicious little cycle of drinking coffee to stay awake, taking sleeping pills to get rest, drinking more coffee to pass the effect of the pills again, and then taking more pills to counteract the coffee.

Now, when a witch suffers from insomnia, what energy or enthusiasm do they have for their magical work? To carry out their spells and rituals? To prepare an altar and honor their loved ones? They're just too exhausted for it all.

Being a traditional healer is something that does not happen overnight by reading books. It is a doctrine that ends up being a lifestyle focused on healing processes and using herbs for medicinal, magical, and even divinatory purposes. Depending on the region, the curandero may rely entirely on herbs, or they may learn to heal using tree balms and even river rocks to channel and draw disease out of the body.

This process I just mentioned can be carried out through dreams. This is done either by sending their own energy from one point on earth to another through various energetic channels or by extracting residual energy from the world of dreams and directing it toward the person in need.

Dream Healing

To achieve a good start working with the energy therapy known as dream healing, you mainly need to keep your mind clear and focused on the person to be healed. Carry out this mystical work at times when you don't feel entirely exhausted, or it simply won't work because your body will not be able to use its own energy to redirect other forms of healing energy toward the individual in question.

When healing, I suggest using a talisman or some kind of amulet. This will allow you to maintain an energetic link with the person you wish to heal. It will be very helpful in your first attempts at healing—or at least while you gain more experience. Perform this energetic work totally focused and without any distraction.

EXERCISE
Dream Healing

To put this ritual to the test, sit cross-legged in a comfortable space, either on a chair or on a soft rug on the floor. Keep your hands together with the palms facing each other to prevent any energy from escaping. Relax your mind with your eyes closed, and as you breathe slowly and deeply, visualize how the healing energy of Mother Earth manifests in shades of green, yellow, and violet and moves from the ground to your feet. Through there the energy is absorbed and distributed to the rest of your body.

Maintain this visualization for ten to fifteen minutes. Keep a slow and deep breathing rhythm, and make an effort to keep your back straight and your muscles relaxed. Release any tension coming into your body without worries. If you suddenly feel you need to move, you are free to do it; don't stress.

Once the meditation time has finished, separate your hands and face your palms in two different directions: one pointing to the ground and the other above your head and pointing to the front. In this way, you let go of all the extra accumulated energy that your body has processed. You release it to not carry it anymore. The energy that feels heavier and more charged will instantly seek the exit back toward the earth, while the energy that was healed from the earth through your body will be lighter and will move upward, seeking to escape or manifest through your other hand.

Maintain this position for about two to three minutes, and then proceed to open your eyes. Get up calmly and notice how your body feels. I recommend you take notes on this. How do your legs feel? How do your arms feel? How do your neck and spine feel? Do your hands feel hot or cold? How do the soles of your feet feel?

Keep this exercise in practice for several days in a row so that you notice how your body is handling it and how the energetic sensation in your body changes.

Variation

We are going to try the same exercise as before in all its simplicity. The only difference is that this time you are going to include an object in the form of a talisman. The object should belong to someone close. They can be a friend or a loved one. Once you have selected an appropriate object, you are going to carry out the entire exercise while keeping it in your hands or inside your workspace.

A Note about These Exercises

All human beings are made up of the same elements and we have the same organs, yet our bodies act and react differently in different circumstances. Your energy system is not the same as everyone else's, so it will adapt little by little to these sessions, reacting in new ways each time. For example, when I practiced a healing exercise in February of 2019 with nine people, all who had attended at least one session previously, the results were as follows:

Two of these people had what they described as a "prolonged deep ringing" in their ears that disappeared a few minutes after the session ended.

Two other people had a prolonged post-session feeling of sleepiness and tiredness accompanied by tingling in the palms of the hands and feet.

Four other people only had a slight tingling in their palms during and after the energy healing work.

Only one person in the session reported a slight tingling in the back of the neck and an icy sensation in the ears.

The method we used was distance healing in a closed circle. Everyone in the yoga room rested on an exercise mat about 2 feet (80 centimeters) away from each other, and each person was holding a photograph of the person to their right. We meditated for about twenty minutes with the scent of eucalyptus and myrrh from various incense sticks in every corner.

To harmonize and balance the energy of the room, we put on a playlist with the sounds of soft drums and flutes that reminds me of the popular music of Peru and Bolivia. This helped create a perfect atmosphere of meditation to relax the senses.

Dream Crystal Healing in Modern Metaphysics

In modern metaphysics, dreams play an important role; they are the means through which students ascend to the nine astral planes and from there are trained by the ascended masters in different disciplines. These healing processes are the result of our energetic evolutionary process, for which we are being trained at this precise moment in the modern era.

From the vision of modern metaphysics—and more specifically from the vision of Christian metaphysics in Latin America—the healing that we carry out during our meditation processes plays an essential role in the evolution of humanity. I believe this daily practice must be done to heal humanity of all its grudges and pains from past war, which will allow the human race to evolve and reach the next step.

In the academic practice of the Christian Metaphysical School of Conny Méndez in Venezuela, the practice of energetic healing sessions, or *Imposicion de manos* (healing with hands over the head of a person), takes us to the metaphysical schools of the seven rays. Each of these seven schools or temples exist in the metaphysical plane and were founded one by one by the great knight Saint Germain in each of his multiple incarnations.

Each of these seven schools is a functional temple of healing and wisdom built with energy blocks. Their walls, floors, and towers take on the appearance of crystals and minerals, such as the blue ray school, which is guarded by the Archangel San Miguel and has walls and towers of lapis lazuli and blue and violet agate, and the school of the gold-ruby ray, which is guarded by the Archangel Uriel and has walls of gold and ruby as high as great mountains.

In the mysterious teachings of Christian metaphysics, schools function as energetic temples that students attend through astral projection for wisdom, personal evolution, and healing. From these points, energy can be redirected to different directions on the planet and to different people to help them in their energy healing processes while they sleep. When these people are unconscious, their energy field is more susceptible and likely to perceive changes and external energy influences.

Dream Magic Insight
RITUAL DE SAN JOSE DORMIDO
BY LAURA DAVILA

Sleep is crucial to our development, health, and well-being, and it is of great importance and vital to our magical and psychic abilities. But what happens when we deal with insomnia and struggle falling asleep, staying asleep, or getting quality sleep? Most studies suggest that insomnia is related to stress and worry about situations totally out of our control. It's a well-known fact that the better we sleep the better we feel, but how can we achieve that when there are so many things that we are worrying about at once, especially in troubled times?

My grandmother was a Mexican bruja who was very devoted to her saints and folk saints—just like a lot of our Latina *abuelas* who saw and experienced magic and religion in a particular and very distinctive way, keeping their faith and their trust in the sacred and at the same time radically distancing themselves from the dogma and hypocrisy of the institution. They were entrepreneurs and matriarchs. They took care of their families. They were pioneers who faced a lot of situations in life that they worried about in countries where the man (not always) helped a lot.

My grandma used to have a lot of saints around her house—some of them at the kitchen, others at the entry—but there was one I felt drawn to, and not in a really nice way. This saint was next to her bed and was always sleeping and relaxed, and it kind of bothered me because in my opinion everyone was working but him.

You may be familiar with Saint Joseph the Carpenter, or with his role as the father of Jesus iconography, but this title that I'm going to introduce you to is not as common as the other ones. The name is Sleeping Saint Joseph.

Saint Joseph is a custodian, a caretaker; his job is to take care of anything that comes to us unexpectedly, just as he did in his life, but he is also a protector.

This ritual is very simple, but it will bring a lot of benefits to your sleep.

You will need:

- Black ink pen
- Paper
- Your favorite essential oil used for sleeping (I use jasmine.)
- Sleeping Saint Joseph statue/image or prayer stamp

Every time you are facing worries or any situation that takes your sleep away and does not let you rest, write a note about that situation. Rub the note with the essential oil and place it under Saint Joseph. Do not forget that in Latin America San José is also known as the Terror of the Demons, so with this ritual he comes to our refuge and helps us fight against the forces of evil and spiritual disturbances while we are sleeping.

TRIBAL TALES
KARAJÁ PEOPLE / INY

The Iny are an Indigenous people of Brazil who have lived since time immemorial in the Araguaia River basin.

For the Iny, the village is the unit of autonomous social and political organization in which the decision-making power lies with the male heads of the extended families. The village is made up of a row of the houses of each extended family along the river in a north–south direction. There is a special house set apart and separated by a ceremonial plaza. It is known as Idjassó Hetô or Casa de Aruanã (House of Men), which is the center of ritual life and where the sacred masks created to be used in ceremonies remain.

The Iny conceive the universe as consisting of three levels:

- The underwater world, which has many names, is where humanity emerged and where the Idjassó live, as do the protective entities and the ancestors of the Karajá and all their deities and very ancient spirits that manifest themselves through the rain.
- The terrestrial world (Araguaia) is the visible world that we inhabit. The only way out is through water, dreams, and death.
- Last is the cosmic world. The terrestrial world gives the rain, and it is where powerful beings live and the soul of the shaman or priest goes. It is their job in life to maintain safe and balanced communication with the cosmic world. Through the Arauaje (dance in the rain), the priests manage to connect with the cosmic world to channel and transmit messages, dreams, prophecies, and healing powers.

Culturally and socially, the row of houses, the plaza, and the men's house are considered spaces analogous to the three worlds. They are three Karajá regional groups as well, and they also represent the trilogy.

According to their myths, their ancestors lived under the seabed of an underwater town where fish were abundant. The ancestors lived among the people (the water also being part of the earth) because they lived in full eternity. Although they had abundant food and a long life, they lived in a small, cold space bounded by walls made of coral and river stones.

Wanting to know the surface world, a young man began an extensive search. One rainy day, he found a passage called Inysedena (the rain portal that connects the physical world with the world of spirits). This passage took him to the island of Bananal. Once there, he was fascinated by the beauty and riches of Araguaia and by the ample space to run and live, as well as the heat of the sun. The young man returned to gather relatives and friends to climb together to the surface.

After some time living on the surface, they found death and death found them. In the earthly world, nothing was eternal. So, they wanted to return to under the river, but the entrance was now closed and guarded by a large snake, Guyii, who was placed there by order of Koboi, the first of men and the head of the people of the waters. Never being able to return, the people settled in the world, seeking to build their houses up and down the river.

After their first generation inhabiting the earth, Kynyxiwe (a hero and deity of the river and rain) arrived and married a Karajá girl. He went to live in her village, and he taught them fishing, hunting, the interpretation of dreams in order to communicate with the ancestors and the sacred dance in the rain.

Kynyxiwe passed away after having many children. Being an old man and the direct bridge between the world of the living and the world of spirits, the priests dance in the rain to connect with him so he can serve as a messenger between both worlds.

For the Iny, dreams represent (as in most Indigenous communities) messages from the ancestors. For them, these messages are created and woven as a network by the oldest spirits and are sent through the sorcerers and priests to serve humanity.

The dreams help them discover who the next shamans or priests of the tribe will be. Dreaming is considered an act of healing and spiritual integration, and having dreams implies that you are connecting with the world of water and receiving messages from the spirits. The dreams received during a rainy night are sacred messages of vital importance.

In their polytheistic traditions, rain is a sacred element that acts as a bridge between the worlds. When the rain fills the rivers and they overflow, it is an omen that the ancestors and high spirits are angry. Rainwater is celebrated but not collected or stored by the people, as the blessings must remain fresh and be respected, not used later. Even so, rainwater can be anointed on the foreheads of children so they have happy dreams where their guardian spirits will be present.

CONCLUSION

You have finished this book! Perhaps it gave you many answers. Perhaps it generated even more questions. Both results are entirely valid.

Dream Witchery was written with the intention of addressing one of the most common topics of magic and sorcery in the Spanish-speaking culture, and I am honored that all the stars have aligned to allow me to be the one who transmitted the message.

Dream Witches are no different from Water Witches, modern witches, Green Witches, and other seekers and practitioners of the esoteric arts. They, like all of those just mentioned, simply climb the same tree but from a different branch, and our witchcraft is like a great tree whose branches do not stop growing or multiplying. Some fall and no one remembers that those branches were there, while others continue to grow and spread, allowing others to climb on them.

The moment you take a practice, make it your own, and put it into work constantly, it becomes your path. Whether you keep it as yours or open it to others is entirely up to you.

The magic of dreams from the Latin American perspective is related to ancestors, our folklore, the morning rituals of the grandmother, and the recipes and traditional medicines of the village healer. It took me years of travel and dozens of journals full of old recipes to make this book. Now this practice is yours. Nurture it with your daily practice, with your own results, with your wisdom, and with your intuition. Bring and guide others; become that new sorcerer and healer who heals those who seek you. But above all, honor yourself as you honor your practice.

Happy dreams and blessed be your steps.

RECOMMENDED READING

Putting this book together was many things but easy. In Latin America, we have infinite esoteric and spiritual traditions that are linked to our Indigenous roots. I was afraid I'd end up doing one of those books that just pretends to be aware of decolonization and Indigenous brujas but, at the end, only rebrands and repackages Western magic and wicca for people of color.

This book required multiple books, night readings, and constant feedback and exchange of information with my family in Venezuela, in Turkey, in Chile, and other places, who sent me photos of the books I should consult and even made corrections to what I wrote.

Here is a list of the books and articles that ended up being useful for my search, giving me more context of different terms, which can have a different use in each different country or guiding me in the process to shape a couple lines. I have divided them up by the language in which they are written.

En Español

Acerca de la institución del kebíchi entre los chácobo del Oriente Boliviano by
   Silvia Balzano

Brujos y Chamanes: Las más Importante Selección de Amuletos y Hechizos by
   Roberto Bustos

"Chácobo 1970: 'Eine Restgruppe der Südost-Pano im Orient Boliviens.'" by
   Heinz Kelm

"Creaciones míticas y representación del mundo: el ganado en el pensamiento simbólico Guajiro" by Michel Perrin

Creencias, ritos, usos y costumbres de los indios catíos de la Prefectura Apostólica de Urabá by Severino de Santa Teresa

"Cronología: Esclavitud y trata del negro en América" by José Luis Gómez-Martínez

Diccionario enciclopédico de la lengua yanomami by Lizot Jacques

"El camino de los indios muertos" by Michel Perrin

"El colonialismo en la crisis del XIX español" by Roberto Mesa

Emberá (Chocó); Literatura de Colombia Aborigen. En pos de la palabra by Fernando Urbina

Emberás: territorio y biodiversidad: estrategias de control en escenarios de conflicto edited by Camilo Antonio Hernández

Estudios fonológicos del grupo Choco by Hoyos Benítez, Mario Edgar Aquirre Licht, and Daniel Guillermo

Fundamentos Morfosintácticos para una gramática Embera by Daniel Aquirre Licht

"Hacer los sueños: una perspectiva wayuu" by Paz Reverol Carmen Laura

Jaibanás: los verdaderos hombres by Luis Guillermo Vasco Uribe

La Guía Latinoamericana de Diagnóstico Psiquiátrico -Versión Revisada- y el Diagnóstico Centrado en la Persona by Cayetano Heredia

"La lógica de las claves de los sueños. Ejemplo Guajiro" by Michel Perrin

La medicina tradicional de los pueblos indígenas de Mexico by Carlos Zolla

Las Capitulaciones de Indias en el siglo XVI by Milagros del Vas Mingo

La trata de los esclavos: historia del tráfico de seres humanos de 1440 a 1870 by Hugh Thomas

Los practicantes del sueño: el chamanismo wayuu. by Michel Perrin

"Los significados sociales de la enfermedad: ¿Qué significa curar?" by García Gavidia Nelly

In English

"Chácobo: Society of Equality" by Gilbert Prost

"A Contribution to the Ethnography of the Karajá Indians of Central Brazil" by George Rodney Donahue

Black Atlantic Religion: Tradition, Transnationalism, and Matriarchy in the Afro-Brazilian Candomblé by James Lorand Matory

The Brazilian Sound: Samba, Bossa Nova, and the Popular Music of Brazil by Chris McGowan and Ricardo Pessanha

End of a World: The Selknam of Tierra del Fuego by Anne MacKaye Chapman

The Formation of Candomblé: Vodun History and Ritual in Brazil by Luis Nicolau Parés

Hain: Selknam Initiation Ceremony by Anne MacKaye Chapman

Manipulating the Sacred: Yoruba Art, Ritual, and Resistance in Brazilian Candomble by Mikelle Smith Omari-Tunkara

The Negro in Northern Brazil: A Study in Acculturation by Octavio da Costa Eduardo

Plants of Life, Plants of Death by Frederick J. Simoons

Sacred Leaves of Candomblé: African Magic, Medicine, and Religion in Brazil by Robert A. Voeks

Slavery and African Ethnicities in the Americas: Restoring the Links by Gwendolyn Midlo Hall

En Français

Culte des Orishas et Vodouns à l'ancienne Côte des esclaves en Afrique et à Bahia, la Baie de Tous les Saints au Brésil by Pierre Verger

Em Português

Cosmologia e sociedade Karajá by André Amaral de Toral

Fluxo e Refluxo: Do tráfico de escravos entre o Golfo do Benin e a Bahia de Todos-os-Santos, do século XVII ao XIX by Pierre Verger

Galinha D'Angola: Iniciação e Identidade na Cultura Afro-Brasileira by Arno Vogel, Marco Antônio da Silva Mello, and José Flávio Pessoa de Barros

Hetohoký: um rito Karajá by Lima Filho and Manuel Ferreira

Iroco: Coleção Orixás by Cléo Martins and Roberval Marinho

Maria e Iemanjá: Análise De Um Sincretismo by Pedro Iwashita

O Candomblé Da Bahia by Roger Bastide

O Pantheon Encantado: Culturas e Heranças Étnicas na Formação de Identidade Maranhense 1937–65 by Antonio Evaldo Almeida Barros

Orixás by Pierre Verger

Os voduns do Maranhão by Maria Amália Pereira Barretto

Ser escravo no Brasil: Séculos XVI–XIX by Katia M. de Queirós Mattoso

Tambor-de-Mina e Tambor-de-Crioula by Oneyda Alvarenga

WITCHERY GLOSSARY

Agague: a long crown made of small feathers that extends to cover the entire back

alapujawaa: sleeping action

Arojie: necklaces made of wild animal teeth

bilocation effect: Multiple methods exist and are used by witches and brujas to enter in different ways in the dreams of others, either to observe the dreams of a loved one or to manifest all kinds of fears during the hours of rest. In Latin America, as well as in Portugal, folklore spells of that teach to disturb the dreams of other individuals are very common. When these "attacks" occur, they are commonly channeled involuntarily by the children of the house.

brujeria: the term that America Latina uses to refer to esoteric-religious practices

brujos: all those who practice some form of Afro-Caribbean esoteric religion

Caima (or Chaima): an Indigenous spiritual worker from the pre-Hispanic period

Carojeoje: priests of the Yuri tribe

Inysedena: the rain portal that connects the physical world with the world of spirits

Jabbe: bells made of teeth and seeds are tied to the ankles to create all kinds of sounds while priests of the Yuri tribe dance around the ritual fire

Javi: entities who act as nocturnal demons made of shadow and animal blood

Jiojio: spirits of the campfire

kabimaras: spirits of the waters and rivers

Kugjo (also Junkgo or Kojgo): the symbolic language of the spirit world that is used to interpret dreams

Lapü: "dream" in Wayuunaiki, the language of the Wayúu

Maleiwa: the creator of everything, especially everything that moves, lives, and breathes, as well as the founder of society and order

Miyakira: the art of painting one's face with the family colors

mou: a bridge formed by trees that connects our rivers with the rivers of the otherworld

Obeba: the spirits of ancestors so old that they are about to be reborn

Oütshii, Outsu, or Jarima: a woman of the Wayúu tribe who is prepared and trained to be the traditional doctor and herbalist

ozunbi: spirits of the rocks and the earth

palero: a practitioner who has been initiated into the Palo Monte rites, a magical-religious and initiatory current that separates itself into several paths and is very popular in South America

Parahuayo: the light of the sun (or the sun god itself)

Piachi and the Alijunas: young maidens of the Wayúu tribe who move around the city, although both terms often also apply to small children and the elderly

Wanülu: the spirit that embodies evil, envy, disease, and death

Yias: visions that the serpent goddess has transmitted through poison

Yimika taai: prediction through dreams

Yoroa: members of the Yanomami tribe anointing the tips of their arrows and blowpipes

Yupu Ushi: ingesting the ashes of the deceased

Yushini: the souls of the dead whose names have been forgotten and therefore do not remember who they were

GUEST SPELLCASTERS

Miss Aida

Miss Aida (Cuba, United States) is a psychic, medium, witch, and author of *Hoodoo Justice Magic: Spells for Power, Protection, and Righteous Vindication,* and *Hoodoo Cleansing and Protection Magic: Banish Negative Energy and Ward Off Unpleasant People,* along with many other books.

Temperance Alden

Temperance Alden is a hereditary folk witch with over eighteen years of practice devoted to witchcraft and Paganism. She founded Wild Woman Witchcraft and is a podcaster and the author of *Year of the Witch* (Weiser Books, 2020).

Oncle Ben

Oncle Ben (France) is a witch, spiritualist, and elder of two different magickal traditions: NY Wica Tradition and the Minoan Brotherhood Tradition. He is also the author of *Les Secrets de Marie Laveau* and *Manuel d'Hellénisme.*

Mawiyah Kai EL-Jamah Bomani

Mawiyah Kai EL-Jamah Bomani is a native New Orleanian writer and spirit woman. She is the recipient of the Southern Black Theatre Festival's 2012–2013 Playwright of the Year Award for her play *Spring Chickens.* Mawiyah is also the author of the plays *Crows Feet, Bourbon, Men of the AmonRa Society,* and *Hair Anthem.* Mawiyah is an educator, eighth-generation witch, Egun medium, and priestess of OYA in the Yoruba system of spirituality. She also is editor in chief of the culture and Afrikan traditional spirituality e-zine *Oya N'Soro*, host of *FishHeadsinRedGravy* podcast, and author of *Conjuring the Calabash: Empowering Women with Hoodoo Spells & Magick*.

Ariana Carrasca

Ariana Carrasca (United Kingdom), also known as the Oak Witch, is a British-Latina folk witch and writer and content creator for the popular YouTube channel *The Oak Witch*.

Phoenix Coffin Williams

Phoenix Coffin Williams (United States) is an archpriest of the Correllian Nativist Church of Wicca. He is also a licensed clinical mental health counselor in private practice in New York state. He is the chief priest of the Temple of Holistic Knowledge. His career and ministry can be defined as activism and advocacy. At present, Phoenix is developing the Blue Door, a program designed to train Wiccan and magickal clergy in professional pastoral counseling, leadership skills, organizational development, conflict resolution, and peer education training from Wiccan and magickal perspectives.

J. Allen Cross

J. Allen Cross (Oregon) is a folk witch, psychic medium, paranormal investigator, podcaster, and author of *American Brujeria: Modern American Folk Magic* and *The Witch's Guide to the Paranormal: How to Investigate, Communicate, and Clean Spirits*.

Laura Davila

Laura Davila (Mexico, United States), also known as Daphne la Hechicera, is a fifth-generation Mexican witch, a long-time practitioner of Mexican *ensalmeria, hechicería, brujeria,* and folk Catholicism. Born and raised in Mexico, Laura has lived in the United States since 2010. Laura identifies as a *bruja de rancho,* or a ranch witch, a term with great resonance in Mexico, indicating knowledge of botanicals and the natural world. She is the author of *Mexican Sorcery: A Practical Guide to Brujeria de Rancho.*

Mira A. Gade

Mira A. Gade (Greece, Turkey) was a folk witch, astrologer, and priestess of Aphrodite in the Aydın Province of Turkey.

Rev. Laura González

Rev. Laura González (Mexico, United States) is a bruja, minister (Circle Sanctuary), priestess (Fraternity of the Goddess), psychic, podcaster, activist, teacher, registered massage therapist (RMT), and published author.

Ella Harrison

Ella Harrison has been a practicing witch for more than ten years and has dedicated herself to the path of German folk witchcraft. She aspires to inspire and educate people about witchcraft and Pagan practices. She holds a degree in social and cultural anthropology, creates content on YouTube and Instagram, and offers workshops and courses on her Patreon. Ella and her husband, Karlis, co-own a small crystal and witchcraft shop called Silver Fern Crystals (ekstones.com).

Dawn Aurora Hunt

Dawn Aurora Hunt (New Hampshire), also known as Cucina Aurora, is the owner of Cucina Aurora Kitchen Witchery, located in Salem, New Hampshire. She is the author of *A Kitchen Witch's Guide to Love & Romance* and *Kitchen Witchcraft for Beginners: Spells, Recipes, and Rituals to Bring Your Practice into the Kitchen*. She is also host of the acclimated podcast series *Conversational Witchcraft* and the popular YouTube channel *Cucina Aurora Kitchen Witchery*.

Emma Kathryn

Emma Kathryn (Nottinghamshire) is a writer for *Witch Way Magazine*; *The House of Twigs* blog; *Stone, Root, and Bone* blog; the *Spiral Nature* blog; and *Gods & Radicals*. She has spoken at a number of United Kingdom Pagan events, including Magickal Women Conference in London, and she has been interviewed on *The Witch Daily Show* podcast. She is the author of *Witch Life: A Practical Guide to Making Every Day Magical* and *Season Songs: Rediscovering the Magic in the Cycles of Nature*.

Aly Kravetz

Aly Kravetz (New York), also known as BronxWitch, is a tarot reader, energy healer, coven leader, and meditation coach. She is also a podcaster and owner of BronxWitch HeadQuarters.

Lorraine Monteagut, PhD

Lorraine Monteagut (Cuba, Colombia) is a witch and astrologer born in Miami, Florida. She holds a PhD in communication from the University of South Florida, where she began her research on bruja feminism and the reclamation of ancestral healing traditions. She is the author of *Brujas: The Magic and Power of Witches of Color.*

Jennifer Sacasa-Wright

Jennifer Sacasa-Wright (United States) considers herself a Craft Witch who follows her path with her husband in Pennsylvania. She founded the free community e-magazine PaganPages.org more than a decade ago and now runs it alongside two wonderful goddesses. You can find her creating her Goddess Dream Dolls and other items for local shops, festivals, and her Facebook page This Witch's Stitches & More. She imparts magick in all she makes.

Hector Salva

Hector Salva, also known as Papa Hector or Houngan Hector, is a brujo, *espiritista*, and author. Born and raised in a family lineage of brujos (witch doctors, healers, sorcerers), Papa Hector was initiated into Haitian Voodoo as a *houngan asogwe*, a high priest of the Asson lineage. He lived and apprenticed for years in Haiti under a number of houngans and *mambos*. Papa Hector is the author of *The 21 Divisions: Mysteries and Magic of Dominican Voodoo* and *Espiritismo: Puerto Rican Mediumship & Magic.*

Maria Elena Urbaneja

Maria Elena Urbaneja (Venezuela) is a medium, bruja, and espiritista. She is initiated in Espiritismo Tradicional Venezolano, Palo Mayombe, and Santeria/Lucumi.

IMAGE DESCRIPTION LIST

Chapter 2: Tree

El Arbol del Diablo (the Devil's tree) is an element that is repeated in multiple stories of Caribbean folklore. In most of these stories, the Amerindians had their own gods and good and bad spirits. Once the conquerors arrived, they brought with them the Devil, the worst of all the spirits. The witches tricked him and locked him up in a tree. In one of the many versions, the Obeah Men of Trinidad and Tobago say that when the witches seek power, they bury gifts and offerings at the foot of the silk cotton trees at night and thus the Devil visits them while they sleep. The bark of these trees is used to

355

make Abás, a type of amulet with sacred symbols that is hung from the doors so that nightmares and demons do not enter.

Chapter 4: Dancing Devils of Corpus Christi

The traditional mask of the Diablo de Yare (Dancing Devil of Corpus Christi) is created by hand for a festival that takes place in Venezuela where people dressed as Devils dance to the rhythm of drums until they reach the entrance of the church. For modern brujos today, this dance symbolizes a ritual to conjure up allied demons.

Chapter 5: Serpent

Guajanari, or Kaonari, is a giant sea serpent spirit with three eyes made of yellow stone, skin white like light, and wings like a bat. It represents the fluidity of the rivers that advance toward themselves through the world. The seas become thin rivers and are then devoured again by the sea. Souls navigate through the waters to return to the aquatic world, and from there, they depart again toward our world. Guajanari is the reason why when the brujas walk around, and inside the Orinoco River they say, "Guajanari take my sorrows, Guajanari drown my miseries." Guajanari is the creator of nightmares and fears, and the waters and dreams are his kingdom.

Chapter 8: Square with Four Symbols

This symbol, although simple and of unknown origin, can be found in grimoires handwritten by witches from the town of Cumanacoa, Venezuela, as well as engraved on trees, large rocks near beaches, and on various murals.

Chapter 8: Pentacle Talisman

The other symbol shown in chapter 8 is drawn on paper and anointed on both sides with a mixture of common sunflower oil, coarse salt, and powder made from eucalyptus leaves. This talisman is then folded in half and sewn with thread to the pillows to prevent witches from entering one's dreams.

Chapter 14: Handful of Herbs

Sahumerio is a magical, traditional, and Indigenous method of spiritual cleansing and protection that has survived for centuries, in which a bundle of dried herbs burns and smokes around the house. For the illustration we use cinnamon, eucalyptus, lavender, rosemary, and cascara sagrada.

Chapter 15: Cougar God

Aemmi, or Azemi, was a lunar deity worshiped in Amazonia by the Kalinago tribe that settled there when they arrived from Barbados and Trinidad and Tobago. Today only carved drawings of him are preserved on the trees, and his history is part of oral folklore. Aemmi was the spirit of a jaguar or a puma (cougar) that stalked at night. One day, the trees turned him into a guardian spirit to protect all those he had scared. He ended up being venerated as a Zemi, a deity or high spirit of the Carib tribes, like a nocturnal god who wanders through dreams and devours nightmares.

Chapter 16: Triangle of Herbs

Blessing decoctions was one of the most archaic forms of sorcery among Amerindian peoples, and it is still practiced today around the Amazon.

Chapter 17: Mask

This image is a representation of a native spiritual worker from Yaracuy (Venezuela) with his face painted in a traditional warrior-priest style. The sorcerer or spiritual worker wears a traditional Amerindian headdress with feathers, which is very reminiscent of a Venezuelan mask of the Dancing Devils of Yare.

"1783. Lavoisier y los estudios sobre combustión animal." *Editorial Médica Panamericana*, 2007.

Arredondo, Alexis A., and Eric J. Labrado. *Magia Magia: Invoking Mexican Magic*. Mobile, AL: Conjure Southern Publications, 2020.

Arrom, José Juan. *Fray Ramón Panén: "Relación acerca de las antigüedades de los indios": el primer tratado escrito an américia nueva versión, con notas, mapa y apéndices*. Mexico City: Siglo XXI Editores, 1974.

Ballaster, Ros, ed. *Fables of the East: Selected Tales, 1662–1785*. Oxford: Oxford University Press, 2005.

Baño, Adrián Hernández. *Transcripción de Toponímicos Indígenas Quechuas en el Estado Falcón (Venezuela)*. Coro, Venezuela: Fundación Hernández Baño, 1998.

Beekes, Robert. *Etymological Dictionary of Greek*. Boston: Brill, 2010.

Cajochen, Christian, Songül Altanay-Ekici, Mirjam Münch, Sylvia Frey, Vera Knoblauch, and Anna Wirz-Justice. "Evidence that the Lunar Cycle Influences Human Sleep." *Current Biology* 23, no. 15 (2013): 1485–8.

Casiraghi, Leandro, Ignacio Spiousas, Gideon P. Dunster, Kaitlyn McGlothlen, Eduardo Fernández-Duque, Claudia Valeggia, Horacio O de la Iglesia. "Moonstruck Sleep: Synchronization of Human Sleep with the Moon Cycle under Field Conditions," *Science Advances* 7, no. 5 (January 27, 2021). DOI: 10.1126/sciadv.abe0465.

Chapman, Anne. *End of a World: The Selknam of Tierra del Fuego*. Buenos Aires: Zaiger & Urruty Publications, 2008.

———. *European Encounters with the Yamana People of Cape Horn, before and after Darwin*. Cambridge: Cambridge University Press, 2013.

———. *Hain: Selknam Initiation Ceremony*. Buenos Aires: Zaiger & Urruty Publications, 2008.

Cross, J. Allen. *American Brujeria: Modern Mexican American Folk Magic*. Newburyport, MA: Red Wheel/Weiser, 2021.

Davila, Laura. *Mexican Sorcery: A Practical Guide to Brujeria de Rancho*. Newburyport, MA: Red Wheel/Weiser, 2023.

de Ovalle, Alonso. *Histórica relación del Reyno de Chile y de las mifiones y ministerios que exercita la Compañia de Jesus*. Rome, 1646. http://www.bibliotecanacionaldigital.gob.cl.

Donner-Grau, Florinda. *The Witch's Dream: A Healer's Way of Knowledge*. New York: Penguin, 1985.

Duviols, Pierre. *La destrucción de las religiones andinas*. Mexico City: Universidad Nacional Autónoma de México, 1977.

Epstein, Isidore, ed. *Babylonian Talmud: Berakhot* (Hebrew-English Edition), London: The Soncino Press, 1984.

Eranimos, Boban, and Dr. Art Funkhouser. "The Concept of Dreams and Dreaming: A Hindu Perspective." *International Journal of Indian Psychology*, 4, no. 4 (September 2017).

Foster, George M. *Cultura y conquista: La herencia española en América*. Mexico City: Xalapa por la Universidad Veracruzana, 1962.

Gould, Robert Jay. *Youkai and Kaidan*. Japan Culture Research Project, 2003.

Grionés, Jaime. *Llewellyn's Little Book of the Day of the Dead*. Woodbury, MN: Llewellyn Publications, 2021.

Kaplan, Aryeh. *Meditation and Kabbalah*. Newburyport, MA: Weiser Books, 1982.

Kardec, Allan. *The Gospel According to Spiritism*. New York: United States Spiritist Council, 2020.

Koch, Peter O. *El Dorado and the Quest for Fortune and Glory in South America*. Jefferson, NC: McFarland & Company, 2021.

Kronfeld-Schor, Noga, Davide Dominoni, Hooracio de la Iglesia, Oren Levy, Erik D. Herzog, Tamar Dayan, and Charlotte Helfrich-Forster. "Chronobiology by Moonlight." *Proceedings of the Royal Society Biological Sciences* (2013).

Leafar, Elhoim. "Elhoim's Column." *Todo en Domingos*. Caracas, Venezuela.

Leitão, José, trans. *The Immaterial Book of St. Cyprian: Folk Concepts & Views on* The Book *as a Cultural Item through the Reading of Folk Narratives*. Seattle: Revelore Press, 2017.

Méndez, Conny. *El Librito Azul: Manual de Metafísica en términos sencillos*. Caracas, Venezuela: Ediciones Giluz, 2006.

———. *El Libro de Oro de Saint Germain*. Mexico City: Grupo Editorial Tomo, 2004.

———. *La chispa de Conny Méndez: Humor y memorias*. Caracas, Venezuela: Ediciones Giluz, 2007.

———. *Metafísica 4 en 1*. Caracas, Venezuela: Bienes Lacónica, 1996.

———. *Metafísica al alcance de todos: Verdades Espirituales en palabras de a centavo*. Caracas, Venezuela: Ediciones Giluz, 2007.

Monteagut, Lorraine. *Brujas: The Magic and Power of Witches of Color*. Chicago: Chicago Review Press, 2022.

Nelson, Mark. *Shamanism: Your Personal Journey to Healing and Self-Discovery*. Woodbury, MN: Llewellyn Publications, 2022.

Newman, Louis J., ed. *The Talmudic Anthology: Tales and Teachings of the Rabbis.* West Orange, NJ: Behrman House, 1945.

Ovid. *Metamorphoses.* Loeb Classical Library. Accessed March 29, 2023. https://www.loebclassics.com/view/ovid-metamorphoses/1916/pb _LCL043.163.xml?readMode=recto.

Röösli, Martin, Peter Jüni, Charlotte Braun-Fahrländer, Martin W. G. Brink-hof, Nicole Low, Matthias Egger. "Sleepless Night, the Moon Is Bright: Longitudinal Study of Lunar Phase and Sleep," *Journal of Sleep Research* 15, no. 2 (June 2006): 149–53.

The Torah: A New Translation. Philadelphia: The Jewish Publication Society of America, 1962.

Torero, Alfredo. *Lenguas de los Andes: Lingüística e historia.* Lima, Peru: Instituto Francés de Estudios Andinos, 2002.

Trachtenberg, Joshua. *Jewish Magic and Superstition: A Study in Folk Religion.* Philadelphia: University of Pennsylvania Press, 2004.

Vaan, Michiel de. *Etymological Dictionary of Latin and the Other Italic Languages.* Vol. 7 of *Leiden Indo-European Etymological Dictionary Series,* edited by Alexander Lubotsky. Leiden, Netherlands: Brill, 2008.

Van Cott, Donna Lee. "Andean Indigenous Movements and Constitutional Transformation: Venezuela in Comparative Perspective." *Latin American Perspectives* 30, no. 1 (January 2003), 49–69.

Varela, Francisco J, ed. *Sleeping, Dreaming, and Dying: An Exploration of Consciousness with the Dalai Lama.* Translated by B. Alan Wallace and Thupten Jinpa. Boston: Wisdom Publications, 1997.

Vorhand, Susan. "Dreams in the Talmud and in Depth Psychology." Deep Insights. Spring, 2013. https://www.depthinsights.com/Depth-Insights -scholarly-ezine/e-zine-issue-4-spring-2013/dreams-in-the-talmud-and -in-depth-psychology-by-susan-vorhand/.